HAITI
STATE AGAINST NATION

HAITI
STATE AGAINST NATION

The Origins and Legacy
of Duvalierism

Michel-Rolph Trouillot

Monthly Review Press
New York

Library of Congress Cataloging-in-Publication Data

Trouillot, Michel-Rolph.
  Haiti, state against nation : the origins and legacy of
Duvalierism / Michel-Rolph Trouillot.
    p. cm.
    Includes bibliographical references.
    ISBN 0-85345-755-7 $28.00—ISBN 0-85345-756-5 (pbk.) ; $12.00
    1. Haiti—Politics and government—1934– 1971.   2. Haiti—Politics
and government—1971–1986.   I. Title
F1927.T76   1990
972.94 dc20   89-27395
                                                           CIP

Monthly Review Press
122 West 27th Street
New York, N.Y. 10001

Manufactured in the United States of America

10   9   8   7   6   5   4   3   2   1

Truth is always revolutionary.
—Antonio Gramsci

To Czerny and Lyonel
To Pierrot and Evelyne

Contents

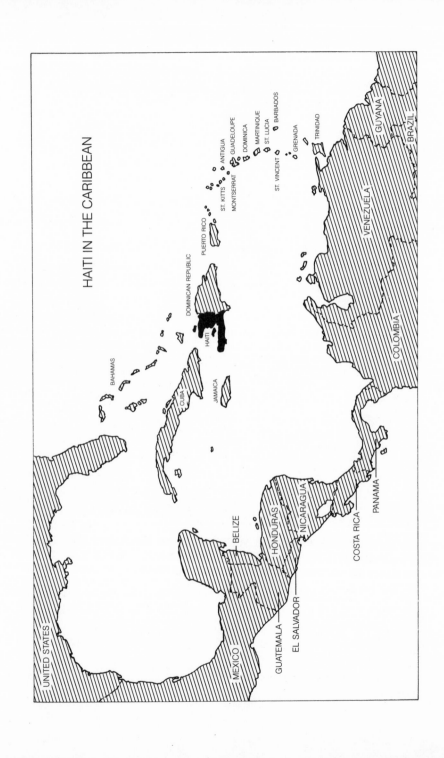

HAITI IN THE CARIBBEAN

Preface and Acknowledgments

When I first returned to Haiti, three days after Jean-Claude Duvalier's departure for exile, I joined in a moment of national euphoria unprecedented in Haitian history. I soon became convinced, however, in spite of the elation that I shared, that few among the urban elites dared to envision concretely the transformations necessary to ensure popular participation in state affairs. While members of the lower classes practiced their brand of summary justice on kin and neighbors associated with the fallen dictatorship, the interim government that replaced the Duvaliers protected the true pillars of the fallen regime, providing them with safe houses or secret means to flee the country. Meanwhile, many traditional politicians and professional members of the petty bourgeoisie used the unusual degree of freedom of expression to position themselves in the upcoming contest for leadership of the state apparatus. Amid genuine demands for democracy, many were those who wanted only to emphasize their alleged anti-Duvalierist credentials or the Duvalierist connections of their potential competitors. State fetishism, the congenital disease of the Haitian urban classes, soon obliterated such fundamental issues as the social basis of Duvalierism, the conditions of its emergence, and the social mechanisms behind the longevity and resilience of the dictatorship. In short, few intellectuals, and no political party, even among the progressive ones, chose to address the multitude of questions that the passing of the Duvalier dynasty posed to the Haitian people. It was to call attention to some of these issues, and especially to the tortuous relationship between state and nation, that I wrote *Les Racines historiques de l'état duvaliérien* in the spring of 1986.

The present book was at first intended to be a translation of *Racines*. But just as the first book imposed itself on me in the course of an entirely

9

different project, so too this work claimed a life of its own. First, as events unfolded in Haiti they encouraged a stronger phrasing of parts of the argument and called for the refining of others. Chapter 7 was revised in the light of current events and I added an entirely new chapter to bring the book up to date. More important, the book in French was aimed at a Haitian audience, mainly the intellectual elite. As such, it drew from a common pool of images, of historical, social, and political references easily decoded by Haitian urbanites. To present the same argument to an international audience unfamiliar with Haiti required more than a linguistic transcription. It also meant filling in hundreds of historical and cultural blanks. It further implied that I make accessible to the reader multiple points of entry into the discussion on the basis of much reduced assumptions about existing understandings. In short, this book required a cultural translation for which the shift from French to English was but a metaphor.

I need not detail here the lessons I learned, as a practicing anthropologist, in this peculiar exercise in cultural translation. But the recouching of the argument in cross-cultural terms forced me to elaborate upon my conceptualizations. The book benefited from my having to set the state/nation dichotomy in English, a language within which the equality of these two words is often assumed. The first chapter in particular was rewritten to underline the relevance of the theoretical issues beyond the Haitian case. Similarly, chapter 4, as rewritten, provides the unfamiliar reader with an introduction to the landscape of color prejudice and social organization in urban Haiti. More generally, the entire book has been recast with an eye for tighter conceptualization and greater empirical background.

Les Racines historiques also bore the mark of the ethical and political stance from which it stemmed. That book was as much a scholarly argument as it was an appeal to certain sectors of the Haitian elites; as such it said as much about its author as it did about his audience. I have not tried to lessen that stance here, but I could not assume the community of interest on which the original appeal was based. Thus the cultural translation necessarily implied a muting of voices, notably the first person singular and the first person plural that are an intrinsic part of the analysis. But if the "I" and the "us" have disappeared from much of the text as rewritten, there remains enough within and between the lines for the reader to catch the dialogue I am engaging in, and indeed to participate if he or she so wishes.

The two books being so intertwined, I cannot but acknowledge here the people and institutions that supported them both. Over the years my exchanges with Michel Acacia, Czerny Brasuell, Jean Coulanges, Pierre Buteau, Lyonel Trouillot, and Drexel Woodson improved my understanding of Haiti and its people; their influence found its way into both versions of the book, although not always in forms they would endorse. Jean-Robert Hérard and the late Richard Brisson, killed by Baby Doc's minions, commented on my early notes on the Duvalierist Executive and its repressive machine. More specifically, Michel Acacia, Louis Buteau, Pierre Buteau, Evelyne Ménard-Trouillot, and Lyonel Trouillot reviewed the original manuscript of *Racines*. While writing that book, I enjoyed a fellowship at the National Humanities Center, with support from the Ford Foundation. Both versions draw on ideas and motifs first sketched in my 1985 essay, *Nation, State, and Society in Haiti, 1804–1984,* commissioned by the Woodrow Wilson International Center for Scholars in Washington, D.C. Finally, the further research for this rewrite was done in Haiti, in 1987, on a faculty research leave from Duke University. I thank all these institutions for their support.

I began my work using as my starting point a translation of the Haitian book done by Craig Charney (for the first half) and Julia Adams (for the second half). I am enormously grateful to them for the work that they did, because without it the finished book would not have been possible. The only reason their names do not appear on the title page is that the final product has been through so many transformations and editings since their translation that I do not feel that they should seem responsible for the final result.

Three friends and fellow anthropologists helped me with the extensive rewriting in English. Katherine Verdery commented on the theoretical framework couched in the first chapter and raised valuable questions about its empirical application in and outside the Haitian case, not all of which I could answer. Sidney W. Mintz read the entire manuscript, providing page-by-page comments on both substance and form. This native continues to be fascinated by that foreigner's deep knowledge of Haitian society, a knowledge matched only by his deeper respect for Haitian culture. Susan Lowes, my editor at Monthly Review Press, went through numerous versions of the text, helping me with the tedious process of cultural translation and reorganization of the material. My warmest thanks to all three.

I have good reasons for bowing here to the awful tradition of concluding a preface by thanking one's kin. First, I am blessed with kin who actually read my work and encourage it. Most if not all of my adult relatives truly supported this endeavor in its various phases. I have already singled out some of them. Second, the argument of this book was first conceived and framed during a period of political apprehension, and its recouching was even more painful than the first time around. As events in Haiti verified some of my worst fears, both my extended familial network and the members of my household soothed my mood. In particular, my wife, Anne-Carine, and my newborn daughter, Canel, provided personal peace of mind and irrational but undying hope. They all deserve my gratitude.

Haitian Chiefs of State

DESSALINES, Jean-Jacques January 1804–October 1806

    (Emperor Jacques I, September 1804–October 1806)

CHRISTOPHE, Henry January 1807–October 1820

    (King Henry I, March 1811–October 1820,
    overlapped regimes of Pétion and Boyer)

PETION, Alexandre March 1807–March 1818

BOYER, Jean-Pierre March 1818–February 1843

HERARD, Charles Rivière December 1843–May 1844

GUERRIER, Philippe May 1844–April 1845

PIERROT, Jean-Louis April 1845–March 1846

RICHE, Jean-Baptiste March 1846–February 1847

SOULOUQUE, Faustin March 1847–January 1859

    (Emperor Faustin I, August 1849–January 1859)

GEFFRARD, Fabre Nicolas January 1859–March 1867

SALNAVE, Sylvain June 1867–December 1869

SAGET, Nissage March 1870–May 1874

DOMINGUE, Michel June 1874–April 1876

CANAL, Boisrond July 1876–July 1879

SALOMON, Lysius Félicité October 1879–August 1888

LEGITIME, François-Denis December 1888–August 1889

HYPPOLITE, Florville	October 1889–March 1896
SIMON SAM, T. Augustin	March 1896–May 1902
ALEXIS, Nord	December 1902–December 1908
SIMON, Antoine	December 1908–August 1911
LECONTE, Cincinnatus	August 1911–August 1912
AUGUSTE, Tancrède	August 1912–May 1913
ORESTE, Michel	May 1913–January 1914
ZAMOR, Charles Oreste	February 1914–October 1914
THEODORE, Davilmar	November 1914–February 1915
SAM, Vilbrun Guillaume	March 1915–July 1915
DARTIGUENAVE, Philippe-Sudre	August 1915–May 1922
BORNO, Louis	May 1922–May 1930
VINCENT, Sténio	November 1930–May 1941
LESCOT, Elie	May 1941–January 1946
ESTIME, Dumarsais	August 1946–May 1950
MAGLOIRE, Paul Eugène	December 1950–December 1956
DUVALIER, François	October 1957–April 1971
DUVALIER, Jean-Claude	April 1971–January 1986
MANIGAT, François Leslie	January 1988–June 1988

Note: This list does not include chiefs of state installed on a temporary basis.

Introduction:
The Problematic of State and Nation

This book is as much about Haiti as it is about the governments of François and Jean-Claude Duvalier, whose combined regimes (1957–86) represent the longest dictatorial sequence in the history of that country. Its aim is to retrace the path that led to the emergence of a form of state control typified by those two dictatorships, to uncover the mechanisms behind their longevity, and to expose some of the problems that Haiti continues to face, even though both Duvaliers are gone. It eschews simplistic answers, both the dogmatic ones favored by some Haitian scholars and the sensationalist anecdotes about "Papa" or "Baby Doc" fancied by many U.S., Canadian, and European authors. Analyses that present the protracted crisis that has torn Haitian society apart during the past thirty years as an aberration, and the hereditary dictatorship that formalized that crisis as the sole offspring of a few malevolent minds, are at best naive. Similarly, studies of Haiti that cannot see the Duvalierist state as an outcome—albeit not an inevitable one—of that nation's historical evolution fall short of the mark.

HAITI AND THE DUVALIERS

The main argument of this book is that the Duvalierist state emerged as the result of a long-term process that was marked by an increasing disjuncture between political and civil society. (The concepts of political and civil society, as well as state and nation, will be defined in the following sections.) The forms of production and the political models that solidified during the first half of the nineteenth century bore the germs of dis-

15

equilibrium. Agricultural goods produced with the simplest means by a growing peasantry constituted the bulk of the country's exports, with coffee being by far the leading product. Peasant crops and imported consumer goods were the mainstay of local economic exchange. Taxes collected at the customhouses and ultimately borne by the peasantry provided the bulk of government revenues. Profits made from the peasantry contributed a large share to the returns garnered by an import-export bourgeoisie that was dominated by foreign nationals and unconcerned with local production. The productive system and the way in which the surplus was extracted foreshadowed an eventual depletion of the country's economic resources.

The political sphere also contained a promise of escalating tensions. While the state turned inward to consolidate its control, the urban elites who gravitated around that state pushed the rural majority into the margins of political life. Peasants were the economic backbone of the nation; yet peasants had no claim whatsoever on the state. Meanwhile, access to the state apparatus was the ultimate goal for most native urbanites—and the state itself the privileged arena for their petty struggles.

The disequilibrium inherent in that combination manifested itself throughout the nineteenth century in waves of political and economic difficulties that became increasingly strong, especially after 1860. Yet there were counterweights that prevented total collapse. State and nation were profoundly at odds, but the process of state centralization remained uneven. There were still domains in which civil society had its say, reserved areas of social relations in which the power of the state was mediated.

The 1915–34 occupation of Haiti by the United States removed those counterweights and aggravated an already explosive situation in two ways. First, it heightened the economic irrationality of the system by increasing both the forced contribution of the peasantry to the state and the dependency on a monocrop. Second, it worsened the political panorama by centralizing the state apparatus (especially the army) and by disarming the provinces, both militarily and economically. While the military, fiscal, and commercial centralization imposed by the occupiers postponed Haiti's day of reckoning for thirty years, it also guaranteed that that reckoning would be bloody.

The U.S.-trained army led the way to totalitarianism when the crisis reemerged in the late 1950s. Between 1956 and 1960, the entire system began to go off its traditional guide rails. The manifest dislocation of civil and political society spurred panic and confusion, especially among the urbanites. Using that confusion and state-sponsored terror, President

François Duvalier succeeded in providing what was, in Haitian terms, an unconventional response to the crisis: the transformation of the authoritarian political model of the past into a totalitarian apparatus. In so doing, he pitted the state against the nation.

By 1965, the Duvalierist state had reshaped the relations between state and civil society and strengthened itself in the process. At the center of the system stood an all-powerful and personalized executive that totally dominated all other branches of government. This modified state apparatus in turn functioned as a superordinate institution that alone defined the conditions of existence of its many subparts (the army, the ministries, etc.), as well as the conditions of reproduction of the formal institutions of civil society (schools, clergy, press, trade unions). It is this seizure of a weakened civil society by the state—which went so far as to subjugate many traditional (regional, religious, and even familial) solidarities—that lets us speak of a *qualitative* transformation. The Duvalierist state aimed to become "total"; its means became totalitarian.

Duvalierism entered into its second phase with the transmission of power from François Duvalier to his son Jean-Claude in 1971, which was accompanied by increased support from the United States and a thorough economic restructuring. By this time the Haitian rulers, in agreement with foreign "experts," had completely dismissed the rural world in favor of a gamble on the returns from cheap urban labor: Haitian labor and U.S. capital together were to spark an "economic revolution." Alas, the rapid spread of light assembly industries, subcontracting work from U.S. firms, simply reinforced the urban-rural polarization. The already huge gap between the haves and the have-nots widened at frightening speed. Inflation and corruption grew as well. The intense economic polarization, factional rearrangements within the Duvalier clique, and the unmediated distance between the regime and the swollen urban masses all contributed to the downfall of Jean-Claude Duvalier in February 1986.

Yet Haiti's problems were not over with Baby Doc's departure, if only because the two Duvalier dictatorships were part of a trend. Haitian intellectuals have claimed since the nineteenth century that Haiti has never had a government worthy of its people. From economist Edmond Paul (1876, 1882) and sociologist Louis-Joseph Janvier (1886) to modern-day historians like Antoine Michel (1932) and Leslie Manigat (1971), Haitian intellectuals have steadily condemned past governments. More recently, foreign observers have sung a similar tune. Since the early 1970s, a string of publications—among which the work of economist Mats Lundahl (1979,

1983) stands out as the best illustration—have repeated the tune, familiar to Haitian ears, that Haiti's major problem has been its governments.[1]

The charge is easy to make, but that is exactly where the shoe pinches: its very simplicity leads nowhere. It is not enough to say that Haitian governments have never been up to their job; it is necessary to know why Haiti continues to produce such governments, and why and how such governments led finally to the Duvaliers. Among my childhood memories, there is the troubling recollection that the adults around me were relieved when the Magloire dictatorship collapsed in 1956. They thought that the worst was past, that the next government could only be better. Two juntas and one carnage later, they sensed that the ordeal was still not over. Soon thereafter, indeed, we had François Duvalier; and from one Duvalier to the next, we learned that there could be worse than the worst.

Middle-class Haitian perceptions, electoral propaganda, and the academic analyses mentioned above share a basic assumption: that the state can be treated as an independent variable. Not surprisingly, these three discourses overlap. Mats Lundahl's words on the "distorted views of the purpose of government held by most Haitian politicians" and the lack of a "political ideology in the Western sense" (Lundahl 1979: 358) are a case in point. Notwithstanding the fact that such assertions grossly display their racist underpinnings when used by less competent minds they all merely repeat the old Haitian tune. In 1915, one Joseph Justin quoted approvingly a 1882 statement by Edmond Paul denouncing "the primitive vision of our governments" (Justin 1915: 8). That Justin was a cabinet minister-cum-scholar quoting a cabinet minister-cum-scholar from a previous generation exposes the academic and political impasse intrinsic to the vision they shared. For they, at least, were not primitive. If the state is indeed an independent variable, Haitians have no choice but to put their faith in the hands of the individual, the family, or the clique displaying the most convincing combination of good will and diplomas—and hope for the best. However charming that fantasy, history past and present suggests its shallowness.

The state is not an independent variable—neither the Duvalierist state nor any other. State forms are constantly created, reproduced, maintained, and modified. Moreover, these processes of reproduction and change are intertwined with the historical evolution of the particular society and culture within which the state functions; their understanding requires an examination of the relationship between state and civil society.

STATE AND CIVIL SOCIETY

The distinction between state and civil society, inherited from the Enlightenment, was amplified at the beginning of this century by the Italian philosopher and journalist Antonio Gramsci (1971: 210–76). In Gramsci's view, the state encapsulates "political society" and represents the moment of force and coercion, while "civil society" is the complex network of educational and ideological institutions in which leadership is more important than force. Most of the institutions that exert direct domination are controlled by the state, whereas civil society encompasses the bodies and sodalities usually termed "internal and private" (Macciocchi 1974). Gramsci (1971: 209) wrote that "between the economic structure and the state with its legislation and coercion stands civil society."

At one level, therefore, the distinction between civil and political society has to do with content. Political and civil society do not exist "out there," but there are actions or things, especially institutions, that can be said to belong to one or the other. For instance, an institution such as the army can be said to be part of the state (political society in the strictest sense), whereas an institution such as the family seems to belong to civil society. At this level, the distinction remains somewhat superficial: the state, for instance, does invade the family if only by legalizing marriage, while in many societies there are military families.

At another level, the distinction has to do with methodology in a broad sense. It represents two ways of dividing up the same elements, two principles of organization of similar institutions or groupings. Here, as in real life, civil and political society can have the same "content." Political society is the polity (the *polis*)—that is, the society at large, perceived as an arena where power, the common good, and conflicting interests are always at stake. It is the wider arena wherein the nexus of coercive institutions (the state in the strictest sense) reproduces itself. In this second Gramscian view, which Catherine Buci-Glucksmann dubs the "enlarged" vision of the state, the machinery of government *plus* civil society constitute the state in the strongest, "organic," sense (Gramsci 1971: 108, 138, 257, 263; Macciocchi 1974: 64–65; Buci-Glucksmann 1969, 1975). Thus Gramsci (1971: 160) comments that "in actual reality civil society and State are one and the same." Political and civil society are "moments" of the same process.[2]

To put it this way is to suggest that there is a fundamental relationship between civil and political society but that the terms of that relationship cannot be taken for granted. This is a perspective that enables us to evaluate major conceptions of the state and to reassess some fundamental ways of thinking prevalent both in folk theory and academic discourse, in Haiti and elsewhere. For purposes of presentation, I will group under the same umbrella views that do not agree on all points in order to concentrate on two major tendencies. My first cluster groups theories that ultimately deny an organic relationship between civil and political society. The second includes theories that acknowledge that relationship but perceive it as predetermined.

THE STATE AS PATERFAMILIAS

The dominant folk theory of the state in Haiti fits into a larger international perspective within which one can place all "paternalistic" visions of the state. Paternalistic theories view the state as an independent and supernatant entity, one that ideally calms the transient tensions of the social organism and intervenes to promote justice on the basis of Reason, understood to be absolute and universal.

This paternalistic conception underpins most theories of the state as an independent variable and is preferred by elites the world over because it gives them a choice role. In Haiti's case, this view rationalizes and reinforces obvious inequalities: politics becomes a reserved domain, a preserve to which the urban elites alone have access thanks to their education and moral values. *They* are to represent the interests of the people, defined, by them, according to the universal principles of Justice and Reason.

Thus, contrary to the assessment of many foreign observers, Haitian elites do not lack a Western vision of the purpose of government. Their speeches and writings conform neatly to an outlook whose fundamental tenets have been repeatedly exposed and criticized in the West. Views of the state as "arbiter" or "paterfamilias" prevailed among leaders of the revolution that led to the birth of independent Haiti in 1804 (M.-R. Trouillot 1977: 199). Those same basic assumptions defined local political debates in the nineteenth century (Paul 1882; Delorme 1873; Janvier 1886). They also underlay both the discourse of the Duvaliers and that of their opponents (Duvalier 1966a; 1969; Honorat 1974; Manigat et al. 1975; Collectif Paroles 1976).

To say that Haitian politicians and intellectuals did not believe in these high ideals, whereas their Western counterparts did, is an ineffectual riposte. First, such a reply would grant to Western politicians a global credit that individual biographies hardly sanction while making all Haitians guilty until proven innocent. Second, and more important, that rebuttal simply pushes the voluntaristic base of the argument further. Of course some Haitian politicians were sincere; of course others were not. The very fact that, here as elsewhere, we may never be able to separate those who were from those who were not says a great deal about the limits of theories that treat the state as an independent variable.

THE STATE AS INSTRUMENT

Paternalistic theories of the state have repeatedly been called into question in the West since the nineteenth century. Visions of the state as an independent variable are still around, but have given way to what I call an "instrumentalist" trend. Here again I am consciously engaging in a gross generalization, but many recent academic theories of the state have roots in the functionalist vision that has dominated Western social science since the end of the nineteenth century. Within this functionalist framework, the state is seen as the precipitate of the many conflicts of interest and power struggles inherent in a heterogeneous society. It emerges as a sort of vector sum, but more importantly, "it functions." It guarantees order and maintains an equilibrium. Opinions vary as to the nature and degree of society's concealed heterogeneity and the efficiency of the state in maintaining or restoring the equilibrium, but the metaphor for the functionalist view is ultimately mechanistic.

Functionalist Marxism—with a good deal of help from Marx, Engels, and Lenin—grafted its own theory of the state onto this vision by introducing class struggle as one piece of evidence that analysts should examine and as one of the problems the state itself must alleviate. This change did little to modify the basic mechanistic perspective, however. The state is still an instrument—"it works"—only now we know "for whom" it works. Its design and its performance ultimately benefit the dominant class that controls it.

Instrumentalist theories of the state represent enormous progress when compared to the many voluntaristic approaches, and most scholars have inherited at least some of their metaphors. We speak of the "state apparatus" and the "state machinery" in part because the state seems to work *within* society. All instrumentalist theories by definition reject a vision of the state as an entity floating above the social order. All assume that the state is *not* an independent variable. But instrumentalist theories tend to replace the voluntaristic "free-for-all" attitude with theoretical stalemates. In their Marxist mode, they deny the possibility that the state may function in ways that do not fit the immediate requirements of the economic structure. In almost all variants, they deny the possibility that the state may occupy a structural position in which it becomes an agent on its own terms—in the economic sphere, for instance. Yet as Gramsci (1971: 208–9) reminds us, if "the state is the instrument for conforming civil society to the economic structure . . . it is necessary for the state 'to be willing' to do this." Similarly, Nicos Poulantzas (1971) has argued for a "relative autonomy" of the state, although critics have questioned the extent of the relativeness he proposed.

Few instrumentalist theories account for any such contingency. Since they reduce the state to either a precipitate of another set of relations or a derivative of another "structure," they are at a loss when the state does not act "as expected." Yet the state rarely acts as expected. Indeed, there is little agreement among politicians and scholars on exactly how the state is expected to act in the dependent countries situated on the periphery of the capitalist world economy.

THE STATE IN THE THIRD WORLD

The conspicuous unpredictability of the state in most of the so-called third world arises from the many inherent tensions to which it is constantly subjected (Goulbourne 1979; Thomas 1984). Indeed, instability is inherent in the social structure of peripheral capitalism (Alavi 1982a). It stems from the very dependency that characterizes these societies and "disarticulates" to varying degrees the social organism (Touraine 1978: 155; Amin 1980: 174).

Societies on the periphery of the capitalist world economy are of necessity outward-looking, if only because they are economically dependent on capitalist centers. Yet states are inherently inward-looking (even if expansionist): they exercise primary control over a definite territory and derive their momentum from the dynamics of coercion and consent within that space. Thus peripheral societies are characterized by a permanent tension between the centripetal forces of the state and the centrifugal forces inherent in dependency.

The historical evolution that led to the peripheral state contributed to an increase in the stresses on that state. The peripheral capitalist state is often a colonial legacy, the result of a political "independence" built upon the remains of a power structure imposed from outside. The ultimate moral and political justification of decolonization notwithstanding, the replacement of a European-led apparatus with a "native" bureaucracy creates as many problems as it solves. The "national" state so created never inherited a blank slate because the preceding colonial entity, as well as the conditions of its demise, limited both the new rulers' possibilities and those of their successors. Not surprisingly, the inherent disjuncture between state and nation, conveniently concealed by the recent notion of "nation-state," tends to increase in peripheral countries.

STATE AND NATION: AN AMBIGUOUS RELATIONSHIP

Most politicians and many social scientists assume a natural and exact interface between state and nation. They view the nation as that entity upon which the state rules—a position that eliminates the search for painstaking definitions. Touraine (1973: 272) calls the nation "the other face of the state," without indicating how or why the state would build itself another physiognomy. The difficulty increases in the English-speaking world, where "nation" is often treated as a synonym of "state" (in contradistinction with most romance languages, for instance). Thus it is no accident that otherwise incisive social scientists in Britain and the United States tend to trivialize the concept. Giddens (1985: 119), for instance, claims that a nation exists "only when a state has a unified administrative reach over the territory over which its sovereignty is claimed," a reduction that makes the concept useless. Likewise, for Wallerstein (1987: 22–23), nations are a somewhat mechanical result of the world system, and nationalism a consequence of administrative uniformity.

Other observers have tried to solve the definitional problem empirically: they associate the term "nation" with a chosen cultural feature, and the analyst's task is to make sure that this empirical feature (or set of features) obtains in a particular situation. In that second viewpoint, language is often the determining cultural feature. Thus in spite of his own warnings against Eurocentric views of the nation, Amin (1980: 19), for instance, suggests that a common language and a centralizing state define a nation.

Yet the suggestion that peoples united by language are, should, or tend to be part of the same polity is itself Eurocentric. Although the legendary correspondence between language and state (as well as language and race) goes back to North African themes as old as the biblical story of the tower of Babel, its recent revitalization is a Western phenomenon. It occurred during the eighteenth-century consolidation of the state in France and Britain, and then spread throughout the modern world. But in those two cases, as elsewhere, the equation language = nation = state was made *a posteriori* through manipulations that required the mass production of a new past (Hobsbawm and Ranger 1983; Worsley 1984: 272–75). In fact, the language that became French enjoyed no special status within the state from the eighth to the twelfth century. It replaced Latin for certain documents only under Francis I (1515–47). At most only two-fifths of the "French" were born French speakers at the time of the French Revolution and half of the population did not understand a word of that language (Calvet 1974: 166). Thus Giddens (1985: 119) is right to suggest that a common language is not a universal feature of the nation.

But Giddens, like Wallerstein, throws the baby out with the bath water. The problem with concepts of the nation that emphasize a specific cultural feature, such as language or a belief in a common ancestry, is not their emphasis on culture-history as such but the search for a cultural feature that would repeat itself *mutatis mutandis* in each and every situation. In other words, "nation" has no fixed cultural content—and that is what makes its cross-cultural conceptualization a difficult one. But in a fundamental way, "nation" has everything to do with culture, for culture and history are its sole constant referents. Claims of nationhood always imply a reference to some past and to the cultural present eventuating from that past. This reference is always a fiction, but only to the extent that all cultural constructs are somewhat fictitious. Cultural constructs always privilege some human-made relationships and features. In that sense, nation is a fiction, as are race, color categories, and descent. And indeed, the features invoked to claim nationhood are as varied as those we manipulate to justify racial distinctions, ethnic boundaries, and color or descent lines.

BETWEEN CULTURE AND POLITICS

The difference between the nation and other cultural constructs is that the nation is a construct that operates *against the background of political power.* Thus any cultural construct becomes relevant to the "national question" when it operates within the realm of politics. Peter Worsley (1984: 251) says rightly that nationality is "ethnicity institutionalized at the level of the state." But if nationality is a cultural construct backed by political power, it does not always dictate nationhood, as both Gellner (1983) and Worsley (1984) seem to suggest. Armed separatists in various places and times are living proof that the state does not always dictate the cultural referent upon which the claim of nation is based. In a more subtle way, members of the Nation of Islam, or of the Aryan Nation in the United States, have taught us that even small groups of citizens can significantly question the cultural references of the most powerful states. Further, the tolerance of cultural heterogeneity within state boundaries was the rule rather than the exception both within and outside of Europe until the eighteenth century; and it took the bourgeois revolutions for states to systematically seek cultural *qua* ethnic homogeneity, a search to a certain extent abandoned in the West after World War II (McNeil 1986; Worsley 1984: 255–75; Hobsbawm 1975: 87–105). Finally, while some observers are now discovering the correlation between cultural identity and claims on the state, those of us who work in the Caribbean have long discovered that this correlation is not a simple one (Debien 1956; Lewis 1983). Nation-building can operate within the state, against the state, or in the name of the state. The nation is not necessarily a cultural construct *backed* by political power. Rather, it is a cultural construct that offers some claim to homogeneity *in relation to* political power.

In this sense the concept of nation involves relations and processes rather than an ahistorical essence. Nation-building is a never-ending struggle; and nations are destroyed as well as made and remade, regardless of the fate of corresponding states. The equation nation = state is unjustified; the equation nation = capitalism (e.g., Gellner 1983) is Eurocentric, as Amin (1980: 20) suggests; and even the equation nation = society is sometimes shaky, although not always for the reasons Amin offers. The nation is the culture and history of a class-divided civil society, as they relate to issues of state power. It is that part of the historically derived cultural repertoire that is translated in political terms. Benedict Anderson (1983: 15) comes close to the point when he defines nations as "imagined *political* communities" (emphasis added). But again, the nation has no "content" and is no more political in nature than any other imagined community. What *is* political is the projection of this community; or, better said perhaps, the field against which this projection operates. The nation is not a political fiction; it is a fiction *in politics*.

As cultural construct, the nation is always open to contest, the potential object of contending fictions. That is not to say that it does not exist, or that "nation" as a category is less "objective" than "class"—or "state" for that matter (Wallerstein 1987). The cultural repertoire that influences behavior and is the object of national debate exists objectively even if it never exhibits the bleak homogeneity often claimed by those who control or seek to control the state. The political power against which this repertoire is projected, as a basis for support or contention, exists also in the "real" world. More fundamentally, individuals often define themselves and their actions in terms of that very translation of culture into politics which, for reasons still unexplained, always seems more powerful than the restricted language of state politics or the straight language of class struggle. More people have died in the name of nations than in the name of any state or class.

Because the practical effects of nationalism are more evident than the constructed reality of the nation, many analysts choose to define "national identity"—or, especially, "nationalism"—rather than to tackle directly the concept of nation. But by starting with the more difficult notion, we gain a deeper understanding of nationalism. Nationalism is not a feeling or a devotion. It is a political claim made on the basis of culture and history. It is a particularly vocal claim among a potentially endless list, but one that aims to create a space for political management. Since the reference upon which this claim rests, the nation itself, is always part fiction, nationalism always appears somewhat "invented." Yet since that reference is always "real," if only because it is part of the lived reality of some members of the nation, nationalism is always anchored in sociocultural reality.

Thus the increased disjuncture between state and nation in peripheral societies does not at all preclude nationalism. In fact, the very opposite is true. The legacies of the colonial past and ongoing dependence often give rise to conditions that favor claims for increased political space on the basis of history and culture. Both the disjuncture between state and nation and the intensity of those claims add to the stresses on the peripheral state.

THEORY AND ITS
APPLICATIONS

The theoretical framework for this book combines an awareness of the tensions inherent in peripheral capitalism with an "enlarged" notion of the state and with the notion of its "relative autonomy." The following propositions, as adapted to the Haitian case, provide the theoretical guidelines that underlie the narrative:

The state is not an independent variable. Its purpose cannot therefore be reduced to the intentions of its current rulers. Rather, in the final analysis the explanation for the role of the state must be sought in social relations (Touraine 1978; Miliband 1973; Poulantzas 1971; Fossaert 1981). In the case of Haiti, we will see how social relations of production—in particular, the ways in which production was organized and surplus extracted— influenced, early on, the character of the state.

The state does not however necessarily take orders from the dominant class or classes. State power is not synonymous with class domination, if only because (1) the class that dominates the political scene—the ruling class—is not necessarily the class that benefits the most from the relations of production (Poulantzas 1971); (2) the dominant class is heterogeneous, and particularly so in the third world (Thomas 1984). That heterogeneity was obvious in nineteenth-century Haiti whenever merchants aligned themselves politically according to national origin or area of activity. In part because of that heterogeneity, the import-export bourgeoisie, which benefited the most from the distribution of the peasant surplus, never became the ruling class.

Thus even though the character of the state is rooted in social relations, it is situated on an axis different from the axis of class domination (Touraine 1978: 138–40). The correspondence between these two axes varies, as does the distance between them. In Gramscian terms, civil and political society do not always align. The complexity of relations of production, the range of cross-cutting divisions (classes, ethnic groups, regional factions, color categories, etc.) in the social structure, the mechanisms of social reproduction— all the convolutions of civil society tend to increase the state's autonomy vis-à-vis class relations (Alavi 1982b; Cliffe 1982; Touraine 1978). The social weight of the bureaucracy, the extent of the state's economic role, the impact of sociocultural norms, and the competition between individual members of the propertied classes also help expand the state's autonomy (Thomas 1984: 74–79).

But the "relative autonomy" of the state, which may extend to the point of open conflict with the dominant classes, does not invalidate the basic argument that the nature of the state is rooted in social relations. Instead it suggests that certain types of social relations more than others facilitate the appearance and sustenance of states that seem to define their own logic. Thus, given the tensions mentioned above, we would expect to find that states in peripheral societies do not necessarily follow the "logic" of the dominant classes, and can even appear erratic against the background of local social relations.

Yet the dominant classes are not benumbed by the state's autonomy. Rather, there is a constant bargaining between the state and the dominant classes. The latter must pay their dues to the state in order to maintain their dominance. The state in turn must reach various compromises even while it limits the reach of representative institutions, including those that represent the dominant classes (Alavi 1982a: 303–4). In Haiti, the state's long-held monopoly as sole employer on the urban scene has reinforced its capacity to oversee representative institutions, such as the Senate, since it could always threaten their non-bourgeois members with unemployment. Yet, as we shall see, even the most vocal "anti-bourgeois" governments had to reach a *modus vivendi* with both the merchant bourgeoisie and the middle-class professionals.

To speak of a constant "bargaining" between the state and the dominant classes is not to establish an analytical equivalence between the two. Rather, the metaphor underlines the proclivity of both rulers and members of the dominant classes to link different forms of social control, to maintain some correspondence between the economic and political spheres. This inherent tendency to bargain explains, for example, why François Duvalier courted the Haitian bourgeoisie even while he moved to further curtail the merchants' political prerogatives. It also helps to explain why the bourgeoisie wholeheartedly supported the second phase of Duvalierism.

The rules that govern the constant bargaining between the state and the dominant classes may vary from one country to another, and even in the same country from one conjuncture to the next. In many peripheral societies, including Haiti, the absence of "a great right-wing party" underlines the fundamental incapacity of the local bourgeoisie to assume hegemonic leadership of the society (Cheresky 1983: 279; Kaplan 1984: 147, 279). Even at the peak of its control of the Haitian political process, the merchant bourgeoisie always operated on the political scene through proxies, in part because it never won the ideological right to govern the nation.

Weaknesses of this sort help give the state—and the middle classes, from which it usually draws its personnel—more room for ideological maneuver. Indeed, the weaker the correspondence between political and civil society, the greater the autonomy of the state in regard to social relations and the more "the rhetoric of the state" can take a direction sharply away from class struggle (Touraine 1973: 272). Thus we should not be surprised to find in many dependent countries a high-pitched political discourse, often with "nationalist" overtones. In Haiti, the weakness of the bourgeoisie, the perception of color and race, as well as the origins of the state itself reinforced the propensity to take a "nationalist" stance.

I use the word "stance" rather than "discourse" to emphasize the concrete basis of what may at times seem to be inane histrionics. To be sure, all states derive the right to dominate their people in part from global recognition within the interstate system (Giddens 1985; Amin 1980). But economic dependency does not imply that third world rulers blindly follow the dictates of their industrialized patrons. Further, the peripheral state, as the European state before, can claim to dominate a nation only to the extent that it lays claim to some "national unity" based on culture and history (Thomas 1984: 119; Hobsbawm 1975: 87–105). It cannot avoid recognizing the existence of the nation, because in so doing it would undermine its own legitimacy. Its right to exist depends on the perceived reality of national integrity and the derived need for the nation to be guided from within.

Thus even at their most servile hour, third world rulers can never completely discard the premises of nationalism, even though their practice almost always acknowledges the reality of political or economic dependence. The same ambivalence is inherent in the middle classes, which fill the state apparatus. Their alleged right to occupy leading positions stems in part from what they claim to be their mediating role within a national community. Speaking of the middle classes who fill the Latin American state apparatuses, Marcos Kaplan (1984: 131) claims that they cannot do so without displaying a "messianic posture," on which their legitimacy is in part based. We will see later how François Duvalier made ample use of a similar posture. Suffice it to say here that the mediative role of the middle classes is not just a fancy of third world politicians; nor is the "nationalist stance" just a smokescreen carefully created to deceive the masses or foreign powers.

In Haiti, the nationalist stance was reinforced by the conditions under which the state was born.[3] Haiti became independent in 1804, well before all the other American states (except the United States), after an exceptional revolution which destroyed both slavery and colonialism at the same time. Yet the Haitian state, unlike many of its Latin American counterparts, does not rest on a solid alliance between the national bourgeoisie and large landowners, if only because in Haiti both classes are quite weak. Instead, certain aspects of Haitian authoritarianism resemble that of more recent states—Ferdinand Marcos's Philippines, Eric Gairy's Grenada, Patrick John's Dominica, or Mobutu's Zaire, rather than, for instance, Stroessner's Paraguay or Somoza's Nicaragua. Yet the Haitian state dates from a period when Paraguay, Chile, and Bolivia (to give only three examples) had hardly even defined their boundaries, and when the United States was less than half its current size. The Haitian state thus combines an unusual historical depth and a fragility typical of much newer entities.

That historical depth and the legacies of a violent anticolonial revolution predisposed the Haitian state to hold even more rigidly to its nationalist posture. Nationalist ideologies have always been dominant in Haiti, nurtured first by the masses themselves, then by the large landowners, and finally, after the decline of that class, by the urban middle classes. Even during the U.S. occupation, when only the rural world resisted with armed struggle, the urban officials who accepted the control of the U.S. Marines reserved exclusive spheres of power for themselves (Corvington 1984). They could govern in part because of that exclusivity—however reduced. For if that exclusivity were to disappear, the occupier could have ruled without even the pretense of a native front. The nationalist outbursts of these officials, however rare, were not just for the benefit of their foreign audiences. Their claims to leadership involved Haitian culture and history, both of which they saw as intertwined in the lived fiction of a national community.

An anecdote will make the point. Philippe-Sudre Dartiguenave was the first Haitian president installed by the Marines, a man whose name is anathema to Haitian nationalists. Yet his private secretary, who describes Dartiguenave as a very religious man with "the faith of the simple," recalls a scene in which the president, weeping alone in front of a bust of Dessalines—the first Haitian chief of state (1804–1806) and a symbol of unyielding nationalism—started to rail against the Marines and "their National City Bank." Speaking of the nationalist hero, the most foreign-controlled of all Haitian chiefs of state said through his tears: "He alone was right" (Danache 1950: 103–4).

I do not find this scene moving. I have no sympathy for Dartiguenave and his secretary. But at the risk of being blamed for sharing their faith of the simple, I do believe in their sincerity. How I would prefer them to be lying! The lines would have been defined so clearly. But the inherent ambivalence of the ruling class matters too much in any thoughtful understanding of third world nationalism and the perpetuation of dictatorships in these regions for us to engage in a futile game of "to tell the truth." Third world rulers are always tempted to claim a close correspondence between state and nation. They maintain that claim even when the state they rule is destroying the nation, and even when their policies accentuate the dependent role of the state. They believe in that correspondence—to a certain extent. More important, may of the nationals to whom they speak are equally predisposed to believe in that correspondence.

One aim of this book is to make it clear that civil and political society were never as close in Haiti as most of the urbanites and even some of the peasants would like to think. It argues further that the disjuncture between political and civil society reached its peak under the Duvaliers. But first, in the chapters that follow, I want to uncover the roots of the ruling class's ambivalence, the contradictory duo of nationalism and dependency that lies at the very beginning of the path we must retrace.

Part 1
The Historical Legacy

1

Nationalism and Dependency: The Genesis of State and Nation

The limits of state power are first and foremost historical. Those who challenge state boundaries often phrase their arguments in historical terms, whether to demand their rights, to lend weight to their judgments, or to register their disagreements. Arguments about state power make a necessary reference to the culture-history that creates the nation, for it is in the presumed existence of the nation that the state in turn finds its claims to legitimacy.

History also plays a role in providing the context within which the state traditionally exercises its acknowledged power. That exercise is limited by the origins of the state, its position in the world system, and the nature of the productive base from which it draws its revenues. In theory, the state can do anything it wishes within its recognized boundaries, since there it has a monopoly on force. Slave societies, Nazi Germany, and South Africa are only extreme examples of the state's monopoly of violence. The limits to the exercise of state power, both internal and international, are thus dictated by the conditions of a state's existence, rather than by any abstract moral code; and these conditions are historically derived.

THE LEGACIES OF FRENCH SAINT-DOMINGUE

Haiti became independent in 1804 after the only successful slave revolution in modern history—an event to which I shall return shortly. But the exercise of state power in contemporary Haiti is constrained by enduring characteristics of the French colony of Saint-Domingue, which preceded the rise of the independent state. In 1697, the acknowledgment by the Spanish Crown of the effective occupation of the western third of the Caribbean island of Hispaniola by a few French adventurers established the first internationally recognized political division of the island: the French colony of Saint-Domingue to the west and the Spanish colony of Santo Domingo to the east. The territory of the Republic of Haiti subsequently expanded eastward, beyond the geographic limits of the former colony of Saint-Domingue, and Haitian governments then attempted by force of arms to push it even further (in 1805, 1822, 1849, and 1855). Nevertheless, the border has its origins in the 1697 division, which was confirmed internationally and which first signified two different colonies within the same island. In fact, within all the Antilles, only Hispaniola and the much smaller island of St. Maarten have inland borders.

French Saint-Domingue foreshadowed some of the limits that still constrain the Haitian state: external limits—territorial and demographic; internal limits—the balance between subsistence and commodity production and the dominance of coffee as a crop. In Haiti today, as in colonial Saint-Domingue, the bulk of the population is black, Roman Catholicism is the dominant version of Christianity, and French is the language of power.

Beyond these rather obvious legacies, three developments during the French colonial period also had a profound impact on independent Haiti: the spread of a peasant type of work organization among the slaves; the rise of an insular identity among the elites; and the spatial progression of land use, moving from the plains to the mountains. The last two developments received an unexpected boost from the sudden growth in the production of coffee during the second half of the eighteenth century: coffee was a colonial commodity whose development has shaped Haiti's history in a multitude of ways.

Indeed, the explosive growth of coffee production jolted the colonial structure so profoundly that some observers described it as a revolution. In 1763, the Peace of Paris restored sea travel between France and Saint-Domingue, sharply reduced by seven years of war. A new wave of immigrants—retired soldiers, petty nobles, craftsmen, people whose ties to the upper echelons of metropolitan French society were palpably weaker than those of the nobles and bureaucrats who had preceded them a generation earlier—came to the colony. Taking advantage of the newly created demand for coffee in Western Europe, these newcomers, along with a growing number of "colored" freedmen (free people of mixed ancestry, generally known in Saint-Domingue as *affranchis* or *gens de couleur*), rushed to the mountains—hitherto neglected by the ruling sugar plantocracy—and established small coffee estates, each with an average of twenty to thirty slaves. Coffee exports increased tremendously from the late 1760s to the late 1780s. By 1789, Saint-Domingue was producing about 60 percent of the coffee sold in the Western world and by the end of the century, it held world production records for both sugar and coffee, becoming—at least from the point of view of the French mercantilists—the most profitable colony in the world (M.-R. Trouillot 1982).

The coffee revolution irreversibly tilted the spatial base of production from the coastal plains toward the highlands, and to a lesser extent from the North to the South. It showed the possibility of profitable agriculture in the interior—an area that contained close to two-thirds of the country's arable land, and up to then an untapped resource. That independent Haiti remained primarily a coffee-exporting nation for more than 160 years is a legacy of these early days.

The coffee revolution also boosted a "spirit of autonomy" (Frostin 1975) already latent among the French slaveowners since at least the 1720s. French planters enjoyed the protection of the French state, but they resented the *exclusif* system that forced them to sell tropical commodities only to France. After the 1760s, the growing demand for coffee in the United States increased the planters' reluctance to submit to the French colonial trade monopoly and they increasingly asked for greater administrative control of local affairs.

But the planter claim to greater control of the colonial polity did not rest exclusively on economic grounds. It also reflected the crystallization, at the end of the eighteenth century, of a peculiar sense of identity, aspects of which would later manifest themselves among the Haitian elites. The immigrants who came after the Peace of Paris and invested in coffee production felt their allegiance to the French state much less intensely than had their predecessors. At the same time, an increasing number of white and mulatto estate owners, coffee and sugar planters alike, justified their pretensions to power by pointing to their knowledge of (and attachment to) the local environment and the insular society, including their enslaved labor force. Having neither the means nor, sometimes, the desire to return to France and indulge in the indolent life-style of the absentee sugar planter, the newcomers and mulattoes who invested in coffee contributed to a strong "indigenist" spirit that, by the end of the century, was even shared by some of those colonists who saw themselves as temporary residents. Their knowledge of local mores gave them, they thought, the right and the ability to manage the local polity, in contradistinction to Frenchmen who resided in the metropolis. Yet the creole (local) manners and mannerisms that some of these planters proudly displayed did not stop them from showing an equal admiration for some of the ideas, motifs, and activities that they associated (rightly or wrongly) with French culture.

The Haitian elites would later inherit many aspects of this ambiguous mélange. Products of a situation that anticipated neocolonialism in the rest of the world by a century and a half, they came to power with a sense of identity that was divided between "here" and "there." The successful revolution (1791–1804) that expelled the French at the end of 1803 imbued them with an enduring sense of national and racial dignity. Thus even the light-skinned members of these elites, who treated local blacks with contempt, associated Haiti's political independence with the universal regeneration of the black race (Nicholls 1979; Price 1900). On the one hand, to be Haitian in Haiti means to be black, and the more "black" one is, the more Haitian one can be. On the other hand—and much like the colonists—Haitian elites up to the present implicitly claim the right to prescribe limits to their local identity, modulating it according to their particular emotional and intellectual attachment to France. There is an apparent contradiction in this combination, but it is one to which, generation after generation, they have become reconciled.

A third, and equally neglected, aspect of the colonial heritage is the complex of economic and social practices associated with daily slave life. The garden plots or provision grounds in which the slaves grew their food in and around the plantations represented a striking exception to the domination of the slave by the system. As elsewhere in the Caribbean, allowing the slaves the use of such grounds conveniently released the planters from the need to provide fully for the workers they owned. But in Saint-Domingue, the uneven topography meant that a substantial proportion of the arable land that was unusable for large-scale plantation agriculture could be used by slave families for the cultivation of food. Furthermore, as the richer planters became increasingly involved in sugar, and as the coffee revolution absorbed both those whites with more limited resources and those free blacks who had hitherto engaged in foodstuff production, ever larger segments of the growing population came to depend on the agricultural and craft products of slave families (Moreau de Saint Méry [1797] 1958). In short, a peasant labor process, equally oriented toward subsistence and the market, emerged in the very heart of the plantation economy (Lepkowski 1968–69; Mintz 1979).

It is impossible to grasp the present-day realities of the Caribbean without recognizing this "reconstitution"—to use Sidney Mintz's term—of the peasantry. The history of the peasantry in Dominica, Jamaica, and Haiti can be read as a continuous struggle between those committed to this labor process and the local and international forces that tried to destroy it, circumvent it, or absorb it. What distinguishes Caribbean countries such as Haiti and Dominica from neighbors such as Cuba and Barbados is precisely the peasant's victory on the terrain of the "politics of production"—the successful establishment of a peasant labor process (M.-R. Trouillot 1988). Understanding this victory (pyrrhic though it may have turned out to be) is to lay bare the roots and consequences of the successful imposition of this peasant labor process by the slaves and, later, their free descendants.

For the slaves of Saint-Domingue, the ideological significance of these provision grounds may have been as important as their intrinsic economic worth. In a system that denied them the most fundamental rights, the cultivation of their grounds remained one of their few prerogatives. In a society in which they themselves were treated as property, the products from these grounds were foremost among the few things that they might control. Accordingly, at numerous times after the initial rebellion of 1791, rebelling slaves did not ask for an end to slavery, but merely for additional days to cultivate their plots (Dorsinville 1965; M.-R. Trouillot 1977). That the Haitian peasant has used every means to cling to a bit of family land should not, therefore, occasion surprise. Peasants of all times and places have given high priority to land; but in Haiti, the acquisition of family land and the laborers' right to the product of the labor on such land were the terms under which freedom was first formulated in the history of the nation.

NOTHING BUT FREEDOM

We can now begin to understand why the Haitian state and the Haitian nation were launched in opposite directions.

Four fundamental traits characterized colonial Saint-Domingue: slavery, dependence, commodity production for export, and the plantation regime. The society embodied internal contradictions that were ultimately irreconcilable: between slavery and freedom, dependence and independence, export commodities and foodstuffs, plantations and garden plots. Racism, segregation, and the more or less effective political isolation of those who were neither whites nor slaves cemented the system.

Until 1790, three increasingly wider circles of loyalty had reduced the tensions inherent in the system: (1) An inner circle of *grands blancs,* the most powerful whites: high officials, representatives of metropolitan trade cartels, and rich planters, often tied together by kinship and alliance; (2) a wider circle of whites that included, on the fringe of that initial center of power, the demographic weight of the *petits blancs* (artisans, overseers, owners of small farms, petty local bureaucrat); (3) a still wider circle that tied owners and middle classes across racial and color lines, reaching out to the limited number of black freedmen and the growing mass of *gens de couleur* (especially the free-born mulattoes and their light-skinned descendants) (M.-R. Trouillot 1977).

Regional variations cross-cut these three circles. Before the coffee revolution, Saint-Domingue was comprised mainly of plantation enclaves situated in and around the coastal plains. The important enclaves surrounding the three port cities of Cap Français (later Cap Haïtien), Port-au-Prince, and Les Cayes came to dominate three socio-spatial entities then (and now) referred to as the North, the West, and the South. These terms do not refer to exact geographical positions but to past administrative units and, most important, to aggregates of social, political, and cultural variation. They have passed into Haitian parlance with these connotations. Then and now, for instance, the area described as the South actually

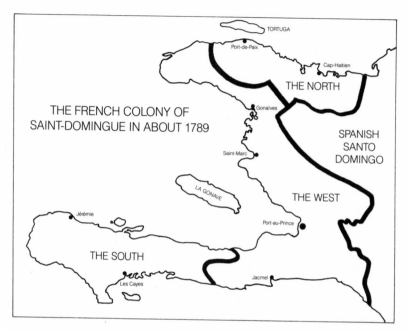

TORTUGA

Port-de-Paix

Cap-Haitien

THE NORTH

THE FRENCH COLONY OF
SAINT-DOMINGUE IN ABOUT 1789

Gonaïves

SPANISH
SANTO
DOMINGO

Saint-Marc

LA GONAVE

THE WEST

Jérémie

Port-au-Prince

THE SOUTH

Jacmel

Les Cayes

comprises the southwestern peninsula, while the North often includes the northwest peninsula. Then as now, the West was sandwiched between the other two, and so its political and social boundaries varied. More important, the South was perceived as the area where light-skinned natives had achieved demographic, economic, and political gains unmatched in the other regions, especially the North, while the North projected an image of economic and political stability. In addition, smaller enclaves surrounding less important coastal towns could be distinguished within the three broad regions.

Saint-Domingue was thus a fragmented place. The difficulty of overland communication between coastal towns and the near absence of contact between interior towns from one enclave to the next increased local particularities. The *grands blancs* tended to operate as a unified front on the local scene but only because their dominance as a group was so often challenged from below. Conflicts between large planters and the governor were nonetheless common from the 1720s on.

But regional characteristics weakened the second and third circles of loyalty. In spite of efforts among the *affranchis* to present a united front, local groups often disagreed on the means to achieve the common goal of equality. Similarly, in spite of the colony-wide prevalence of a racist ideology, local whites reacted differently to the actual integration of freedmen. *Petits blancs,* in particular, responded to colony-wide policies and trends primarily in terms of their local impact, which of course varied greatly, especially after the coffee boom and the economic rise of the *affranchis* in the late 1760s. In short, local variations always cross-cut colony-wide solidarities in the three circles mentioned, even though the metropolis (through its top political and administrative appointees, the *gouverneur* and the *intendant*) did its best to maintain both cohesion and hierarchy among the free.

But by 1789, the metropolis itself was in turmoil, and by the summer of 1791 factions within all three of these circles had begun to oppose each other, at times violently. Such open conflict resulted in turn and in part from the general breakdown of the mercantilist system, from the ongoing revolution in France, from the growing discrimination against the mulattoes, and from the increased assurance of both mulattoes and "small whites," as they succeeded economically through their involvement with coffee (Tarrade 1972; Frostin 1975; Debien 1956; M.-R. Trouillot 1982). As events in France evolved, each faction publicly echoed the proclaimed metropolitan ideal of "Liberté, Egalité, Fraternité," though with its own (privileged, and hence contested) interpretation (James 1962). *Gens de couleur,* for instance, saw in the French Revolution the justification of their claim to full political equality. While some white colonists contested the metropolitan revolution, others saw it as an opportunity to push forward their demands for more autonomy. On August 22, 1791, the slaves of the North entered the debate by burning some of the richest plantations in the northern plains.

It may never be possible to reconstruct the story of the preparations for the uprising, or to describe accurately the organization achieved in secrecy by the forerunners of the Haitian revolution (but see Fouchard 1981; Manigat 1977). The positions taken by various rebel groups on such issues as the slave provision grounds and allegiance to the French or Spanish crowns suggest that there was an initial period of uncertainty during which new leaders were born and issues reformulated. Further, it took time for the rebellion to lose its regional character. Whatever the case, within two years of the first uprising there emerged a solid revolutionary vanguard that possessed the necessary attributes of a political party: a leadership and a mass following; a non-negotiable goal; and a strategy to achieve and protect that goal. The goal was unconditional freedom for all the slaves of Saint-Domingue. The strategy was permanent military control of the colony by an army dedicated to that goal. The early leadership included slaves and freedmen alike. On August 29, 1793, under the supreme command of Toussaint Louverture, they stated that goal in the famous Declaration of Camp Turel: "I am Toussaint Louverture. . . . I want Liberty and Equality to prevail in Saint-Domingue. . . . Join us, brothers, and fight for the same cause." From 1793 to 1801, they implemented their strategy (James 1962; M.-R. Trouillot 1977; Dorsinville 1965). By 1797, after four years of struggle during which he played Spain, England, and France against each other, Toussaint had become general-in-chief of Saint-Domingue, with the reluctant approval of the French government. By 1799, he had neutralized the leading *gens de couleur* of the West and South, his final major challenge. In 1801, he conquered the neighboring Spanish colony on the eastern side of the island and proclaimed a constitution that made him governor for life.

In retrospect, it is easy to see that the major weakness of Louverture's party, and the fundamental contradiction of his regime, was the leadership's failure to face the fact that the goal of unconditional freedom was incompatible with the maintenance of the plantation system, despite the massive exodus of white planters. Up to 1802, in the name of the state, revolutionary generals brought back into cultivation many plantations abandoned by their white owners, encouraged white planters to remain on others, and imposed on a population devoted to the peasant labor process a repressive labor system that Haitian historians have baptized *caporalisme agraire* ("militarized agriculture").

To the newly liberated masses, the work regimen instituted by the revolutionary state was not so different from the slavery they thought they had left behind. Some objected by escaping to the mountains; more objected through political apathy. Not long after Napoleon's troops (led by the First Consul's own brother-in-law, General Leclerc) landed in Saint-Domingue in January 1802, Toussaint was treacherously kidnapped and exiled to France. The masses remained indifferent. Jean-Jacques Dessalines (a former slave and a Louverture follower since the early days), seconded by Henry Christophe (a free black born in Grenada) and

Alexandre Pétion (a mulatto and former member of the French invading troops), reorganized the revolutionary forces. A new goal was set: the elimination of the white presence, without which, they believed, freedom could never be guaranteed. Dessalines led the new army from victory to victory and, on January 1, 1804, proclaimed the independence of Haiti, the first—and for some long decades the only—independent nation in the American hemisphere, where the notion of Liberty applied equally to all citizens. France refused to recognize the new state until 1825; and we will explore later the consequences of this denial. But for the Haitians, liberty had finally been won.

There were major misunderstandings, however, as to what this liberty meant—misunderstandings that had started even before Louverture and his followers took over the state apparatus. The black leaders who arose in the battle against the slaveowners were in complete agreement with the masses of slaves on one point and one point alone: that slavery should be abolished. Beyond that, there were sharp differences between the majority of the population (including some of the higher ranking officers in Louverture's army) and those who gave the party its final direction, including Louverture himself. And after 1799, as more *gens de couleur* and whites came to occupy prominent positions within the Louverture administration, the gap widened.

Hence even though state and nation were taking shape at the same time and as part of the same revolutionary process, they were launched in opposite directions. State and nation were tied by the ideal of liberty, but the nation measured its liberty in Sunday markets and in the right to work on its garden plots. The Louverture party, on the other hand, embryo of the state-to-come and ferocious defender of this same liberty, was firmly attached to the plantation system. The leaders wanted export crops; the cultivators wanted land and food. The leaders wanted a country with plantations expanding on hundreds of acres; the cultivators dreamed simply of larger garden plots. And even though both groups admitted the need for cash crops, those who did the actual planting and harvesting did not wish to do so on plantations controlled by others. In that situation, "independence"—the promise of a world without the French masters— barely papered over a deep misunderstanding. The politicians and ideologues who emerged during the struggle were busy sketching the themes of a nationalist discourse while the emerging national community, pushed into the background, was beginning to shape a peasant world view of its own.

Political independence only increased the gap between leaders and producers, because while it confirmed the end of slavery, it also confirmed the existence of the state, that embodied the gap. And it did so in the most unfortunate manner, for the state itself was weak and those who controlled it divided. The most fundamental divide was between *anciens libres* and *nouveaux libres*—between those who were free before the beginning of the revolution and those who had gained their freedom during the war. For historical reasons, the former were mostly *gens de couleur*—that is, mulattoes and other phenotypes thought to be light-skinned—and their progeny; the latter mostly black. The disagreements were about politics, but also about land. Dessalines, who became the first chief of state of the independent country, ruled it despotically, first as governor for life, then as emperor (October 1804–October 1806). Many *anciens libres* (including some who, like Pétion, had backed the French counterrevolutionary forces before joining Dessalines) had taken important positions in the new state apparatus and resented the emperor's power. More important, they resented his economic policies, even though they agreed with him that the plantation system should be maintained.

By 1804, following the seizure of properties that accompanied the massacre and exodus of the French masters, the state had become the most important owner of cultivated land in the country. Dessalines wanted it to remain so. His aim—at least insofar as it can be inferred from the many laws he promulgated—was to have the state act as supreme landlord, with the generals and high officials acting as managers or lessees of government property. In contrast, most *anciens libres* wanted a plantation system based on private enterprise. Some even claimed legal rights to plantations supposedly bought or inherited from their French kin, a move sharply opposed by Dessalines and his closest followers.

Tensions grew rapidly during the first few months of Dessalines' regime, and within the leadership color soon became the favorite idiom of the rivalry between *anciens* and *nouveaux libres*. Dessalines tried to defuse the color issue: for instance, Article 14 of the Imperial Constitution of 1805 states that all Haitians were to be referred to "only by the generic word *black*" (De Pradine 1886: 49). The emperor also tried to marry off his daughter to Pétion, the most prominent figure among the mulattoes, and forbade references to skin color among members of his staff. In spite of such sincere, if somewhat naive, efforts, it was clear that a *"mulâtre* party" was taking shape among the leadership. Not all of its members were light-skinned individuals, however, and not all mulattoes sided with it. Boisrond Tonnerre, for instance, Dessalines' trusted private secretary and the probable architect of many imperial policies, was a light-skinned *ancien libre,* educated in France, who fanatically believed in the Jacobinist principle that legislation could transform the most cherished customs.

Nevertheless, most *anciens libres* were against Dessalines, and not just because many shared the color prejudice prevalent in colonial Saint-Domingue. It seems likely that the *mulâtres'* greater familiarity with Western customs and values led them to judge the manners of the former slave who was leading them as unbecoming to a chief of state. Some clearly viewed Dessalines' social policies as "uncivilized." Ironically, many such policies, including freedom of religion, equal rights for children born out of wedlock, and marriage and divorce laws favorable to women, have since become hallmarks of "civilization." But when they were formulated by Dessalines and his trusted Jacobinist legislators Juste Chanlatte and Boisrond Tonnerre, such views were anathema to those who thought they held a natural monopoly on civilized behavior. Words like "barbaric" and "barbary" come out repeatedly in the many official and unofficial judgments that the light-skinned generals passed on Dessalines' rule (e.g., De Pradine 1886: 152–69; Ardouin [1853–60] 1958, 6:71–85). Some mulattoes openly condemned him for having ordered the massacre of most of the whites still present in Haiti in the spring of 1804. Not surprisingly, growing rumors of a conspiracy against Dessalines linked the plot to the *mulâtres* (Madiou [1847] 1981: 210, 234–35).

These rumors did not deter Dessalines from pursuing his economic policies. By February 1804 he had annulled all transfers of property made after October 1802, dismissing with a stroke of the pen hundreds of mulatto claims to valuable plantations. In 1805, amidst rumors of a growing conspiracy against him, he ordered the verification of all land titles, a move that particularly hurt the *anciens libres* of the South. And in 1806, he personally went across the South to make sure that properties occupied without valid title or claim were returned to the state. Meanwhile, dissatisfaction was spreading among the masses, who resented Dessalines' version of "militarized agriculture." In October 1806, an insurrection began in the South and spread rapidly to the West, with the secret approval of Henry Christophe, who was military commander of the North. Dessalines then moved out of his headquarters in the central area of the country, hoping to crush the rebels in the South. This last act of bravado cost him his life: he was killed in a roadside ambush on October 17, 1806.

Thus less than three years after its official birth, the Haitian state was in crisis. Christophe, the most senior officer in the army, became Haiti's second chief of state, but the legitimacy of his regime was soon contested by the *mulâtres* of the West and South, who then seceded, creating a new republic under Pétion. For the next fifteen years, until their reunification in 1820, the two polities diverged sharply. Christophe had himself crowned king and created a largely dark-skinned nobility in the North. His kingdom flourished economically, mainly because he imposed his own feudal version of "militarized agriculture" with an iron hand.

The *mulâtres* who ran the republic in the West and South could not afford to take so authoritarian a stance toward the black masses without having their legitimacy questioned on the basis of color and origin.

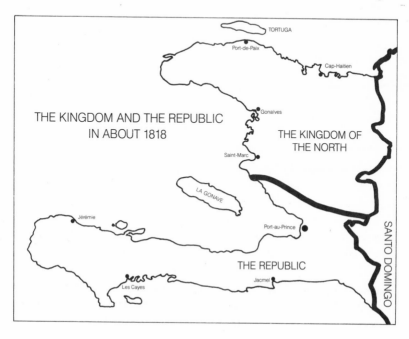

Repeated rumors of an impending French invasion to restore slavery made them uneasy. This unease was shared by Christophe, but the huge economic surpluses generated in the North made it possible for him to maintain his kingdom in a state of military readiness. In the West and South, on the other hand, the solution to the French menace and to the ceaseless threats of an attack from the North was political rather than military: the leaders tried to gain support by accommodating the masses. They surrendered land in order to win control of the state. Thus Pétion initiated a land distribution program which, although it in fact turned the best properties over to members of the elites (especially the mulattoes among them), nonetheless had a tremendous ideological impact on the peasant masses. By the time he died in 1818, Pétion had become a popular leader: the people nicknamed him "Papa bon kè" ("Father with a good heart"). Christophe, on the other hand, committed suicide two years later in the midst of a popular uprising that was provoked in large measure by his economic policies. Pétion's friend and successor, light-skinned General Jean-Pierre Boyer, reunited the two states and underwrote the political and economic preeminence of the *mulâtres*. He centralized the state apparatus, and, in early 1822, led Haitian troops in a successful invasion of the Spanish colony in the eastern part of the island, where they abolished slavery.

Boyer tried his best to revive the plantation system, undermined by Pétion's land reforms and the peasantry's reluctance to work for wages. But he too was forced to make occasional land grants to maintain his power. In any case, by 1825 the peasants, increasingly secure on the land they owned, rented, or simply squatted upon, had found new ways to avoid the plantations. Still, the regime was clearly controlled by *mulâtres,* who openly flaunted their color prejudice (Nicholls 1979: 71–73). Boyer maintained power until 1843, when he was deposed by a coup led by disgruntled southern planters. Residents of the eastern part of the island took advantage of the confusion that followed Boyer's departure, and a year later Haitian troops were forced out of the eastern part of Hispaniola, which was to become the Dominican Republic.

This brief account makes clear the degree to which the first Haitian leaders, regardless of color and origin, fundamentally agreed on two principles, even though they fought about almost everything else. First, slavery as an institution was to be forever abolished from Haiti and from anywhere else the Haitian state could reach. None of Haiti's first statesmen wavered on this issue after 1802. Second, all agreed on the need to maintain large-scale export-oriented plantations and a labor system that would produce results similar to those of the slave regime. Conflicts among them revolved around the issue of who would control the foreign-oriented economy that rested on these estates. Whenever they granted or sold land to peasants (as opposed to redistributing plantations among themselves), they did so for reasons of political expediency—as Christophe himself, a staunch proponent of large-scale agriculture, was forced to do in his last years; or to raise money in an emergency—as Boyer did to cover part of the indemnity imposed by the French in 1825 in return for their recognition of Haitian independence. The great mass of the former slaves, on the other hand, had no clear economic program. Nevertheless, illiterate though they were, they knew that the plantation system was close to slavery and they rejected it.

To be sure, in the absence of any alternative to plantation agriculture and neocolonialism, the choice facing the new leaders was not an easy one. If the peasant labor process was allowed to predominate, it could easily lead to a huge drop in already declining exports, and the new state badly needed foreign currency. At the same time, an export-oriented strategy could easily keep the country in a state of economic dependence. One suspects that Dessalines and his radical advisers were aware of all these dangers, which is perhaps why they aimed at diversification of exports and quick accumulation within the state sector. But the policies of the short-lived empire were not implemented long enough for us to guess at their potential effectiveness. Christophe's thirteen years of rule are easier to judge. He also seems to have opted for quick accumulation, based on an exploitative labor system run by the state and the landed nobility it had created. It worked: the kingdom of the North was rich by standards of the times and, just before it crumbled, the agricultural surplus was large enough to support the development of formal education, the arts, and a growing stratum of artisans (H. Trouillot 1974). Nevertheless here, as in Dessalines' empire, success was possible only through the economic exploitation of the black labor force. At the same time, the pseudo-liberalism of the West and South after 1816 augured decreasing produc-tivity and economic contraction. Indeed, in just a few years, Boyer's regime squandered more than 150 million francs in gold that his generals had found in Christophe's coffers. U.S. sociologist James Leyburn (1941: 320) quotes figures that suggest that sugar production declined from 47.6 million pounds in the first year of Dessalines' regime to 2,020 pounds under Boyer in 1825.

Haiti's early leaders thus faced a dilemma whose dimensions are clearly revealed if we put them in the context of the times. An authoritarian labor system was more likely to lead to increased productivity in the export sector and generate local accumulation of capital. On the other hand, militarized agriculture, and even milder forms of the plantation system, conflicted with the masses' vision of freedom and thus with the fundamental principle of liberty around which the nation was built. But great as it was, this dilemma was exacerbated by the Western powers' efforts to reestablish Haiti's economic dependence. If Haitian leaders showed contempt for the masses, European and U.S. leaders showed contempt for all Haitians, leaders and masses alike, and a total disdain for the independence they had so courageously won.

OSTRACISM AND PROFITS

The birth of an independent state on the ashes of a Caribbean colony was seen as a major threat by racist rulers in Western Europe and in the United States. Given the climate of the times and the general acceptance of Afro-American slavery in the white world, the Haitian revolution was equal, perhaps, to such modern-day events as the Vietnamese victory, the "loss" of "French" Algeria, or the rise of a socialist Cuba a few miles off the coast of Florida. Accordingly, the United States and most European governments imposed a diplomatic and political blockade on the new state. But profit and *raison d'état* were nevertheless reconcilable, and some merchants from Britain, France, Germany, and New England continued to trade with Haiti whenever it was in their best interests. Indeed, the international context favored the foreign traders by reducing the bargaining power of the Haitian middlemen, who were allowed no official representation in the countries they traded with (*Le Télégraphe* 1819). On the other hand, British merchants had secured a privileged position as the leading representatives of several foreign firms before France's conditional recognition in 1825. In 1807–8 no less than eighty British ships landed in Haiti, as well as numerous ships of other nations flying the British flag. Immediately after France's conditional recognition, Britain established diplomatic relations with Haiti; so did Denmark, the Netherlands, and Sweden. France finally extended full recognition in 1838. The price was heavy: the Ordinance of 1825 imposed by the French government of Charles X, with the complicity of the Haitian rulers, entailed a heavy indemnity to be paid by the Haitian people to their former masters.

The two international powers that did the most to isolate Haiti until the second half of the nineteenth century were the Vatican and the United States. In spite of repeated Haitian demands, the Vatican refused to establish an independent diocese in Haiti. The contempt of Rome cost Haiti dearly, both in terms of its internal development and in the international arena. First, it crippled the Haitians' chances of building a solid and wide-ranging system of formal education. In Catholic Europe, as in the current and former colonies of Catholic nations, religious orders have always been the backbone of the formal educational system. Starting from scratch, with a population just liberated from slavery, Haiti badly needed the help that the missionaries could have provided. Saint-Domingue never had a formal educational system, of course, and only a few of the richer mulattoes had been schooled in Europe. Both Pétion and Christophe had established primary and secondary schools in the areas they controlled, but those institutions were aimed primarily at the urban elites (*Le Télégraphe* 1821–23). By the time church schools were finally created, after the 1860 Concordat in which the Vatican formally recognized Haiti, these urban elites had already tuned the educational system so that it would serve their needs exclusively.

The absence of formal ties between Rome and Haiti reinforced the disdain of many white foreigners who saw in the Pope's reluctance to associate himself with Haiti's rulers (who, after all, claimed to be Catholic) further proof of the "savagery" of the people whom they ruled. Vatican indifference clearly hampered Haiti's political and economic integration into Latin America. Given the United States' vocal refusal to admit Haiti to the community of American states, only papal support might have encouraged the new governments of Catholic Latin America to challenge the U.S. position.

By 1822, the United States had formally recognized all the countries of the Americas that had liberated themselves from Spanish tutelage. But a succession of congressmen, senators, and presidents had vehemently argued against recognition of the Haitian state. They were successful even though relations between the revolutionary leaders and many U.S. merchants and officials had not been antagonistic. The Louverture state had traded openly with the United States, and a contingent of free blacks from Saint-Domingue (which included Henry Christophe) had fought for U.S. independence against the British at Savannah. But the United States was inclined to forget this past, both because of the virulence of its racism and the importance of slavery to its economy, and because the Haitian contribution to U.S. independence was less influential than many Haitians want to believe.

Latin America's attitude toward Haiti sprang from a different history. For one thing, its debt to Haiti was harder to deny: when a victory against Spain had seemed unattainable, Pétion had repeatedly granted aid to Bolívar, the leader of the independence movement. Hence when the United States finally agreed to preparatory talks for the 1825 hemispheric Congress of Panama, the Federation of Colombia raised the issue of Haiti's status among the American states and the desirability of its presence at the congress. The United States replied that it disapproved of Haiti's participation and that its delegates at the meeting would argue against the recognition of Haiti by *any* Latin American state. Meanwhile, congressional representatives from the U.S. South questioned the very idea of a U.S. delegation to the congress. In the end, neither Haiti nor the United States participated. Anxious to please the U.S. government, an ungrateful Bolívar refused to invite Haiti, while the sole U.S. observer conveniently arrived after the congress had adjourned, deferring most of its work for a second meeting to be held the following year in Mexico (Léger 1930: 146–52). Bolívar's dream of hemispheric cooperation was not realized until 1899, long after his death, when the congress was finally held in Washington. By then, slavery had been abolished even in the United States and Haiti was among the participants—because the all-powerful host had invited it.

In the meantime, of course, most Latin American countries had established diplomatic relations with Haiti. Nevertheless, the initial rejection by the United States and Latin America—and the fact that Bolívar did not keep his personal promise to Pétion to end slavery in the territories liberated from Spanish control—intensified Haitian feelings of frustration and isolation. More importantly, the tribulations of the aborted Congress of Panama had established an unequivocal precedent: Ibero-America's attitude toward Haiti would thereafter be shaped by that of its powerful northern neighbor.

The U.S. attitude toward Haiti may also have hardened the position of the European governments toward the black republic. In a world where diplomacy remained a side effect of military and economic might, European nonintervention in the affairs of the Americas implied—even before the Monroe Doctrine—tacit recognition of U.S. dominance over the continent. An American state whose existence was not officially sanctioned by the United States remained something less of a state in the eyes of Europe, formal diplomatic ties notwithstanding. Both abuses and pressures by European governments and foreign merchants of diverse origins, directed at Haiti and Haitians throughout the nineteenth century, must be seen in that context. So must the numerous attacks against the Haitian people in the international press of the time.

Isolation was a con game, and one in which the United States was the biggest winner. For while the U.S. government openly ostracized the new republic, U.S. merchants made substantial profits from their trade with it. Indeed, Haiti's very proximity to the United States made the latter an ideal source of foodstuffs and textiles for its citizens: by 1821, U.S. merchants were supplying nearly 45 percent of Haiti's imports; England was in second place, with 30 percent; and France was a distant third, with 21 percent. Yet if the United States sold much, it bought little. In the same year, 1821, it bought only 25 percent of Haiti's exports, and the trade imbalance between the two countries accounted for nearly 79 percent of Haiti's trade deficit. The unevenness grew with the years, as Haitians purchased more U.S. goods. By 1851 Haiti's imports from the United States surpassed in value those of Mexico, and U.S. trade with Haiti was greater in volume than U.S. commerce with most Latin American states. Yet U.S. recognition of Haiti was delayed until 1862, when the Union's need for cotton, increased by the Civil War and the movement against slavery, emphasized the desirability of formal contacts.

The establishment of formal diplomatic ties between the two countries in 1862 improved the already significant edge enjoyed by U.S. firms over those of other countries in the Haitian import market. Meat and dairy products, wheat and breadstuffs, fish, wood, soap, and tobacco led the list of commodities entering Haiti via New England. Two years after formal recognition, Haiti's 1864–1865 trade deficit with the United States was six times higher than it had been in 1861 (Georges Adam 1982: 38). In the last quarter of the century, more U.S. vessels reached Haiti than those of all the European states combined. Moreover, Norwegian, English, and Russian ships landed cargo and passengers from North America in various towns of the republic. By the early 1890s, trade with the United States accounted for nearly two-thirds of Haitian imports, measured in both value and tonnage (Vibert 1895; Bureau of American Republics 1893; Turnier 1955).

The U.S. control of the Haitian import market was possible in part because of the low price of the products the United States sold to Haiti. U.S. products, made and sold with an efficiency unknown in France and threatening to surpass that of Britain, could enter the home of the average Haitian consumer. Their initial price advantage was reinforced by the short distance between Haiti and the United States, which greatly reduced the cost of transportation.

Yet U.S. control of the Haitian import market did not afford the political influence that many parties in Washington expected. To extend this influence, the U.S. government sent a series of diplomats to Port-au-Prince to watch over U.S. interests. Republican administrations in particular sent what passed for the best of the black intellectual elite of the post-Civil War period, including Frederick Douglass and Henry Watson Furniss. But given the ambiguity of Haitian social categories and the interplay of social, economic, and phenotypic factors in determining status in Haiti (Labelle 1978; Nicholls 1979), it is likely that these intellectuals were viewed as either *grand blancs* (rich/powerful whites) or *gros souliers* (boors), or some odd combination of the two. At any rate, they were perceived as *blan* (the Haitian word for white/foreigner). If the political influence of these diplomats grew considerably from 1867 to 1915, it nevertheless did not go beyond secret deals, suspicious transactions, and support for palace coups (Padgett 1940; Gaillard 1984; Price-Mars n.d.). U.S. policymakers and diplomats, white and black, in Haiti and in Washington, underestimated the importance of cultural values in Haitian life, including those of the bourgeoisie. In Haiti, economic and political deals are sealed with personal ties, a fact best exemplified by Dessalines' desire to marry his daughter to Pétion. U.S. representatives, already turned off by the elites' predilection for Latin cultures, did not integrate themselves within Haitian society. Even the black diplomats from the United States were unable to establish long-term links with the elites—let alone the masses—or to make any mark on the country's social life.[1] In sharp contradistinction, German merchants, whose numbers grew rapidly in the second half of the century, married Haitian women and entered into the intellectual and artistic life of both Port-au-Prince and the major provincial towns. They gained, as a result—intended or not—considerable political credit, and reduced U.S. influence accordingly.

The French presence placed other limits on U.S. hegemony. While France was declining as a power in the international arena, it still bought most of Haiti's exports, particularly its coffee. In addition, French bankers financed two important loans, in 1875 and 1896. Accordingly, the French government used Haiti's dependence on French markets and French finance for political leverage. The French diplomatic corps, like the U.S. corps more recently, spared no effort in making the Haitians feel a need for their presence. Furthermore, the formidable alliance created by the representatives of France and the new Catholic clergy (composed primarily of French priests who had arrived after the signing of the Concordat) used the elites' admiration for French manners and customs, and their reverence for the French language and literature, to build their cultural influence.

Although U.S. control of day-to-day political life was sharply curtailed by the rival impress of the French and German residents, U.S. influence received a spectacular boost at the end of the century with the "Syrian invasion"—the influx of new migrants from the Levant who took on an important role as intermediaries in local trade, and later as importers. According to Joseph Justin, the first Syrians, "ill-clad and destitute, disembarked on [Haitian] beaches" in 1890 (Justin 1915: 61). In fact, in Haiti the term "Syrian" covers a variety of people from the Levant belonging to different ethnic, national, and religious groups, among whom individuals of Lebanese origin predominated. At first they were peddlars, carrying cheap goods on their heads from port to village, from one village to another, from one part of the city to another, serving both the peasantry and the poorer urban classes. Later on, using contacts in New York and Chicago, they accumulated enough credit to move into the import trade. Their ranks swelled accordingly, and by 1895 they numbered around 2,000 (Plummer 1981; Gaillard 1984: 278–79).

The demographic and commercial growth of the Levantine community soon spread panic in the ranks of its Haitian and foreign competitors. French, German, and native "Haitian" traders—born in Haiti of foreign parents, many of whom staunchly retained their foreign passports while passing for Haitians—were eager to cast the first stone at the "invaders." The press questioned their civic spirit; the populace physically attacked their stores. A succession of laws and regulations was promulgated in an attempt to put a stop to their immigration and to limit their numbers and activities. As a result, in 1905 a large number were forced to leave, taking with them an estimated $2 million in capital (Justin 1915: 62; Plummer 1981: 531).

But this exodus came too late to enable non-Levantine merchants to reduce U.S. commercial domination. The U.S. State Department and its representatives in Haiti had used both the Levantine invasion and the violent reaction it provoked to transform the immigrants into a political and economic clientele partial to U.S. commercial interests. Diplomats like William F. Powell and Henry Watson Furniss did not hesitate to put the imperial power of the United States at the service of the Levantines by supplying some with U.S. passports and others with access to U.S. sources of credit. In return, the Levantines played a role that few whites from the United States were willing to take on: with their new passports and connections, they constituted a community whose physical existence guaranteed the permanence of U.S. residents in Haiti, outside the walls of the U.S. embassy.

The short-term result of the Levantine invasion was to give added impetus to the U.S. offensive against indigenous Haitian commerce and craftsmanship. According to Plummer (1981: 532), Haitian consumption of U.S. products doubled between 1903 and 1911 thanks to the Levantine presence. Of course, the comings and goings of the Levantine peddlars and their establishment of commercial businesses on the coast only confirmed the U.S. hold on the import sector. But in doing this, the Levantines also undermined the activities of the minority of Haitian importers, already weakened by the Western European presence. Meanwhile, other Haitian, French, and German merchants focussed on export activities. After all, as noted above, the bulk of Haitian exports went to Europe.

In retrospect, then, Haiti at the turn of the century was a country poorly fitted into the world system, torn by its dual and fragmented dependence on France and the United States, both of which were, at the same time though for different reasons, unable and unwilling to integrate it fully within their spheres of influence. The first, geographically remote and itself a declining force among world powers, remained the favorite client of Haiti's exporters, the guiding light of its intellectuals, and the usurer of its treasury. Yet the proximity and the increasing military and economic strength of the second could not be ignored, despite a historical and cultural estrangement. In the interstices left by this uneasy and incomplete enfeoffment of the small nation's resources, Spain, Britain, the Holy See, and especially the Germany of Wilhelm II cut shares for themselves.

As the first testing ground of neocolonialism, Haiti experienced the somber implications of that policy for the third world very early. As a neocolony of two industrializing countries, it collected from neither the now-expected (even if meager and unsatisfactory) returns of the post-colonial order. Foreign aid was not fashionable—not even in the name of strategic interests; nor were development programs. The United Nations did not exist; nor did the World Bank, the IMF, the Organization of American States, or the British Commonwealth. Haiti's trajectory was against the current; its very existence defied the geopolitical odds. It was an agricultural exporter, yet imported primarily agricultural products—indeed, a peasant country where food topped the list of imports. It was a country born of a revolutionary war, yet one subordinated to the military powers of Europe and the United States. It was an American state, the second in the hemisphere, yet one where the doctrine of nonintervention by Europe applied only when it was convenient to the United States. At a time when European nations were extending their sway in Africa and when U.S. forces were occupying the Philippines, Cuba, and Puerto Rico, Haiti stood alone with Liberia and Ethiopia, black states in a modern international order where political independence was associated—as if in nature—with whiteness. It was a country without natural allies, an international anachronism. Despite formal acknowledgment of its independence, the menace of foreign warships continuously reminded its citizens of their impotence on the world scene. Haitian territorial waters were violated more than twenty times in the second half of the nineteenth century by warships of various foreign powers, backing with their cannons the claims of their citizens or governments—notably in 1862 (Spain), 1865 (Britain), 1868 (United States), 1871 (Germany), 1883 (France, Spain,

England, Germany, Sweden, and Norway), 1891 (United States), 1897 (Germany). No longer a colony, yet a country standing outside the international political order conceived by the West, Haiti could not fully benefit from its hard-gained independence in a world that was not ready to accept the implications of its existence.

The class relations that lie at the roots of the current Haitian crisis—and those that therefore underlay the Duvalierist state—can only be understood against this backdrop of political ostracism and commercial dependence. It is to these relations that we turn in the next chapter.

2
A Republic for the Merchants

The generals who laid the foundations of the Haitian state between 1804 and 1843 did not create the political isolation from which the country suffered or the economic dependence that limited its options. Yet within the limits imposed by the foreign powers, Haiti's leaders chose their responses, and those choices were crucial for subsequent history. They chose to establish a system that would perpetuate the country's dependence while imposing an unjust burden upon the majority of the population. A cornerstone of that system was a fiscal policy that persistently siphoned off the meager resources of the peasantry, so that this peasantry came to finance the state while having no control over it.

ON THE COFFEE TAX AND OTHER INJUSTICES

In early March 1807, General Guy-Joseph Bonnet led the self-appointed senate of the republic created by the *mulâtres* in the West and the South in approving two pieces of legislation. The first was to name Alexandre Pétion president of the republic; the second was to approve a tax package. The two major features of that package were a new emphasis on the customhouses as collection centers for all sorts of revenues, and the differential treatment accorded sugar cane and coffee, the country's major exports.

Dessalines' tax system, barely modified from that of French Saint-Domingue, had required owners of agricultural properties to contribute one-fourth of their production (called a *quart de subvention*) to the state as a "territorial levy," collected most often in kind. To this Dessalines added, in 1806, a 10 percent tax on all goods entering or leaving the country (Ardouin [1853–60] 1958, 7:11; De Pradine 1886: 9, 136). Bonnet's package eliminated the *quart de subvention* and turned the "territorial levy" into a de facto export duty on all agricultural commodities, sugar and coffee included, to be collected at the customhouses. The schedules varied, with coffee duties more than twice those imposed on equal weights of sugar. The law also introduced an "export tax" on a number of specific items. Coffee was high on that second list as well, while sugar and its derivatives were exempted (De Pradine 1886: 241–43; Ardouin [1853–60] 1958, 7: 5). In short, under various guises, Bonnet's tax package amounted to a new fiscal strategy heavily dependent upon coffee export duties. It was thus the first in a series of steps taken against the interests of the growing peasantry, and set the tone for Haiti's economic policy for the next two centuries.

Just as the less prosperous among the whites and the freedmen of Saint-Domingue had found an economic alternative in coffee, so a growing number of the postrevolutionary peasants and small landowners had turned to that crop for similar reasons. It required little start-up capital, its cultivation and processing required much less labor than did sugar cane, and it sold well on the export market. In contrast, the generals had seized the sugar plantations, which they ran as their own properties, even if—nominally at least—they were held in the name of the state (H. Trouillot 1960, 1963). Thus the new law was clearly shifting the burden of state financing from the major planters, producing sugar, to the peasants and small farmers, producing coffee. Indeed, historian Beaubrun Ardouin, a staunch defender of Pétion and an ideologue of the *mulâtre* party in the 1840s and 1850s, states flatly that the new taxes tended to "facilitate *la grande culture,*" that is, the plantation system (Ardouin [1853–60] 1958, 7: 5).

Despite this preferential treatment for plantation agriculture, the plantation system continued its decline in the South and the West during Pétion's regime, and receded in the North once Christophe was gone. Boyer's 1825 Rural Code, which tried to reestablish "militarized agriculture," was little more than a sign of the leaders' deep-seated despair at their inability to make the cultivators return to the plantations. Unable to control the masses at home and stymied in the international arena by France's refusal to recognize Haiti's independence, Boyer finally accepted

Charles X's Ordinance and the indemnity of 150 million francs that it imposed. To refill the coffers of the state, he arranged for a loan from French bankers, printed new paper currency, sold state-owned properties, and, most importantly, once again raised those export duties that hit coffee production and those import duties that fell disproportionately on the average consumer.

The pattern set at the beginning of Pétion's regime was reinforced during Boyer's lengthy tenure. From then on, successive Haitian governments were to draw the majority of their revenues from indirect taxes, most of which were collected at the customhouses. Import and export duties provided the bulk of customs revenues, supplemented by various additional fees. The relative importance of import and export taxes varied according to the commercial context—with particular governments emphasizing one or the other; within the export group, coffee taxes occupied first place. By 1810, at least 73 percent of all government revenues were collected at the customhouses, with export taxes and fees providing more than 50 percent of the national budget. In 1837, import and export duties officially accounted for over 52 percent of government revenues, with import duties making up 33 percent and export duties 19 percent—and this without taking into account various other taxes and fees on export commodities, including the "territorial levy." Figures for 1842 show that while import and export duties accounted for 62.5 percent of government revenues (36.5 percent for imports and 26 percent for exports), total customs duties amounted to at least 92 percent. "Territorial" levies provided 30 percent of this, making export taxes account for 66 percent. By 1881, import and export duties accounted for 98.2 percent of state income. By 1887, the *entire* government budget depended on customs duties, and by 1909, more than 95 percent of government revenues came from multiple taxes collected at the various ports on a single crop, coffee (Benoit 1954; Ardouin [1853–60] 1958, 7: 66, 93; H. Trouillot 1963: 75; Un Patriote Haïtien 1887: 5; Justin 1915: 50). The state was spending, but it was the peasant who was footing the bill.

Most peasants were not even aware of the size of that bill. As Ardouin—who fully supported the system—suggests, the peasants were unwitting taxpayers. Ardouin writes that export duties were collected "without the taxpayer ever suspecting it; no one directly asked them for anything while [the tax on] their products had been paid through commerce, by the middlemen or the merchants, by way of the sums that the exporters were obliged to turn in to the Treasury for the 'territorial tax' and the 'export duties' proper" (Ardouin [1853–60] 1958, 10: 13).

The trick of indirect taxation, as opposed to direct deductions from income, is that its injustice is built into the system and hence is not easily visible; thus it rarely occasions the interminable debates to which income taxes, for instance, give rise. By definition, indirect taxation ensures that citizens do not contribute to the upkeep of the state according to their means (Eaton 1966: 214). If the state takes an equal amount of money from each citizen, and all citizens do not have equal incomes, then the state takes a disproportionate share of the income of the impoverished masses. The greater the variation in incomes, the greater the injustice. Indirect taxation also creates opportunities for the tax to be shifted to someone other than the individual from whom the state collects it. Most countries impose some form of indirect taxation, but in the Haitian case indirect taxation, and particularly the various fees and duties collected at the customhouses, have been the principal source of government revenues since Pétion's regime. Whenever the state increased the fees and duties on coffee, the exporters (who paid them) passed the charges on to the *spéculateurs* (licensed middlemen, who are limited in number), who in turn imposed them on the peasants by reducing the price paid them for their produce. Competition among exporters could have given the peasants some bargaining power and eased their burden by forcing the exporters to absorb some of the taxes. But the exporters acted as a clique, and their small numbers, as well as their political connections, gave them a virtual oligopsony with rich opportunities for price fixing. The bulk of the 304 million gourdes that constituted government revenues for the year 1842 came from only fifteen import-export firms, four of which paid more than a quarter of those revenues (H. Trouillot 1963: 75–77). In short, the peasants had little bargaining power in the export market.

Injustices also occurred in the case of imports, in part because during the first half of the nineteenth century a very small number of firms, sometimes the same ones that dominated the export chain, controlled the import market. Further, the luxuries imported for the urbanites were taxed on the basis of customs schedules that discriminated in their favor. For example, at the turn of the century the import duty on a pair of opera glasses was the same as that on five gallons of kerosene; the duty on a copper bathtub was the same as that on a barrel of wheat (Bureau of American Republics 1893).

The injustice was so obvious that many of Haiti's liberal intellectuals were denouncing it long before the arrival of the present wave of international experts from the World Bank, the IMF, and the United Nations, all of which are now pressing the Haitian government to institute a fairer tax policy. In 1843, some of the politicians who took part in the coup against Boyer promised, in their liberal manifesto, to redress the inequalities of the tax system. Not only was their reign a short one, but it was soon apparent that neither they nor the governments that succeeded them really wanted to modify the system. The tax issue was dead until the 1870s. Then, liberal economist Edmond Paul (1876) wrote a book entitled *De l'impôt sur le café* ("On the coffee tax") in which he denounced the unfair burden that these taxes imposed on the peasantry. In 1902, Hérard Roy, summarizing previous critics, voiced similar allegations:

> Our ill-founded tax laws weigh heavily on the most numerous classes of the population, whose productive faculties are paralyzed and whose means of subsistence are limited as a result. . . . On the other hand, import duties, though applying to everyone, fall inequitably on different consumer goods, further burdening the neediest classes because they are too high on essential commodities. (Roy 1902: 44–45)

A former customs director and secretary of state for finance and commerce, Roy knew well whom the state lived off:

> Only those who sit in their offices and feel none of the suffering of the people, who pay no taxes on the lovely clothes they order from the best Parisian clothiers, or on what they eat and drink every day, only they say that it is possible to increase the taxes on basic consumer goods. They do not know that the customs duty on a frock-coat is seven piasters, while that on a barrel of wheat is four and one-half, or that the duties on everything else that the poor consume are equally high. (Ibid.: 22)

Thirteen years later, Joseph Justin, whose passion for the West and free trade had not stilled his reason, went further: "It must be said in all sincerity that in Haiti, the most productive, the most useful class is surely the peasantry. After all, is it not this class alone that pays taxes? Is it not they who bear all the nation's costs?" (Justin 1915: 24).

But these were the voices of a few liberals, and signified little, especially since those liberals themselves took little action to redress the injustice when they ran the affairs of the state. The fact of the matter was that the state had chosen to live at the expense of the nation—and in this choice lay the seeds of future divisions.

THE DANAIDES BARREL

The funds collected by the state did not stay long in the Treasury, which resembled the bottomless barrel that, in ancient Greek mythology, the daughters of the King of Argos were forever doomed to refill. The Haitian state did not accumulate its revenues, and the money taken from the peasants was not transformed into capital. Such a process of accumulation might have been beneficial to the nation, at least for a time, if it had helped to launch infrastructural projects or to promote health and education.

But the chance for capitalist accumulation within the state sector died with the murder of Dessalines. The emperor's projects—unknown to the masses, treated with contempt by historians, and rejected by the dominant coalition of soldier-landowners linked to the foreign merchants—were never realized. Christophe taxed the northern nobility heavily, but the capital accumulated from those taxes and from the surplus exacted by force from the peasantry was squandered by the light-skinned generals who finalized the terms of economic exchange between the state and the nation under the presidencies of Pétion and Boyer. These men had to make concessions to keep themselves in power. They granted land to a suspicious peasantry, but then heavily taxed its products. They granted monopolies to foreign traders and limited the bargaining power of Haitian middlemen. They redistributed the peasant surplus among their cronies, and they provided luxuries to their families and friends. In short, they opted for wasteful expenditures and increased dependence. The merchants were the prime beneficiaries of these choices.

Between 1807 and 1843 the political leadership established a relationship with the merchants that was to outlast the individuals who forged it. The rulers patronized the merchants in many ways. First, they bought from them, in the name of the state, the imports used by a rapidly growing civilian and military apparatus. Many government officials also bought in bulk from the importers for resale on the local market, establishing retail stores managed by their wives. Finally, following a practice common at least since Dessalines, political and military leaders bought for themselves, with state money, the luxuries they thought they deserved. And the traders who benefited the most from the leaders' reckless spending were the consignment merchants, the majority of whom were foreigners.

In the first decades of the nineteenth century, foreigners were forbidden to engage in retail activities, but they could act as consignment merchants or wholesalers. In principle, the consignment system, barely modified from the trade practices of Saint-Domingue, allowed the captain of an incoming boat to consign his load to a licensed wholesaler who would in turn sell the goods to the state warehouse or to local retailers and collect a commission. Ideally, competition limited the power of any one consignment merchant, first by allowing captains to choose freely the wholesalers to whom they delivered their goods, and second by allowing the managers of the state warehouse and private retailers to bargain over prices. Further, consignment merchants, like the major exporters, were generally allowed to establish offices only near the wharfs of a few designated port cities: hence the name "Bord de Mer"—seashore—which came to designate the merchant bourgeoisie. Thus in principle this three-layered system favored open competition.

In fact, despite all these regulations, the system was plagued by graft, corruption, and secret transactions, with captains and wholesalers often serving as fronts for the same European or U.S. firms. Further, many consignment merchants found it convenient to enter into partnerships with Haitian politicians. Other importers simply used local politicians as fronts. The merchant sector was dominated by foreigners, since Haiti had no ships of its own, and few natives had the capital and contacts necessary to set up a wholesale firm. The legally sanctioned division between *haut commerce* ("high commerce")—that is, import- and export-oriented wholesale activities—and *petit commerce* ("little commerce")—that is, the retail distribution of imported and local goods—paralleled differences in the national origins of the individuals who engaged in the various trading activities. Dessalines had tried in vain to curb the power of the foreign merchants. First, only Haitian or U.S. firms could obtain a consignment license and incoming vessels had to be assigned to all licensees in turn. Second, extensive regulations made it difficult for merchants to carry away currency; instead, they were forced to take, in return, a diversified load of local goods, mainly cotton, sugar, and coffee (De Pradine 1886: 116, 126–33). These policies were loathed by merchants and lasted barely a few months. They were dismantled by Pétion, who bowed to the foreign merchants' demand for "freer" commerce (Ardouin [1853–60] 1958, 7: 13, 66, 89; De Pradine 1886: 337–49).[1]

Consignment merchants furnished the bulk of the foreign goods used by the civil establishment and, most important, supplied the growing army. Nineteenth-century budgets show army supplies and salaries absorbing a large part of the government's resources. To be sure, an adequate defense force was necessary in the aftermath of independence, especially with constant rumors of a French invasion. But since the days of Louverture, military rank had functioned as a mechanism for socioeconomic advancement, and after 1825, with the French threat receding, the army became a fustian network of political sinecures, utterly useless for the protection of the country when it was menaced by the very same individuals who furnished its uniforms.

The Bord de Mer also provided the luxuries with which the political *nouveaux riches* festooned themselves. Dessalines spent state money not only on himself but also on his numerous mistresses, one of whom reportedly sent her bills directly to the treasurer of the southern province. Half a century later, Maxime Raybaud, the French consul in Haiti, reported that in 1847 President Soulouque (1847–59) had ordered, from Paris, "a green coat that cost no less than 39,000 francs, just equal to current government spending on education" (d'Alaux 1856: 222). Writing under a pseudonym, the diplomat was making fun of Soulouque, a curious character who compensated for his plebeian manners with ostentatious luxuries and earned the scorn of Westernized Haitians and foreigners alike—especially after he crowned himself emperor in 1849 under the name of Faustin I. Daumier made him the target of one of his cartoons, while Marx derisively used him to ridicule Louis Bonaparte. Hence Raybaud's contempt was no exception. But what the French diplomat conveniently ignored were the enormous profits made by French merchants, in Haiti and in Paris, on those luxurious and useless imports. Indeed, from Soulouque's green coat to the luxury cars of Duvalier's cronies, the Bord de Mer shamelessly pocketed its commissions on eccentricity. The merchants' prices reflected both the monopoly they enjoyed and their knowledge of fiscal and administrative corruption. Corrupt bureaucrats rarely objected to the high prices of goods sold to the government. Similarly, even though luxuries were most often bought by private individuals, the merchants were well aware that those individuals were using government money and they raised their prices accordingly. They sold to citizens, but it was the state that paid the bill, directly or through intermediaries.

Throughout the nineteenth century, the international context favored the foreign merchants in the race for the Treasury's riches. In addition to their easier access to foreign credit and markets, the foreigners enjoyed the protection of their consulates in Haiti. Better still, they themselves often became consuls. Thus, the repeated violations of the country's territorial waters by foreign warships always received their approval—when not done expressly at their request.

The tradition of foreign nationals calling on their government's forces to settle disputes dates from the Boyer regime. It was in July 1823 that some British businessmen, charged with counterfeiting by a conscientious justice of the peace, appealed for aid to Sir Edward Owen, commander of the Royal Navy in the West Indies. Owen declined to make a show of force in Haitian waters—perhaps for fear of provoking a scandal, perhaps because the Haitian army was still a force to be reckoned with; but he nevertheless conveyed his concerns to Boyer in His Majesty's name. The case then faded away. Less than ten years later a British businessman, John Hearne, one of those implicated in the case and a friend of both Pétion and Boyer, was appointed consul to the King of Sweden and Norway.

The moral of the story is clear: the foreign trader has always operated in Haiti with the assurance that he can call in a foreign power if necessary. When the protection of one power has appeared doubtful or insufficient, he has not hesitated to seek the aid of another. This was true in 1823; it remained true in 1903, when the Levantine merchants threatened to use the military power of France and the United States to settle their disputes with the government. And it was true throughout the intervening period. Some merchants rejoiced at Haiti's many insurrections because they gave them numerous opportunities to claim exorbitant damages from the state. Others committed arson, burning their own stores and then claiming indemnities, and they were usually backed by their consulates. The French diplomat Maxime Raybaud wrote that at least seven of the British and

German merchants involved in political intrigues under Soulouque's regime were supplied with protective consulships (d'Alaux 1856: 97). And Raybaud, who reported these facts under cover of a pseudonym that allowed him to denigrate the Haitian state and people, did not hesitate to menace the government with *his* country's naval might (d'Alaux 1856: 124–28). He even went so far as to threaten Soulouque with an indemnity if *Haitian* stores in which there was French merchandise were touched by thugs allegedly working on behalf of the government. The history of trade in Haiti has thus been marked by the constant use of force by the agents of dependence. With their metropolitan relations, they were able to put the state in a vise: profit on one side, the cannon on the other. Moreover, their contempt for Haiti let them do it with a clean conscience. Profit and contempt went hand in hand.[2]

Profits did not come solely from "honest" trade or from fraudulently gained indemnities. At times the merchants became usurers and speculators. The French, for instance, drew the largest share of the commissions for handling foreign loans to the state. And when the state, impoverished by corruption, had trouble paying its bills, the merchants did not hesitate to advance their own funds, also on usurious terms. Minutes of a senate meeting on October 2, 1808, describe how foreign and Haitian merchants were invited to the senate house in Port-au-Prince to listen to a plea for contributions to the military campaign against Christophe. One of the guests, a Haitian merchant, offered an alternative suggestion: the government should increase taxes rather than suggest "voluntary" contributions. British merchant Robert Sutherland, speaking in the name of the foreign merchants, offered a third proposal: the merchants would lend money to the government. It was Sutherland's suggestion that was adopted (De Pradine 1886: 501–2; Ardouin [1853–60] 1958, 7:47). From then on, merchants repeatedly lent money to the state, receiving huge interest payments in return. In 1882, for instance, the trading house of H. Etienne and Co. turned a profit of 7,190 piasters on a loan of 12,000 piasters, an enormous gain made virtually overnight.

But the Haitian merchant's suggestion of 1808 was not forgotten. As the state turned increasingly to borrowing from merchants and foreign governments in order to pay its on-going expenses, it used export taxes extracted from the peasantry to pay off its debt. The text of the agreement accompanying one of the earliest of such loans (in 1827) shows how explicitly the link was made: "For the next thirty years, all the revenue of the Republic of Haiti, that is, all the duties, taxes, and contributions that have been or may be established, will be used to ensure the payment of the interest and the reimbursement of the principal of the present loan." Each subsequent domestic or foreign loan led to increased customs duties, reducing the peasants' income from export crops while raising the cost of the imports on which they depended. Government dependence grew accordingly; so did the arrogance of the foreign merchants. According to one committee of inquiry, "in 1892, all the funds generated by the export duties on coffee, cacao, and logwood were committed to ensure the service of the loans whose origin had been the immoderate expenditures of the administration" (Bruno et al. 1909: 19).

By December 1899, when the government begged once more for money from the richest merchants, one of them was bold enough to suggest that the customhouses be put under the supervision of a "Council of Creditors," so that the merchants could deduct what was due them at the source. Others, a touch more conciliatory, simply suggested that their embassies participate in running Customs (Roy 1902: 38–39). Bridling at these suggestions, the state's representative clung to a traditional nationalistic rhetoric, and the merchants abandoned their proposals. But a month later, an accord providing for a 300,000-gourde loan from *haut commerce* to the government barred the state from touching, "for any reason whatsoever," the revenues provided by an increase in the duty on coffee, which was to go directly toward repayment of the loan (ibid.: 41–48). In short, throughout the nineteenth century, Haitian politicians turned the state Treasury over to foreign merchants and condemned the peasants to refill, day and night, the bottomless barrel of the Danaïdes.

POWER AND PROFIT

Personal antipathies notwithstanding, nineteenth-century Haiti was dominated by an alliance of politicians and merchants in which the latter played the leading role. Whether or not the foreign merchants could enter the national palace, they dictated economic policy, inasmuch as the state complied with their most important demands. To be sure, such demands were often formulated in personal terms, particularly in the period from 1807 to 1843, when many of the merchants' ties to Pétion and Boyer enhanced their visibility. Pétion was barely in power before he invited his friend Jacob Lewis, a New York-based merchant who had left Haiti after a dispute with Dessalines, to return. Lewis did so, and immediately requested money that he felt the state owed him for supplies captured by Dessalines. Pétion then issued a presidential decree ordering that all export crops from the plantations of Dessalines' widow be turned over to Lewis (Madiou [1847] 1985: 233; De Pradine 1886: 362–64). John Hearne, counterfeiter and consul, was one of the most powerful men in Boyer's republic. Rich merchant families—the Sutherlands, Prices, Bernards, Brouards, and Milroys—had the ear of the presidential palace during both Pétion's and Boyer's regimes. Soon after Pétion's death, his mistress Magdelaine Lachenais (who immediately became Boyer's official mistress) invited foreign merchants to a requiem mass to offer "further proof of your friendship to the family of the deceased." Boyer sent a personal note requesting the presence at the funeral of several members of the largest merchant establishments. Visitors to Haiti did not fail to note the existence of a second power alongside that of the state. Just as British visitor John Candler (1842: 82) described Hearne as one of the "barons" of Port-au-Prince, so Frenchman Eugène Aubin, disembarking at the provincial port of Saint-Marc sixty-six years later, called the consignment merchants the "lords of the town" (Aubin 1910: 262).

But the power that these lords exerted did not depend upon their personal ties to the political elites. Rulers could change, enmities could replace friendships, but the corporate position of the richer merchants remained untouched. Indeed, during the reigns of Soulouque (1847–59) and Salomon (1879–88) and into the 1890s, relations between the leaders of *haut commerce* and the rulers of the day lost the intimacy of the earlier part of the century and at times became openly antagonistic. That did not prevent the merchants from imposing their wishes; it only increased the number of military threats.

Similarly, the merchants were not particularly disturbed by the national-ist discourse of the political elites—such talk was a principal entertain-ment of the urban intelligentsia. Boyer's acceptance of Charles X's Ordi-nance—presented to the people under a cloak of victorious rhetoric—had revealed the extent to which the rulers' nationalist stance could accommodate major concessions to foreign powers. Moreover, resident foreigners were in a good position to see the fundamental division that pitted the peasant masses against the educated urbanites. A few foreigners may have taken the elites' nationalism and the threats that sometimes accompanied it seriously, but most knew that such gestures also served to conceal a familiar alliance in which they played the leading role.

All of which is to say, then, that the bonds between the political oligarchy and the merchants are best seen in structural terms. The alliance was grounded in the relations of production—property relations, labor relations, and relations of distribution—that characterized Haitian society; in the mechanisms through which the state extracted surplus from the peasantry; and in the ways in which that surplus was redistributed. From a structural viewpoint, the state functioned as an economic agent (extracting and redistributing the surplus) for the benefit of the local agents of dependence. These agents in turn exported most of the surplus, together with the local goods. As a result, capital accumulation by either the state or the strata that furnished its personnel (army officers, landowners, and professionals) was well nigh impossible. Social mobility outside the state structure remained marginal, and the state was permanently weakened by its inability to unite political and civil society. Finally, because of that fundamental weakness, the governments that succeeded each other and were expressions of that state were necessarily authoritarian, for they had to use repression to check the civil society that they were unable to control through persuasion. But their inherently undemocratic ways of maintaining power left them open to coups, insurrections, and rebellions.

If this sounds utterly bizarre, it is because it *was* indeed a strange compromise. The commercial bourgeoisie, although it included some Haitian citizens, was fundamentally opposed to the consolidation of the state, uninterested in the fate of the nation, and the Haitian leaders knew that. The Haitian leaders also knew that the foreign powers did not respect Haiti's revolutionary past, and certainly did not care to contribute to a political independence of the sort that the local leaders themselves cherished. Their nationalist stance was not a mere facade: they believed in independence. But if the cost of maintaining power and continuing to enjoy the spoils of the state was the plunder of the nation, they were quite willing to sacrifice the nation. The alliance thus rested as much on the permanence of the needs of the state as on the frailty of the regime in which it was temporarily incarnated. Merchants fed on the political, financial, and military instability of the state, and had an objective interest in the rate of political succession, since every regime offered them a new and greedier clique of customers. Keenly aware of the profits to be made from political turnover, the Germans, for instance, became experts at financing "revolutions."

The alliance was thus unbalanced, unequal in principle; but it became increasingly unsteady under the growing weight of the parasites that surrounded it. First among these were the landlords, whose early decline as a dominant class had paralleled the emergence of the alliance.

THE DEFEAT OF THE LANDLORDS

Historically, the alliance was created by generals who owned or controlled plantations, in their own names or on behalf of the state. Haiti's first ministers, senators, and presidents—all of whom were high-ranking officers—were by and large disillusioned landlords who turned to the state and transformed it into a machine to drain off at the customhouses the surplus that they could not extract from the peasantry on the plantations. However, that choice, which prompted the rise and consolidation of the alliance between merchants and landlords, was a partial admission on the part of the landlords of the defeat of their original project, the reestablishment of the plantation system.

There were a number of reasons for this defeat. Haitian historians like to point to the most visible one: the war of independence. The cane fires of 1791 and the devastation that followed the encounters between the revolutionary army and the French expeditionary troops sorely damaged plantation properties. But while there is as yet no detailed economic analysis of the twelve years of combat, the widespread belief that the plantations were totally destroyed is a later exaggeration. We know that some plantations continued to function profitably under Toussaint, under Dessalines, and in the kingdom of the North. The physical damage was real, but there were no technical barriers to reconstruction. Furthermore, the biggest drop in production was recorded several years after independence, not immediately following it (Franklin [1828] 1971: 325–30).

Lack of capital was a more serious problem. Haitians had little access to cash or credit, and fear of French infiltration led to property laws that severely limited foreign investment: the Imperial Constitution of 1805 forbade "any white, of whatever nationality" from owning land in Haiti (De Pradine 1886: 49). Moreover, it is doubtful that foreigners would have invested in plantations even without such laws: the international context discouraged them from risking fixed capital in Haiti, and commerce offered a quicker and surer return.

Finally, and most important, the peasantry had made up its mind: it clung to its control of the labor process and refused to be regimented by the landlords. The former slaves, remembering their pre-1791 garden plots, associated liberty with the possession of land. Toussaint, Dessalines, and Christophe faced massive resistance when they tried to institute their respective versions of "militarized agriculture." And resistance was not limited to cultivators: Toussaint's program was secured only after the execution of his adopted nephew, Moïse Louverture, one of his most trusted officers who had nevertheless sided with the cultivators and encouraged their refusal to work on the plantations. A few years later, General François Capois, the hero of the final battles against the French, was killed by Christophe in part for refusing to enforce the despotic agricultural regulations promulgated in the North. Yet Toussaint, Dessalines, and Christophe were able to succeed for a time with their repressive policies thanks to their national prestige as military heroes and to their dark skins, which offered them some protection from the anger of the masses.

In contrast, until the official recognition of Haiti's independence by France, Pétion and Boyer could not afford to alienate the black masses, whom they would need if it became necessary to defend the country. Pétion thus had cause to trumpet his "agrarian reform," even if it only confirmed some of the rights that the peasants had already acquired, while carefully reserving the best land for the president and his closest *mulâtre* supporters. Beaubrun Ardouin, who as a planter had wept over Pétion's agrarian reform, nonetheless admitted that it "saved the country." After Christophe's suicide, the generals contemplated the possibility of once more using force to send the cultivators back to the plantations, but the nightmare of French warships suddenly appearing in the harbor precluded the full implementation of such a drastic policy. It is no coincidence that

Boyer published his Rural Code after negotiations with Charles X's representatives had finally ensured that the French invasion would not happen.

Nevertheless, as noted earlier, the Rural Code was in fact a measure of desperation. By 1825 the die was cast, and none of the landowning generals truly believed that they could reestablish the large plantations—even though they tried to do so with all the force they could muster. James Franklin, who visited Haiti in the 1820s, claimed to have seen Haitians working at bayonet-point on the plantations of Generals Inginac, Leurebours, Gédéon, and Magny (Franklin [1828] 1971: 334). Yet even Franklin, who had been present at the Code's proclamation in 1826, doubted that it could be enforced. There were limits to the language of the bayonet unless it was supplemented by the restoration of slavery, which was unthinkable. The sense of a national community born during the struggle against slavery protected the masses from the excesses of militarized agriculture. Further, the peasantry, conscious of its new-found liberty and stubbornly holding onto its rights, was not responsive to the lure of money. When it had to choose between a higher income and direct control of the labor process, it chose control. Those landlords who offered a monetary bonus in addition to the cultivators' legally required share of the product saw their proposition stubbornly rejected (Franklin [1828] 1971: 333). Even on Plantation Thor, which Boyer had inherited from Pétion (along with his office and his mistress), only 2 percent of the 2,000 acres were planted in sugar in 1827 (Franklin [1828] 1971: 349). And if the president himself could not manage to secure enough labor, what could be said about most of his subordinates? Here is Senator Beaubrun Ardouin:

> I am also the owner of a coffee plantation, and I have been able to see what is happening on my plantation and all around me. I know how many cultivators lived there twenty, fifteen, and ten years ago. I have seen their numbers shrink . every day, and my income decline each year. Where are they, these farmers who produced the thousands of pounds of coffee that I delivered to the merchants? On new properties they have founded for themselves and their families. Could I have stopped them? (Ardouin n.d.)

Ardouin was not exaggerating: there was nothing he could have done. Candler visited Ardouin's estate and noted how in a brief period it had lost twenty cultivators. Candler added:

The few remaining labourers on Fourcy not only take their half of the 10,000 lbs. of coffee which the plantation yields, but appropriate to themselves almost the whole of the provisions which the land furnishes, sending down only a few of the rarer vegetables, beans, peas, and artichokes, to their master, for his table at Port-au-Prince, and supplying his need when he comes to reside for a few days in the country. This he knows very well, but has no alternative, but to bear it quietly. (Candler 1842: 144)

Of course, the defeat of the landlords was not total. But the sudden growth of small-scale landholdings, the establishment of *de moitié* ("half and half") sharecropping as a result of cultivator pressure, and the landlords' absenteeism meant that ground rent inevitably lost first place as a mode of extraction of peasant surplus. Ardouin, never at a loss for words, summed up the situation in a few: "The subdivision of property has displaced welfare" (Ardouin n.d.). As a result, the Haitian elites had to look to other sources for their income.

POWER TO THE LANDLORDS

Confronted by the peasants' refusal to furnish surplus through ground rent, many of the light-skinned landlords chose to tie themselves to the foreign merchants. Some served as fronts in the retail trade. Some set up service, transport, and insurance firms tied to *haut commerce*. Others used foreign help to establish their own wholesale firms. General Bonnet, for example, the architect of the 1807 tax package, was one of the first to see the way the wind was blowing, but he was not the only one to consolidate his commercial ties. However, the paths to commerce were both more attractive and more accessible to the elite group of light-skinned officers associated with the ruling *mulâtres* than to their darker counterparts: they spoke fluent French and they had been educated in Europe or had better knowledge of Western customs and practices. And we should not dismiss the possibility that the white merchants had established a hierarchy in their racism, favoring lighter Haitians. We know the diplomats did so (e.g., St. John 1889).

Despite the visibility of the *mulâtres,* the majority of the generals who owned large holdings were dark-skinned officers who had moved up through the ranks under Toussaint, Dessalines, or Christophe, and few of these made the transition to *haut commerce*. As the plantations declined under Pétion and Boyer, and as profits from politics became surer than ground rent, many threw themselves into the pursuit of power. Curiously perhaps, the transition of many black landlords from plantation to politics was facilitated by some of the *mulâtre* leaders who had been entrenched in the senate since the days of Pétion. From 1844 to 1849, these leaders, among whom were the ever present Beaubrun Ardouin and his brothers, connived to install a series of dark-skinned presidents—Philippe Guerrier (1844–45), Jean-Louis Pierrot (1845–46), Jean-Baptiste Riché (1846–47)—in order safely to consolidate their own power. With their ties to commerce and what remained of their properties, these *mulâtres* easily manipulated their dark-skinned puppets. Haitian historians have labelled this strategy *politique de doublure* ("government by understudies") and have noted that it turned against its architects when Soulouque, hand-picked by Beaubrun Ardouin in 1847 because he looked like an idiot, arrested, killed, or exiled the very individuals who had put him in power. Yet even after 1847 and until 1915, most Haitian presidents were dark-skinned and most came from the continuously disintegrating landlord class. As time passed landlords became rulers—and often nothing but rulers.

The two categories did not merge completely, however, for several reasons. First, some landlords continued to draw part of their income from the ownership or control of land. Few generals or politicians voluntarily abandoned agriculture in the early nineteenth century, and even those who sold some land to the peasants tried to retain control of the best properties. Others refused to sell at all, either because land ownership brought them prestige, or because they held properties in areas where the labor market was more favorable, or because they had enough political clout to coerce the labor force. Some of these properties were worked without interruption until the beginning of this century (Candler 1842; Aubin 1910). As late as 1938, Armand Viré, an expert water diviner who visited the countryside at the request of several local planters, noted the existence of "properties of several hundreds or several thousands of hectares," some producing only one commodity (Viré 1942: 139).

Landlords can thus be distinguished analytically from the agents of the state apparatus by their ability to extract additional surplus from the peasantry through various forms of sharecropping. One of the greatest gaps in Haitian social research is the lack of figures documenting the extent of such practices and the amount of land involved. The groundwork for such research was laid some twenty years ago by Haitian economist Gérald Brisson, who was later killed by the minions of Papa Doc. Brisson, a Communist, showed how "bourgeois statistics" had been manipulated and suggested that the concentration of landowning has been much greater than official figures indicate.

Brisson's revision of "bourgeois statistics," however, misses its target. What is required to correct the prevalent belief that Haiti is a country of idle yeomen whose indolence and backwardness have led them into poverty is an analysis of production relations that shows what happens to the surplus. The precise measurement of this surplus requires direct observation: good old-fashioned fieldwork of the kind made familiar by anthropology, rural sociology, or agricultural economics. To be sure, Brisson's demonstration that landlords and state together held title to six times more land than the hundreds of thousands of small-scale peasant proprietors, who controlled 69 percent of all agricultural units, is useful. But he also conceded that only about 7 percent of the land on the large estates was being exploited (Brisson 1968: 18)—which would suggest that the amount of surplus drawn from them was relatively low. Moreover, field research by Madian-Salagnac's team has shown a dual process of parcellization and recombination (*Recherches Haïtiennes* 1980), which suggests that a real critique of "bourgeois statistics" requires a diachronic, historical dimension.

Finally, systematic fieldwork also suggests that the landlords' access to the peasants' surplus is further reduced by the intricacies of the labor process and local perceptions of rights and obligations, in ways not directly related to the amount of land that each peasant legally owns (Murray 1977; Woodson n.d.). Peasant control of this process makes it hard for most landlords to collect the half share of the crops harvested from their land that is supposedly their due (Woodson n.d.). As early as the nineteenth century, direct observation showed that the peasants had devised ways of producing and distributing that circumvented the official rules on sharecropping (Franklin [1828] 1971; Mackenzie 1830; Candler 1842; St. John 1889).

This does not prove that ground rent has completely disappeared. We still see this form of surplus circulating on the urban scene when the most prosperous landlords transmit part of it—just how much is unclear—to the merchant class. Indeed, it is because of this surplus that it is analytically useful to separate landlords from rulers. Moreover, those landlords who were associated more with agricultural production than with politics— and some were (Vibert 1895)—reacted differently to decreases or inter- ruptions in export-oriented activities. Finally, and expectedly, the rural residents among them maintained ties with peasants unknown to the urban oligarchs. But the social difference that such ties created, as well as the landlords' distinctive position vis-à-vis the export market, manifested itself at the national level only at times of political crisis.

It is thus fair to say that the landlords have remained, since the 1840s, in the shadow of the alliance of rulers and merchants, never again becoming an autonomous social force. Even as individuals, they were somehow anachronistic. Whenever one of them reached the top echelons of society, it was as an ally of the merchant bourgeoisie or as an official within the state apparatus. Whenever any one of them distinguished himself during the nineteenth century and the first decades of the twentieth, it was always, on the political scene, as a member of the oligarchy.

THE URBAN PARASITES

While most landlords tried to make the transition to politics, few succeeded. Many joined the other, more numerous groups of parasites who jealously latched onto the alliance between rulers and merchants. Professionals, retailers, soldiers, and state employees are the most impor- tant among those parasitic categories. Professionals and retailers differed in education, language, and the circles in which they moved, but their paths ran parallel, for both groups swam in the wake of the alliance. Many professionals had either fallen from power, lost out in the export-import trade, or risen out of a peasant past they were trying to forget. Most retailers had similar origins, at least until this century. Professionals and retailers saw themselves moving, pendulum-fashion, from one mediocre job to the next, surviving from one season to the next, hoping for political fortune to propel them into the ministry of their dreams, the embassy of their choice, or the field of *haut commerce*. Although few achieved these dreams, their objectives, their transient situation—self-defined as it was—and their position as intermediaries put them on the side of the alliance. They lived off the system, unable to influence it as a group until and unless—as individuals—they ventured onto the political scene.

The second set of parasites was, all things considered, little better. They also slipped into the interstices of the system, into the many gaps between the alliance and the peasantry. They included the ever growing mass of state employees, lower ranking army officers, and soldiers. Thanks to their position in the state apparatus, they benefited from the surplus drawn from the peasantry by the government they served. In return, they kept the peasantry at a distance from the state. When force was necessary, the soldiers furnished it. For their part, civilian employees joined with the professionals and the Roman Catholic clergy to create an ideological buffer zone between the peasantry and the alliance. If both army recruits and civilian employees of the state redistributed some of the funds to their peasant clients and relatives, it was always in unequal shares and with the added value of their own political allegiances.

Although the parasitic groups helped the alliance, their demographic growth created unexpected problems, especially for the oligarchy. First, as these groups swelled in size, they became unmanageable from the rulers' point of view. Second, they became increasingly parasitic. They were a buffer; they became a dead weight. The army offers a perfect example of the effect of this parasitism. In about 1840, its standing force included 33 colonels, 95 lieutenant-colonels, 825 captains, 654 lieutenants, 577 sub-lieutenants and ensigns, 6,815 noncommissioned officers, 19,127 soldiers, and 25 medical attachés—for a total of 28,151 personnel paid from army funds—as well as an additional 15 brigadier-generals, 63 colonels, 48 lieutenant-colonels, 9 captains, 1 lieutenant, and 20 medical attachés, most of whom enjoyed agreeable sinecures in nonmilitary positions (Candler 1842). This army probably cost the state more than 1.5 million gourdes per year; and its total cost continued to rise even when the real value of individual salaries fell.

The nobility of Faustin Soulouque's empire offers another example of such parasitic growth. The counts and barons of Haiti's second empire had incomes that were ridiculously low compared to those of Christophe's nobility, but while Christophe's kingdom knighted only seventy-seven men during its first four years, the empire created four hundred in a single week (d'Alaux 1856: 208)! This spawning of an impoverished nobility cost the Treasury far more than did the feudal elite of the North. In other words, as the number of parasites grew, their total cost to the state increased enormously, even though their individual incomes declined. True to form, even after the republic was restored, successive governments tapped the peasants' resources more and more deeply to support the growing groups of parasites.

The peasantry bled the more because even at best productivity was stagnating. The cultivators' isolation contributed to the lagging development of production techniques. The landlords for their part did not worry about agricultural efficiency, having abandoned the politics of production for the politics of state power. Finally, the ruling oligarchy and the agents of dependence had no interest whatsoever in changing production methods, since as far as they could tell these did not affect the mechanisms of surplus extraction. To be sure, they would have benefited from a net increase in export-oriented production, but they were not willing to foot the bill for technical improvements. First, they did not control the labor process. More important, opportunities for quick returns were numerous enough to turn them away from long-term investments.

While productivity was stagnating, the proportion of citizens engaged in nonproductive activities was rising. The parasitic groups grew more rapidly than did production, and even more rapidly than the peasantry itself. This was in part because the peasantry reproduced itself within its own social and geographical frontiers, while the parasitic groups were augmented by individuals who had fallen from power or dropped out of *haut commerce,* as well as by peasants who had "come down" from the countryside.

A NATION DIVIDED

This socioeconomic organization divided the nation sharply into two markedly distinct groups: the agricultural producers and the urbanites clustered around the alliance of rulers and merchants. The urbanites generally agreed that there was something they called *l'arrière-pays* ("the hinterland"), a catchall term that included the bulk of the population. But the economic structure—in particular, the prevalent system of surplus extraction—meant that wealth could be pumped out of the peasantry without the urbanites ever coming into contact with, or even seeing, them. The nation met its masters only through intermediaries, and only at points of exchange. This physical separation influenced the gestation of distinctive cultural patterns in the first half of the nineteenth century as much as the international blockade imposed on the republic. For most practical purposes, the Haitian peasant was as isolated from the country's other classes as Haiti was from the rest of the world. The Haitian expression *mounn andeyò* (literally, "people outside") that urbanites use to describe the peasantry is as telling as the French *arrière-pays*. It signifies both an acknowledgment and an implicit approval of the split. Few urbanites ever wondered how a majority of the nation could be seen as being "outside." Peasants in turn often refer to powerful individuals, especially urbanites, as *leta* ("the state"), regardless of their actual ties to the state apparatus. In short, both sides acknowledge that a split exists.

This social and spatial split gave rise to cultural divergences so blatant that empiricist observers, such as the U.S. sociologist James Leyburn (1941), couched them in terms of a caste distinction between peasants and elites. Jean Price-Mars—the founder of the Haitian school of ethnology and himself a critic of the elites—rightly criticized this approach. The danger of taking Haiti for a caste society lies not in the observations upon which that analysis is based—Haiti is undeniably a society split in two—but in focussing on the split between elites and masses, rural and urban, *mulâtre* and black, French and Creole, or Christian and Vodoun believer, we run the risk of masking the exchanges and contacts underlying these oppositions.

The dualist approach typified by Leyburn leads to a failure to identify classes and class fractions within and outside the peasantry, and to neglect the dialectics of social reproduction. Though Haiti is split in two, it does not consist of two societies. On the contrary: the very mechanisms that have produced the split keep the two parts in an unequal but complementary relationship. The isolation of the peasantry is a good example of this dialectic of divisions and complementarity. The peasantry's isolation arose from its avoidance of the plantations and was maintained by the alliance insofar as it benefited the town dwellers. Yet the peasants' isolation was never so absolute as to forestall contacts that benefited the urban classes. Further, the peasants themselves rarely aimed at total isolation, if only because they clearly approved of some form of economic exchange. Hence while the country's economic structure and the organization of political society always implied the isolation of the peasantry, at another level the fact that this same peasantry helped, biologically and economically, to keep the growing circles of urban parasites afloat broke this isolation. What the dualist sociologists—especially from the United States—have missed is the depth of the peasant penetration of urban civil society, a penetration made possible, ironically, by the peasantry's isolation.

In the nineteenth century, as now, the distribution of agricultural products depended on weekly or seasonal trips by members of the peasantry into the urban areas. Peasants came to the *bourgs*—interior towns that serve primarily as relay points in the export chain—to deliver the major commodities to middlemen, often rich peasants, who would then take the produce to a major port. Similarly, market women of peasant origin came to both coastal and interior towns (or to their peripheries) to deliver produce through an intricate and efficient system that, until recently, provided a large share of the urbanites' food (Mintz 1960a, 1960b, 1961). They then took back to the majority who remained in the villages of the hinterland most of the imported items they consumed. Through such daily or seasonal to-and-fro, repeated for generations, the peasants mounted the ramparts of the cities. In addition, crowds of peasants have long come down from the hills to serve the urban parasites; many return infrequently, if at all, to the hinterland, although they maintain ties there. Today as yesterday, the majority of cooks, nannies, housekeepers, seamstresses, craftsmen, gardeners, houseboys, and *restavèk* (child domestics exploited by city families in return for room and board) have peasant roots. The peasants' comings and goings across the great gulf that divides the nation has meant that, in the long run, they have come to occupy part of the social and cultural terrain, a point to which I shall return more extensively in chapter 4. Suffice it to say here that the complexities of this cultural terrain did not conceal the fact that the structures of the merchants' republic divided the nation and reinforced the peasantry's political isolation. Unless these fundamental relations changed, that imbalance was bound to lead to a crisis. The next chapter looks at how and when this crisis developed.

3

The Recurring Crisis

The central social imbalance in Haitian life was felt as early as the first half of the nineteenth century, and took the form of chronic political instability. The structural positions of the actors, the cultural context, and the historical evolution of the society made the urban political scene the principal arena in which the crisis was to play itself out. The dissociation of political and civil society was softened on the cultural front by the impact of peasant culture and values on the urban scene. Urbanites could always point to, and at times engage in, practices that sustained the vision of a "community." In economic terms, the gap was wider, but its immediate effects were less likely to provoke open conflict as long as the masses were more or less satisfied with their control of the labor process. Hence the first manifestations of the crisis were likely to be political. The chronic instability of Haitian political life, as manifested in the rhythm of political succession, numerous constitutional crises, and recurring armed feuds is so obvious that Haitian and foreign observers alike have tended to inflate the role of politics in shaping the course of the country's history. They often see the stages of historical evolution in terms of changes of regime, to a degree that masks underlying continuities. The point is that the state's importance came not from the power vested in individual regimes but from its role in the extraction and distribution of peasant surplus.

THE LIMITS OF THE SYSTEM

Let us first examine the most basic contradiction, that between the productive forces and the methods of surplus extraction. At the bottom of the social scale, but vitally important for the entire nation, was a peasantry divided into several strata: landless people, sharecroppers, small proprietors, and rich peasants. Together, these men and women did the work and furnished almost all the country's wealth. But their techniques of production stagnated. The attempts at innovation that followed independence (for instance, the unsuccessful efforts by a few black immigrants from the United States to introduce the plow) failed to modify a labor process that had been inherited from the provision grounds of colonial Saint-Domingue. Land fertility declined accordingly. Statistically, peasant productivity today is only equal to that of 1843, if not lower. The touchstone of Haiti's socioeconomic system has thus been a peasantry that worked more and more but produced less and less, as population increased and the availability of fertile land decreased.

Further, as we have seen, most of the fruits of the peasantry's toil were seized by the alliance of rulers and merchants and transferred abroad. The landowners took the rest for themselves. None of these three groups reinvested the surplus they expropriated: there was no local accumulation of capital, either in private hands or within the state sector, and no major effort to improve the forces of production.

It is not difficult to see how this system led to ruin. Some 150 years ago, the U.S. physician Jonathan Brown visited Haiti and wrote: "In this state of things it is seen that the country is saved from utter want and political dissolution solely through the spontaneous productiveness of its soil" (Brown [1837] 1971, 2: 263). Brown's apprehensions were well founded. There was, built into the system, a moment when the rulers and merchants would have siphoned off so much from the peasantry that there would be nothing left to take without forcing the majority into abject poverty. This was the first critical threshold.

A second threshold, linked to the first, was also on the horizon. The state's role in the extraction of surplus and its monopoly of the labor market carried with it two complementary functions: it enabled the state's managers, and some of their subordinates, to climb the social ladder; and it redistributed a part of the surplus drawn from the peasantry back to the state's civilian and military employees. The largest part of these urban groups' expenditures went to the importers and local artisans, but some returned to the peasantry or to those connected with it, through purchases of Haitian goods, food, and gifts, and through the mechanisms of socioeconomic patronage.

The effects of these complementary functions were contradictory. On the one hand, the redistributive effects somewhat alleviated the plight of many peasants. On the other, social climbing by state employees, limited as it was, increased the numbers and needs of the nonproductive groups. But since the productive base and the social relations surrounding it remained unchanged, the needs of the state apparatus grew faster than its capacity to redistribute. There would thus come a time when the merchants and the oligarchy would be unable to control the rate of growth of the urban parasites, when the sponging function of those groups would render irrelevant the unequal redistribution they performed. This was the second crisis point.

Behind these two thresholds lay the permanent threat of what Kaplan (1984: 15), working from Latin American data, has called a tendency toward "entropy" or "decreasing returns" on the part of national institutions, especially in third world countries. As the alliance increased the peasants' isolation, national institutions—particularly the Christian churches, but also the press, the judiciary, and the schools—showed themselves less and less capable of bridging the gap between political and civil society, or papering over the dichotomies through which this gap became tangible: governors vs. governed, urban vs. rural, Creole vs. French, Christianity vs. Vodoun, etc.

The third aspect of the crisis was more directly political in nature. We have seen that the socioeconomic structures, and the historical and cultural context in which their effects were felt, implied a separation between the peasantry and the urban world. This separation produced two contradictory tendencies: the political marginalization of the peasantry and the concentration of urban demands in the narrow sphere of governmental decisions.

Nicos Poulantzas (1971: 68–69, 120–22) has noted in more general terms that a lack of intensity in the economic class struggle often has an inverse effect on political battles. It frequently leads to a "fetishism" of the state, to the primacy of *la politique* ("politics" in the most restricted sense) over *le politique* ("policy," conceived as a much larger field of administrative and economic issues). Alain Touraine (1973: 268) has described the same paradox in the following terms: "A blocked political system pushes a good part of all political and class relations back inside the state. If it is completely closed, political life is replaced by rivalries between individuals, clans, cliques, and interest groups within the state itself."

In Haiti's case, we are looking at a political system that was doubly blocked: first by the marginalization of the peasantry, and second by the intensification of partisan struggles within political society. The peasantry's struggle to maintain a labor process favorable to its interests forced the oligarchy to seek access to the peasant surplus outside the confines of this labor process. Thus as the peasantry reinforced its control over the use of its labor, the surplus—indirectly extracted via the tax system and the process of commodity exchange—became the pivot on which production relations turned. However, in the course of its daily labor, the peasantry never directly confronted the system's ultimate beneficiaries—the top state officeholders and, above all, the merchant bourgeoisie. Hence, even though the peasants might have wondered about the causes of their poverty, they knew few individuals on whom to place the blame. Indeed, they were more likely to accuse a fellow villager of worsening their lives than an exporter or an official they had never met. The problem was aggravated by the total lack of political institutions that could have allowed the peasantry to express its views to the state or the Bord de Mer. As time went on, the peasants increasingly withdrew from the political arena, while the urban dwellers, in contrast, threw themselves ever more ferociously into it. Partisan struggles necessarily became more complicated with the growth of the parasites—particularly the professional petty bourgeoisie— who had their eyes on positions in the state apparatus. Indeed, with no path to salvation outside the state, the number of individuals who wanted to be president or minister had to grow, as did the number of those who wanted lower level public sector jobs. When the candidates' qualifications were more or less equal (and equally minimal), the choice was political. Thus politics played an even greater role than usual in the choice of state personnel because the professional petty bourgeoisie was unable to reproduce itself outside the state. From the viewpoint of the middle classes, politics was more than a game with high stakes—it was a profession. For many of them, indeed, it was the only one they could practice. Hence there had to come a time when the numbers of jobseekers would far exceed the resources, as well as the needs, of the state apparatus.

The implications of this situation were disastrous, given the other problems that faced the nation. As economic problems grew worse and social contradictions intensified, those who controlled the state paid scant attention to them, so busy were they in shoring up their own positions, under increasingly difficult conditions, within the state apparatus. Politics took first place, excluding the peasants but increasing the intensity of urban competition in an ever shrinking arena. There was thus a third threshold, when the pretenders to the spoils of the throne would become too many for any faction to remain in power without the incessant validation of that power through violence.

GAGS AND GUNS

The positions of the actors, the history of their emergence, and the nature of Haiti's social divisions all tended to make politics the arena in which the society's basic contradictions found expression. The total absence of contact between the peasant producers and the ultimate beneficiaries of the system—the local and metropolitan agents of dependence—restricted the ability of the greater part of the nation to express its demands. The use of French as the language of power reinforced the peasantry's institutionalized silence. The tradition of "government by understudies," revitalized during the last decades of the nineteenth century, added another layer to the veil that already covered the mechanisms of indirect control. Color prejudice complicated both the reality and the appearance of power. Militarism reinforced the state's visibility within the nation.

We have seen that the strategy of Louverture's party had required a formidable army whose main task was to impose and maintain unconditional freedom in Saint-Domingue. Even before independence, the rebel slaves saw themselves first and foremost as a people united behind a military–type organization. The awareness of the nation came through this organization. The army thus played a crucial unifying role in the formation of the nation as a self-conscious community fighting for a new political order (M.-R. Trouillot 1977; Dorsinville 1965; Lepkowski 1968–69). But the militarism that guaranteed first freedom and then independence, the dual objective of the national community, also helped to reinforce the state, and within it the role of an executive with aspirations for greater and greater power.

From the time of the Louverture regime until the U.S. occupation in 1915, all of the strata of Haitian society (except the merchants) were represented within the army. Even in its most revolutionary days, the army offered social and economic mobility to its officers and the redistribution of income to its lower ranks and their families. Before 1915, there had been only five presidents who were not career army officers, and three of these had been honorary generals, while a fourth had served as head of a peasant armed band. The only true civilian in the group was also one of the first chiefs of state to create a secret police force along paramilitary lines (Price-Mars n.d.).

Thus the army played a cohesive and redistributive role, but at the same time the militarism that it imposed on the country reinforced the separation of state and nation. Not only were issues debated just at the time that problems had become so serious that they could no longer be postponed. But the ad hoc solutions were always military in nature: arrests, assassinations, rebellions. The importance of the political sphere thus reinforced the size and importance of the army, and this in turn reinforced the role of the political sphere in national life.

THE PRIMACY OF THE EXECUTIVE

The civilian machinery of state also contributed to the reinforcement of the role of the political arena in the daily lives of the urban population, and in much the same way. After all, the civilian state apparatus had social functions similar to those of the military, although without the pomp or the coercive power that went along with military uniforms. The state's near-total domination of the job market reinforced the control of the Executive, enormously enlarging the impact of politics on the day-to-day existence of the urbanites. The most qualified professionals—who, in other circumstances, would have asked nothing more than to be allowed to practice their professions—had to accept this forced initiation into pork-barrel politics or risk starvation. It was not François Duvalier who wrote the rules concerning the omnipotence of the Executive in Haiti, although he certainly pushed their application to the limit. It was Beaubrun Ardouin—historian, politician, and respected member of the *mulâtre* oligarchy—who had the dubious honor of being the first to proclaim them more than a century before Papa Doc.

In 1843, some time before the end of Boyer's government, more than one hundred residents of the southern town of Jérémie—the overwhelming majority of that town's political elite—awarded a medal for "devotion to the motherland" to Hérard Dumesle, a politician and civil servant who had protested injustices committed by the government. Boyer immediately had Dumesle fired, and Ardouin, then a senator, publicly approved his dismissal. Under cover of anonymity, a "private citizen" attacked Ardouin's position in a tract whose title—rather long, as was customary at the time—nonetheless bears noting: *Apologie des destitutions pour opinions politiques ou Dogme de l'obéissance passive prêché aux fonctionnaires publics, par un Sénateur et réfuté par un citoyen privé* ("Apology for dismissals for political opinions or the dogma of passive obedience preached to public servants by a senator and refuted by a private citizen"). Ardouin replied with a riposte in much the same vein, entitled *Réponse du Sénateur B. Ardouin à un écrit anonyme, intitulé Apologie des destitutions...* ("Response by Senator B. Ardouin to an anonymous piece, entitled Apology for dismissals...").

The response by Ardouin—who is, we should remember, considered one of the pioneers of Haitian liberalism—clearly shows that the "private citizen" had not misinterpreted the senator's attitude to Dumesle's dismissal. Ardouin's position is precise and goes beyond the immediate case to establish a principle: a state employee is the political servant of the state that provides him with his daily bread. Whatever his rank in the administration, whatever the circumstances, he remains linked to the regime in power for the duration of his employment. According to Ardouin, the employee may not become involved "in any activity which the government *may* disapprove: in so doing, he exposes himself to dismissal" (my emphasis). At most, he may offer his resignation, though according to Ardouin, this is a "negative" form of opposition. A civil servant should fall into poverty by resigning rather than become a perjurer by keeping his post. The principle was widely followed, although it was formulated by one of the rare Haitian intellectuals who held a public post without worrying about the attitude of the rulers of the day. Ardouin was part of the oligarchy that put governments together; further, he had other sources of income. Nevertheless his outlook, at least on this point, was shared by most members of the urban strata: participation in the civil service, at any level, implied tacit if not vocal approval of the Executive, and dissenters should resign or expect to be fired.

They were fired, of course, more often than they resigned. From the nineteenth century to our time, the state has always been the principal buyer on the Haitian labor market. Only the minority of civil servants who, like Ardouin, were also landowners or had contacts in the Bord de Mer could resign to defend their honor. Similarly, many resignations, especially under François Duvalier, were primarily tactical—ideological preparation for emigration by those whose qualifications made it possible for them to find work elsewhere. But, as Ardouin's anonymous critic noted, in the majority of cases the "doctrine of passive obedience" reduced the public servant to a "choice between conscience and poverty." Henceforth, every state employee would be, in principle if not in fact, an automaton serving the government of the day.

Not all Haitians were ready to accept this state of affairs, and certainly Ardouin's critic virulently rejected it:

> With what can one reproach an accounting officer if his books are accurate, if his agency is running well, if his conduct is honorable? With what can one reproach a magistrate if he administers justice impartially, if he follows the Constitution and the laws that he has sworn to observe and enforce? With what can one reproach clerks of the court, process-servers, or office clerks if their files are in good order, their registers up to date, if they serve the public promptly? (Un citoyen privé n.d.)

But Ardouin's critic did not prevail. From 1843 to the present, I doubt that there has been a single accountant dismissed principally or solely because his books were wrong, a single magistrate named or fired principally or solely on the basis of his ability to administer justice, a single clerk hired or moved principally or solely because of the way he or she served the public. From 1843 to the present, every decision concerning the nomination, promotion, or dismissal of a public servant has involved political factors, because even at the bottom of the ladder these individuals fall under the patronage of figures higher up, who themselves serve, or are close to, the chief executive. The lowering of public employment to the level of servile adherence to the policy of the Executive of the day thus does not depend solely on the intentions of employer and employee. It has deep roots in the social positions of the actors and in the state's monopoly of the job market. But it implies, in turn, the daily presence of politics in the lives of people who in other circumstances would gladly have left politics alone. The state is the source of their daily bread, and they fight for the state, against the state, or within the state in order to have their place *in* the state. The civilian state apparatus, like the military machine, puts politics in the foreground of urban life.

From all this sprang two contradictory tendencies that eventually led to a breaking point: on one side, the political marginalization of the peasantry, a marginalization that paralleled its sociocultural isolation; and on the other, the coalescence of all the urban strata in the political sphere. Conditions were thus ripe for the crisis to manifest itself in the political arena. Earlier in this century, a native intellectual and politician declared, in words that resonate today: "In Haiti, we reduce all the problems of society to political problems. . . . However, the state is not the society" (Laroche 1908: 16).

THE MAINSPRINGS OF THE SYSTEM

The political disturbances of nineteenth-century Haiti did not, however, escalate into a disaster of Duvalierist magnitude, and for many reasons. The first and easiest explanation is demographic. Modern analysts with a Malthusian bent draw attention to the geometric growth of the population and the impact of this growth on the country's natural resources. The relation between human and natural resources certainly played a catalytic role in the development of what Pierre-Charles (1979) has called the "uninterrupted crisis" of Haitian society. The stagnation of the productive forces doomed the system to eventual breakdown. But demography is not a neutral science: its powers of explanation can only make sense within a socially determined space. Haiti's population growth is a handicap, but only within the context of the production and distribution relations imposed by the ruling alliance. Moreover, it should be remembered that the contradictions inherent in the system had reached a critical point as early as 1867, well before the population upsurges of the twentieth century.

The key difference between the two centuries is the nineteenth-century presence of corrective forces, of social and economic mechanisms that limited the intensity of the structural crisis and channeled the ways in which it manifested itself. They acted as counterweights by limiting the process of economic and political centralization implied by the social structure. Three such corrective factors deserve special attention: militarism, regionalism, and the heterogeneity of the individuals making up the dominant alliance. Although we must distinguish them analytically, in reality they worked together. Hence it is most useful to analyze their operation by considering a specific historical case.

The case we will examine is the set of events spanning the years 1866 to 1870, whose key episodes were the accession to power and subsequent execution of President Sylvain Salnave. It is an exemplary conjuncture for many reasons. First, the country's economic situation had recently worsened considerably. Coffee exports were at their lowest since 1861, in part because some producers had turned to cotton, for which there was an unusual demand in the United States. But the end of the U.S. Civil War in 1865 had led to a 75 percent drop in the price for Haitian cotton in just a few months. The Treasury was nearly empty. By 1868, the local currency had fallen so low—with exchange rates plumeting to 1,000 gourdes to $1 (U.S.)—that people had baptized it *zorèy bourik* ("donkey's ear"), indicating its low value. Second, the government's inability to control the countryside had been obvious since the last months of Geffrard's administration, and disorder increased when Salnave took over in June 1867. In fact, Salnave spent most of his eighteen months in power fighting one regional rebellion after another. Third, foreign powers, notably Germany, Britain, and the United States, threatened to intervene militarily in order to protect their citizens or to defend "civilization," violated Haitian waters many times between 1867 and 1870, and took part in secret arrangements with one or more of the political contenders. By all accounts, this was a crucial period during which Haitian society seemed ready to explode. In many ways it did, but it recovered; and we shall see why.

By the end of 1866, the long reigns of Soulouque (1847–59) and Geffrard (1859–67) had exacerbated the tensions that had been mounting since the 1820s. The relative stability that these two governments enjoyed had increased the dominant alliance's ability to suck the surplus from the peasantry and the propensity of the elites to gorge themselves on luxuries.

The army's ranks had been enormously inflated and the costs of corruption increased by Soulouque's military campaigns against the Dominican Republic in 1849 and 1855. Geffrard reduced the size of the army by half but did not reduce the costs of corruption, in part because of his need to check—or flatter—influential blacks in the capital and the larger provincial cities in order to compensate for his ties to *mulâtre* segments of the elites. The civil administration swelled, but still not rapidly enough to meet the demands of all the intellectuals and professionals seeking new or higher positions.

In other words, by 1866, after two extremely centralized governments, the underlying contradictions outlined earlier were growing. Between 1861 and 1866, Geffrard had to deal with at least one armed revolt a year, all led by disgruntled army officers. Discontent was also spreading among the street vendors, the *madan sara* (wholesale market women), the urban unemployed and underemployed, and the less isolated sections of the peasantry. Most of those groups, especially the urban poor, began to back a charismatic officer, Major Sylvain Salnave, reputedly the most fearless of the rival army chiefs and the leader of a provincial revolt in the North. Salnave also enjoyed the support of a significant number of populist intellectuals and the cooperation of some landlords in his native province. In March 1867, after still another provincial uprising, Geffrard suddenly went into exile. A constitutional assembly was quickly brought together, but for once the people in the street had spoken: vendors, unemployed, craftsmen, and especially market women in Port-au-Prince came out waving bouquets and handkerchiefs in an unusual show of support for Salnave, who made a triumphant entry into the capital with his northern troops and was proclaimed president by the populace.

MILITARISM

The first point to emphasize is the influence of the armed forces, both on the form in which the crisis manifested itself and on its temporary resolution. Salnave entered Port-au-Prince at the head of an army, and his nomination by a National Assembly was mere protocol. Similarly, the "election" of his successor, Saget, by a Senate as quickly put together as the preceding assemblies, would have had absolutely no importance if it had not been approved by the generals in Port-au-Prince. In two years, two constitutional changes had modified the name and composition of the Legislature, but made little difference to the way power was first won and then lost. The bayonet, not the Senate, put presidents in power; the bayonet also ousted them. The first lesson of the events of 1866–70, then, is that the armed forces—the regular army as well as forces raised by military landlords—played a key role both in shaping the crisis and in defusing it.

The military could play such a role partly because it sustained and reinforced the heterogeneity of those who controlled the state apparatus. For political, administrative, and military reasons, not all of the officers were stationed in Port-au-Prince. Though the army had supposedly been unified under Boyer, its main regional divisions acted as semiautonomous bodies, at least insofar as their allegiance to the local commanders was stronger than their sworn obedience to the chief of state. The force of arms, preferably turned against Port-au-Prince, remained the principal asset in the race for the presidency, but a regime needed a delicate balance to survive: on the one hand, it had to maintain some unity among the numerous military chiefs scattered around the country; on the other, it had to keep the most ambitious ones at a distance. Small disputes among high-ranking officers could easily bring down a regime that threatened to accumulate power more rapidly than it redistributed it.

In the nineteenth century, then, militarism encouraged the redistribution of political power. The rebellion of a local chief in a distant province profoundly troubled the central authorities, partly because the provinces, no matter how near, enjoyed a degree of economic importance and independence that they have since lost. Between 1865 and 1869, successive rebellions in the provinces shook the presidencies of both Geffrard and Salnave, far more than subsequent army rebellions or armed invasions would shake François Duvalier. By November 1869 anyone but Salnave, who was famous for his bravura, might have decided it was time to leave. But Salnave had nerve: he postponed his departure—and paid for it with his life. Thus we can reject the theories that attribute the Duvaliers' long survival to the stamina of one man or the ferocity of one clique. Given their reputation for ferocity, an astonishing number of Haiti's dictators calmly left for exile when it became clear that their time had come. In short, it was not the determination to hold onto power that Haiti's nineteenth-century presidents lacked. Their departure from office can only be understood by analyzing the effects of the redistribution of executive power within the army.

The divisions among the generals reflected, in addition to conflicts over power, oppositions between spatially differentiated groups of landowners and rich peasants. For example, sharecropping was more common in the North and an independent yeomanry more evident in the South. Further, within the three broad regions (North, West, and South), internal characteristics created differences of allegiance and political loyalty. In addition, gunpower was not the prerogative of the regular army alone. Retired or ousted officers, political leaders and local landlords, sometimes financed by urban merchants, put together small armed bands that were effective within their limited regional spheres and that sometimes gave critical support to rebelling regular troops. Haitian historians have only begun to sketch out a more complete picture of political life in the provinces (e.g., Price-Mars n.d.; Péan 1978; Turnier n.d.), but there seem to have been intricate networks of allegiance reaching as far down the social ladder as the richest segments of the peasantry. We still do not know the actual composition of the armed bands (called *cacos* in the North) that backed one or another cause in the countryside, usually under the leadership of one or another "general," but it is clear that they rarely if ever claimed to fight to satisfy peasant grievances (except during the U.S. occupation). The important point for now is that political opposition always emerged from a local base and always included a military component. Just as opposition to Geffrard reached a critical level with the provincial revolt led by Salnave, so a *caco* rebellion in the northeast marked the beginning of Salnave's end. And many other times, both before and after 1869, the march of a provincial army on Port-au-Prince marked the end of a regime.

Thus, no matter how much militarism cost the nation—and everyone agrees that there are better ways to replace governments—the regionalism it reinforced through a decentralized organization and the pretensions it nurtured among high-ranking officers helped to moderate the power of the state.

REGIONALISM

Regionalism and militarism went hand in hand, but the regionalism of the nineteenth century did not simply duplicate the country's military and administrative divisions. Within regions and provinces, the principal coastal towns—Cap-Haïtien, Gonaïves, Saint-Marc, Port-de-Paix, Les Cayes, Jérémie, and Jacmel—were all relatively independent. Together with Aquin, Miragoâne, and Petit-Goâve, which were also open to foreign trade, and the minor ports of Anse d'Hainault, Fort Liberté, and Port-à-Piment, these towns challenged the hegemonic tendencies arising in Port-au-Prince. Coffee was exported from all the port cities, with Port-au-Prince often handling the largest share; but other crops reflected regional specialization. At times Jérémie exported more than half the country's total cacao, Gonaïves and Saint-Marc most of its cotton, and Port-de-Paix and Cap-Haïtien half of its logwood (Moral 1961). In fiscal year 1890–91, more than 70 percent of total customs revenues were collected from the provincial towns (Bureau of American Republics 1893). Thus within the territory delineated by the state lay a more complex geographic ensemble: a space filled with many units which were themselves comprised of smaller entities—what Haitian geographer Georges Anglade has called the "Federation of the Provinces."

The expression may be stretching the point, and Anglade himself (1982: 23) admits that not all the regions were of equal importance. Nevertheless, his phrase underlines a neglected aspect of nineteenth-century Haitian reality. The ten largest provincial ports stood at the top of small regional pyramids that integrated seacoast and hinterland via the inland towns. If all of these pyramids tilted toward Port-au-Prince, they were nevertheless not under the capital's thumb. Moreover, within these pyramids themselves, partly because of the vitality of spatially differentiated subgroups within the peasantry and partly because of their isolation, there was enough leeway at the nodal points to allow for the relative autonomy of any part. *Bourgs* (inland towns), for example, could turn to *their* hinterlands to seek food or export commodities. Thus in 1868–69, during the civil war against Salnave, Haiti was in effect divided into three states—one in the North, one in the South, and the one headed by Salnave in the West—but the two provincial ones were no worse off than the one centered around the capital.

Geographical isolation greatly contributed to the economic and political autonomy of the regional pyramids. Haiti's rugged terrain had placed limits on centralization since colonial days by impeding the completion of a national road system. Even in the early twentieth century, communication between the coastal towns was easier by sea than by land. Regional armies often skirted the mountains to make their way to Port-au-Prince to install the president of their choice, but their very existence rested on the partial isolation of their own regions, as well as on their capacity to raise funds independently through legal or illegal means. Further, naval support often made the crucial difference between the success or failure of a regional invader. That in turn depended upon his taxing capacity or on the extent of his contact with the local merchants, and these in turn varied in part according to the economic specialization of the region. In short, the relative autonomy of each regional pyramid and its sub-units acted as a brake on the development of political centralization.

CRACKS WITHIN THE ALLIANCE

Regionalism also impeded the cohesiveness of the merchants since many had to contend with local interests in the areas in which they operated. Moreover, in the political arena, merchants and consular agents were often divided according to nationality. Thus the British made no attempt to hide their support for Geffrard, while the United States half-heartedly backed Salnave, at least until he took power. And some years after Salnave's death, at the turn of the century, German financial assistance to the "revolutions" led by Simon and Leconte in turn irritated the United States.

These national rivalries both reflected and intensified differences that stemmed from the fact that all these foreigners were taking their pieces of the cake in different ways. Georges Adam (1982) differentiates among the state's suppliers, its financiers, and the foreigners and Haitians who were exclusively engaged in commerce.[1] He suggests that each group had a different economic aim during the presidencies of Geffrard and Salnave. For instance, the inflation that marked Geffrard's reign, or the devaluation under Salnave, did not affect each group in the same way. We can add that the divisions between importers and exporters grew during the latter part of the century. As more Haitians joined the merchant ranks, and as the Levantine offensive led to sometimes violent clashes among importers, it became increasingly difficult for the merchants to express themselves, as a group, in the political arena.

In conclusion, the heterogeneity of the merchants and the rulers, militarism, and regionalism all hampered a centralization process that was being generated by the unequal distribution of wealth and power. The dominant alliance's political and economic control was limited by pressures that: (1) prevented the homogenization of either of the two groups within it; (2) limited their capacity to accumulate power, alone or jointly; and (3) limited their capacity to use their power according to a united strategy. From time to time, the conflicts among the merchants allowed greater leeway to the middlemen or producers. Similarly, the conflicts among the rulers periodically gave the peasantry a chance to catch its breath, and even allowed some of its members to have an impact—indirect and controlled—on the political scene, as when localized peasant groups joined one or another of the troops attacking Port-au-Prince.

Salnave's era was followed by a short period during which Haiti came as close as it ever has to an effective parliamentary experience. Some members of the urban elites, tired of the domination of an Executive led by ignorant generals, rallied around two liberal politicians, Boyer Bazelais and Edmond Paul, and formed the Parti Libéral, a relatively unstructured organization that nevertheless took control of the legislative branch of government. The Libérals, most of whom were associated with the more Westernized *mulâtre* elite—in spite of the fact that some were phenotypically black—emphasized competence, economic liberalism, and, most of all, the need to limit the power of the Executive. The remainder of the legislature soon gathered around the Parti National, an even looser organization whose members shared only a vague affinity for the kind of populism embodied by Salnave. To the Libéral leit-motif, "Power to the most competent," the Nationals replied. "The greatest good to the greatest number." The generals remained undaunted by these legislative and ideological quibbles and, with the lukewarm support of the Nationals, held onto an Executive whose greatest asset remained the force of arms. In the event, the Parti Libéral lost its impetus when two of its leaders ran against each other for the presidency in 1876 and the winner turned to the Nationals. By 1883, what remained of the Parti Libéral had finally realized that power rested on military strength. But this realization came at their own expense: most were killed during an unsuccessful invasion to which President Salomon (1879–88) reacted with the utmost brutality. Electoral democracy had been but a passing dream.

Hence Haiti went out of the nineteenth century much as it had gone through its first decades, on political crutches. As before, corrupt governments competed in their incompetence and their brutality. As before, most of these regimes were cut short by a successful insurrection originating in one or another province. As before, a limited few, more adept at centralizing power, managed to hold long enough to affect the nation significantly. By far the most notable of such regimes was that of Lysius Félicité Salomon, leader of the Parti National. An educated landlord from a southern political family, Salomon had been a diplomat, minister of finance under Soulouque and an early backer of Salnave, whose populist tendencies he shared. He also had (and believed in) the competence so cherished by his Libéral enemies. Salomon introduced a certain degree of efficiency to public administration, which became more sensitive to the needs of the growing black middle classes. In addition, the debt to France was finally paid off, and Salomon took that opportunity to reduce coffee taxes and promote public education, no small feat in Haitian history. He also made conditional land grants to those peasants who were willing to plant export crops—a policy that achieved only partial success because of the stiff conditions imposed on the grantees.[2]

The productive base remained unchanged, however, as did the relations of production maintained by the alliance. Neither Salomon nor the military landlords who followed him wanted to tamper with the foundations of the merchants' republic. Indeed, the merchants themselves were becoming increasingly arrogant in their demands, in part because productivity was not improving, in part because conflicts along national lines were increasing among the small group of resident foreigners. The tensions between the German merchants, who were tied to the local elites, and the U.S. diplomats, who were willing to fall back on military intervention, reflected larger international games but profoundly affected Haitian political life. After a few undistinguished regimes—Simon Sam (1896–1902), Alexis (1902–8), and Simon (1908–11), Haiti went through six presidents from August 1911 to July 1915. Four of these were killed in office, including Vilbrun Guillaume Sam, whose body was cut in pieces on the street by an elite-led mob on July 28, 1915. That very same afternoon, a contingent of 330 U.S. soldiers landed in Port-au-Prince. By the end of the next week, most Haitians realized that a foreign military occupation had begun. It was to last nineteen years.

THE U.S. INVASION

The official reason for the occupation was that the obvious political anarchy in Haiti gave the United States the moral duty of protecting the lives of foreigners, including its own citizens.

However, we should not ignore the fact that the invasion took place exactly one year after the beginning of World War I, at a time when the U.S. embassy was increasingly nervous about German influence on Haitian politics. As noted before, German merchants financed various Haitian political groups and had established strong links with the urban elites. In 1883, the then German crown prince visited Port-au-Prince and welcomed Salomon and the *crême* of Port-au-Prince's aristocracy on his frigate. In the early 1900s, German-dominated firms were still more important than U.S. ones, despite the fact that many of the new Levantine merchants used capital originating in the United States. In 1915, with German and French governments occupied with the war in Europe, Washington's policymakers no doubt believed that military occupation would quickly establish U.S. political and economic dominance. Further, such dominance was part of a larger Caribbean plan: U.S. Marines invaded the neighboring Dominican Republic only a few months later. U.S. interest in Haiti had grown with plans for establishing a base in the northwest of the country or on the neighboring islet of Tortuga (1890–1891); with private loans from U.S. firms to various Haitian governments (1900–1911); with the development of export-oriented banana plantations controlled by U.S. citizens (1910); and with U.S. involvement in various public works projects, including a railway system (1890s–1915). Not surprisingly, plans for the invasion were in the works at least a year before the events that precipitated it.

The occupiers' first political act was to install a puppet president, Philippe-Sudre Dartiguenave (1915–22), whose "election" by the Senate occurred under the watchful eye of one hundred armed Marines. Their first economic decision was to take over the customhouses. Their first military order was to disband the Haitian army. Then, on September 16, 1915, they imposed a Convention (Agreement) that gave them the right to police the country and to control public finances for ten years. From then on, the occupiers took charge of most branches of the administration, with Haitian officials, including ministers of government, sometimes learning of important decisions only when they were publicly announced. Having seized the national bank and the customhouses, the occupiers could easily stop the enforcement of the few decisions Haitian officials made without their approval. And they did, at times, in spite of the Haitians' constant complaints.

Most educated urbanites disapproved of the Convention from the start. Opposition was so vocal that Dartiguenave had difficulty filling high-level positions with individuals who would have been his first choice in different circumstances. The urban youth and the press, in particular, openly criticized both the president and his U.S. "advisers." But words had little impact on a presence that had imposed itself by force of arms, and many intellectuals were simply jailed or intimidated. A few attempts at armed rebellion in Port-au-Prince were quickly crushed. Finally, in April 1916 the Marines dissolved the Senate and in March 1917 they extended the Convention for another ten years beyond its expected expiration date.

Resistance took a different route in the countryside. In the North, and in the central areas just north of Port-au-Prince, officers in the disbanded army, landowners, and peasants formed many centers of armed resistance. Most of the rebel units claimed allegiance to Dr. Rosalvo Bobo, an unconditional nationalist who had vainly opposed Dartiguenave in the preceding "election." They were quickly crushed by a joint force composed of the Marines and the new Haitian army that the Marines were creating. Armed resistance did not die, however. New rebel units were formed in 1917, and in 1918 Charlemagne Péralte, a landowner and officer in the disbanded army, emerged as the national leader of all the units that were engaging in guerrilla warfare against the official forces. Péralte's prestige grew with his early victories, and after the Marines began to require forced labor on public works from the peasants, in 1919, thousands of peasants joined the resistance. Some historians claim that at their height Péralte's troops, spread across the central plateaux and in the North, numbered 15,000 (Millet 1978: 95). In late 1919, however, with the help of a paid Haitian informer, the Marines set a trap for Péralte. He was killed in cold blood by Marine Captain Hermann Hanneken, who received the Medal of Honor for his feat. Péralte's body, tied to a door as if to a crucifix, was put on display by the Marines to intimidate the population. Benoit Batraville picked up the leadership of the guerrillas but had fewer men than Péralte. He was killed in an ambush in May 1920. Armed resistance died with him.

UNHEALED SORES

A detailed balance sheet of the U.S. occupation remains to be drawn up, despite a growing number of studies of that period (Balch 1927; Castor 1971; Schmidt 1971; Millet 1978; Gaillard 1973–84; Nicholas n.d.; Langley 1980; Corvington 1984). Nevertheless, a convincing general picture has emerged. Most observers agree that the achievements of the occupation were minor; they disagree only as to the amount of damage that it inflicted.

The occupation stabilized the currency and briefly reduced administrative corruption. These two achievements in turn contributed to a reduction in the foreign debt, although at the price of depriving the country of the capital it badly needed. The "absolute priority" given to the debt, which had been consolidated in U.S. hands in 1922, left Haiti starved for development funds (Lundahl 1979: 371–72). During the Depression, Haiti had the dubious honor of being one of the few solvent countries in the world—a peculiarity that primarily benefited its U.S. creditors. To the occupation's credit must be added the fact that the Marines' presence temporarily ended the military coups that had marked presidential succession struggles since the early nineteenth century.

Beyond these qualified achievements, the occupation's main effect was damaging because it exacerbated the contradictions embedded in the socioeconomic structure, reinforced traditional conflicts, and broadened the dimensions of the crisis by centralizing the system. This centralization in turn swept away the feeble restraints remaining from the nineteenth century. For Haiti, in the end the game was not worth the candle.

The U.S. occupation exacerbated Haiti's economic problems in two ways, both of which ran counter to its stated intentions. First, it increased, rather than reduced, economic dependence by enlarging the role of coffee as an export; second, it also increased the injustice inherent in the fiscal system by raising the share of the value of imports and exports sucked up by the state through customs duties. A year before the Marines' departure, the U.S. financial adviser admitted failure on these two crucial points: "This report has shown that comparatively little visible progress has been made either in diversifying exports or in shifting the principal source of revenue from customs duties to internal taxes" (De la Rue et al. 1930–33: 76). Even so, the adviser was being generous: his own statistics revealed that the situation was far worse in 1933 than it had been in the early days of the occupation. Between 1916–21 and 1932–33, coffee went from being 67 percent of exports (by value) to 78 percent, increasing the dependence on one commodity despite the creation of a few plantation enclaves where other crops were cultivated. For the duration of the occupation, coffee accounted for 74 percent of all exports. Further, it was the United States that benefited most from Haiti's trade deficit, because the United States remained first among the sources of Haiti's imports—although it sank to sixth among the buyers of Haiti's products (after France, Great Britain, Denmark, Belgium, and Italy).

In the final years of the occupation, customs duties provided 80 to 83 percent of government revenues—an improvement over the last decades of the nineteenth century but no better than the percentage achieved by the governments of Boyer or Christophe. More important, import duties increased in relation to the value of merchandise, imposing a greater burden on producers and buyers alike. Import duties doubled, from 23 percent of the value of merchandise bought in 1916-17 to 46 percent in 1932–33. Over the same period, export duties went from 19 percent to 28 percent of the value of merchandise sold. In other words, the tax burden on the peasantry and the lower classes was heavier under the occupation than it had been during the nineteenth century. In addition, the occupiers imposed special levies on common articles, such as salt and matches, which led to price increases felt most deeply by the poorest classes. The occupation thus reinforced the country's most important economic problems: dependence and the extraction of a massive quantity of peasant surplus by nonproducers.

Yet the disaster went far beyond the two areas acknowledged by the financial adviser, for the occupation also accelerated Haiti's economic, military, and political centralization, leaving the rest of the country unable to restrain the hegemonic tendencies of the "Republic of Port-au-Prince." It signalled the beginning of the end for the regional economies. The centralization of customs collection reduced corruption and facilitated the loading and unloading of ships, but it also meant an increased role for Port-au-Prince. By fiscal year 1932–33, Port-au-Prince furnished 47 percent of customs receipts (69 percent of imports, 23 percent of exports), compared to less than 30 percent in 1890–91. This centralization contributed to the homogenization of merchant and political groups in the capital, and to the reinforcement of their power. Also, as Haiti was pressured to declare war on Germany in 1918—one year after the United States officially entered the conflict—German merchants were imprisoned and their properties confiscated. U.S. control of the commercial sector was then complete, even though prominent merchants were now Haitians or Levantine immigrants and even though most exports still went to Europe. Economic centralization also contributed to the growth of urban parasitic groups, as many provincials rushed to Port-au-Prince, hoping to grab choice places in the state apparatus. This growth of parasitic groups had—and continues to have—an enormous impact on Haitian politics.

Economic centralization went hand in hand with administrative and military centralization, and even with the passage of time it is not easy to determine which caused the most harm. Yet observers as different as James Leyburn and Paul Moral have both put the new balance of military power as among the occupation's most important consequences. Here we will examine the crucial effect of changes in the military on the balance of forces within the state and on the use of state violence against the nation.

AN ARMY TO FIGHT THE PEOPLE

The official pretext for the occupation was to end political anarchy and to establish democracy and civil liberties. Yet in fact the occupation only reinforced the oligarchy's conviction that power comes out of the barrel of a gun—except that, in this case, the gun was in foreign hands. All the absolutist practices for which the Haitian generals had been criticized—and justly so—were legitimized anew by the U.S. military. The list is long: it includes, among other things, the imposition of martial law (on September 3, 1915), the use of military tribunals for the trial of civilians (191 such cases in 1920 alone), the intimidation or illegal imprisonment of journalists, the dissolution of the legislature, the indiscriminate killing of peasants, and the nomination of excessive numbers of soldiers to top-ranking positions in the civilian administration. Even in the United States, the *New York Times, Atlantic Monthly, New Republic, Independent,* and *Nation* echoed the controversies to which these practices gave rise (Blassingame 1969; Schmidt 1971).

The renewed militarization that the Marines imposed on the state apparatus included the formation of a Haitian *gendarmerie* (later called *Garde*), the predecessor of the current army. After an uncertain start, its ranks swelled rapidly. By 1937, the new military apparatus, controlled from Port-au-Prince and filling the functions of both army and police, had 4,653 members (Calixte 1939; McCrocklin 1956). The complete disarming of the peasantry by the *Garde,* the strengthening of the power of the *police rurale,* and the centralization of the new military force all contributed to the concentration of political power in Port-au-Prince. Their effects were all the more strongly felt because the Marines prevented the development of regional solidarities within the new force. Hereafter, as Hans Schmidt (1971: 235) rightly notes, "Political strongmen in Port-au-Prince were able to control the entire country more effectively than ever before."

This concentration of power was particularly dangerous because it was wielded by men who shared an extremely narrow sense of Haiti as a nation. We cannot overemphasize this fundamental political difference between the *Garde* and the army that was dismantled by the Marines. For all its flaws—and despite the fact that it had killed as many Haitians during the second half of its 122-year-long history as it had Frenchmen during the war for independence—Haiti's first army saw itself as the offspring of the struggle against slavery and colonialism. It had first taken up arms against French troops and slaveowners, and long after independence it still included veterans of the victories against General Rochambeau's French forces. It took into its ranks immigrants and sons of immigrants of every sort, men whose patriotism—however defined at the time—was never in question. Its most important postindependence campaigns were the four—however unfortunate—engagements against the Dominican Republic. In short, it was primarily an army that claimed to fight foreigners and to defend the national community. Because of its stated role, because of its origins, and because of Haiti's position in the world, the nineteenth-century Haitian army believed it had been assigned a national mission, even though history may have proved it wrong.

In sharp contrast, the Haitian *Garde* was specifically created to fight against other Haitians. It received its baptism of fire in combat against its countrymen. And the *Garde*, like the army it was to sire, has indeed never fought anyone *but* Haitians. Its most important campaign was its participation alongside the Marines in the war against the peasant nationalists led by Charlemagne Péralte and Benoit Batraville, when Marines and *Garde* together killed at least 6,000 peasants. Another 5,500 cultivators died in the forced labor camps that the *Garde* ran for the occupiers (Moral 1961; Millet 1978; Schmidt 1971).

But the *Garde* did not turn its arms against peasants alone. From the earliest days of the occupation, the new form of state violence it represented was also applied against urbanites, and this repressive role intensified as time went on, especially when the occupiers found a growing number of individuals willing to join the *Garde*.

This point must be emphasized: the young men who joined the new armed forces could not have had any doubt as to what was expected of them—not after the murder of Péralte, not after the killing of Batraville. On December 14, 1929, the *Garde* arrested more than one hundred people (many of whom were students) who were taking part in a demonstration supporting a student strike at the agricultural school in Damien. Yet a few months later the occupiers had no trouble filling the first really "American" class in the military school, which reopened under Marine auspices in 1930. The names of the recruits who played important (if infamous) roles in the politics of these last three decades are too numerous to list here, but the military school's class of 1930–31—the first trained in politics and crowd control—included Paul Magloire, Léon Cantave, and Antonio Kébreau. These three men were to succeed each other as commander in chief between 1951 and 1958. As such, they were the first three routinely to raise the specter of the army over the civilians of Port-au-Prince. The truth is that anyone who entered the military school in the 1930s had a taste for violent solutions; the Marines ensured that such a taste would be systematically cultivated and transmitted to succeeding classes.

In the end, then, the U.S. occupation worsened all of Haiti's structural ills. Only the centralization of the army managed to create a transient veneer of political stability. But, as we shall see, Haiti was to pay dearly for this veneer: certainly today's chaos is no less severe than the troubles that the occupation was supposed to end.

The occupation also aggravated some of Haiti's social problems, notably color prejudice. Racial discrimination against blacks and their descendants began in the French colony of Saint-Domingue long before the first manifestations of U.S. racism on Haitian soil. Similarly, many Haitian *mulâtres* did not wait until 1915 to consider themselves closer to the ideal race and thus superior to blacks. But whether or not the Marines who invaded Haiti were predominantly from the southern United States— which is a subject of debate—it is certain that their behavior, both as individuals and as a group, reinforced color prejudice. The Marines helped install three light-skinned presidents closely associated with the *mulâtre* faction of the elites. U.S. administrators clearly showed their preference for light-skinned Haitian officials. Even Leyburn, who has tried to suggest that the U.S. Marines *may* not have been guilty of color prejudice—an admittedly extreme extension of the "innocent until proven guilty" thesis—concedes that there were few dark-skinned Haitians in the important ministries. He adds: "This return to political power of the colored element was one of the most sweeping transformations effected by the Marines" (Leyburn 1941: 101).

It was, however, a light-skinned president, Sténio Vincent, who made the Marines' departure the top priority of his government. A former member of the Senate and a charismatic speaker with populist tendencies (he was one of the first presidents routinely to make official speeches in Haitian), Vincent came to the presidency in 1930, the winner of the first election in which the Marines did not interfere. From then on, he steadfastly negotiated the withdrawal of the U.S. forces from Haitian soil. In Washington, some officials were tiring of the occupation, unable to remember what the point had been in the first place. Others quietly admitted that the entire venture had been a failure. Black Americans also turned against the occupation in increasing numbers, a sharp change from the early position of many black intellectuals, including Henry Watson

Furniss. The NAACP, a long-time critic of U.S. actions in Haiti, intensified its protest. In 1931, the Hoover administration returned most of the ministries to Haitian control. President Roosevelt personally helped speed up the process of withdrawal, and by the end of 1934 the last Marines had gone and the Haitian flag flew once again on all government buildings.

At the end of Vincent's tenure, however, the U.S. embassy and that of the Dominican Republic—also firmly under U.S. control—joined with members of the Haitian elites who were dissatisfied with Vincent's populism to "encourage" the election of Elie Lescot. Lescot was light-skinned, like his three predecessors, but much more a *mulâtre* than even Dartiguenave. The prominence of light-skinned people in the administration, a legacy of the occupation, reached its height during his presidency. In January 1946, students took to the streets demanding greater civil liberties and new legislative elections. Middle-class intellectuals sprang to the head of the popular movement, emphasizing the social injustice that, in their view, Lescot's regime had exacerbated. In the midst of a series of strikes and riots, a group of army officers, led by Major Paul Magloire, forced Lescot to resign. A military junta, with Magloire as its strongman, took over and quickly organized legislative elections. The new Legislature, with the blessing of Magloire (who had decided to go with the tide), elected one of its *noiriste* members, Dumarsais Estimé, as president of the Republic. Estimé, a provincial schoolteacher and typical representative of the new middle classes, thus found himself the uncontested leader of the "Revolution of 1946."

4
Culture, Color, and Politics

Both witnesses and participants found it easy to describe the so-called Revolution of 1946 as a victory of "black power" over *mulâtre* domination (e.g., Bonhomme 1946; 1957; Collectif Paroles 1976). Similarly, the Duvalier regimes, especially that of the father, have often been referred to as black power regimes. Yet the label is misleading. In both cases, though color was an idiom of politics, the members of rival groups could not be immediately identified solely on the basis of their phenotype. There were dark-skinned individuals both for and against Estimé, and light-skinned individuals both for and against the two Duvaliers. Further, the grievances expressed in 1946 were not aimed simply at color prejudice; some called for a sweeping reevaluation of the social and cultural practices and values that typified Haitian urban life.

Part of the difficulty in dealing with color and politics in Haiti is that while the "color question" cannot be separated from Western cultural influence and a worldwide hierarchy of races, religions, and cultures, at the same time it cannot be reduced to a mere avatar of Western prejudices. Indeed, few Haitian practices and beliefs can be considered derivatively Western. In the social perception and use of somatic differences, as in most domains, the cultural influence of the West is constantly being challenged, even if only partially by local practices, beliefs, and values.

A second difficulty stems from the fact that in Haiti conflict between color-cum-social categories does not simply reflect an opposition between social classes, however defined: the dominant classes are not composed exclusively of light-skinned individuals; nor do all such individuals belong to those classes. A third difficulty is the widespread disapproval of discourses and practices that hint at institutional discrimination on the basis of color—or "race"—alone. Models of discrimination on the basis

109

of appearance, drawn from the experiences of South Africa or the United States, lose their meaning in Haiti because the social postulates on which they are based (and which are, in turn, maintained by discrimination) simply do not apply. Neither do traditional models of racial conflict. There are no bomb threats for moving into the "wrong" neighborhood, no graffiti slurs on school walls, no lynchings, no street wars. Haiti never had a "color riot," let alone a "race riot."

An underlying proposition of this chapter is that the beliefs and practices that Haitian urbanites refer to as the "color question" do not operate in a social vacuum, to the exclusion of all else. Instead, color-cum-social categories operate in various spheres of urban life as part of different strategies of competition and struggle. They materialize most vividly in the familial alliances typical of certain urban classes and they are often a favored idiom of politics. But they also function as referents for sociocultural oppositions outside of the immediate political arena. It is this complexity that explains the fact that references to the "color question" could bestow upon Estimé, in 1946, and Duvalier, in 1957, the legitimacy they then claimed for themselves. To discover the roots of this legitimacy, which François Duvalier inherited from Estimé, we must first turn to the international hierarchy of races, colors, religions, and cultures, and to the ambivalent response of the Haitian elites to the cultural domination of the West.

THE "COLOR" COMPLEX

Those who persist in claiming that the West is *merely* capitalist will have difficulty acknowledging that the international division of labor is paired with a hierarchy of races, colors, religions, and cultures whose complexity cannot be reduced to labor-market segmentation. Ethnocentrism preceded the creation of a European proletariat, let alone an international one. It is fair to say that ethnic identity even foreshadowed the advent of class-based societies. The comparison between "us" and "them" implies, among other evaluative criteria, the existence of what H. Hoetink (1967) called a somatic norm-image, a physical ideal of beauty. All things being equal, "we" are always more attractive than "they."[1] At the very least, we are closer to what human beings really should look like.

But things are not always equal. Because of the differential accumulation of technology, as well as the institutionalization of a combative posture that marked the evolution of Mediterranean peoples well before the rise of capitalism, what came to be called the "West" gave itself a distinct identity. The West defined itself, so to speak, in the course of a history punctuated by internal and external conquests, a history engaged almost from the start in a legitimizing discourse. These conquests and this discourse preceded the north-south social fissure of the Mediterranean from which Europe, as we now know it, was born. Aristotle had already formulated the hypothesis, echoed in fifteenth-century Spain, that some men were inferior and therefore fated to be slaves. Diodorus Siculus found the Ethiopians "primitive," and from Pliny the Elder's imagination sprang monstrous subhumans in the heart of black Africa—men without mouths, noses, voices, or eyes, unspeakably ugly monsters.

No doubt other cultures developed similar themes of exclusion of the Other. But as I said earlier, all things were not equal, for the accounts that have come down to us are those of Diodorus and Pliny, along with those of myriads of Westerners, from the Renaissance to the present. I would thus hesitate to argue that capitalism alone allowed Europe to spread and systematize an unflattering image of others. At any rate, that spread and that systematization brought qualitative changes in the European social perception of somatic differences. If ethnocentrism was ever naive, it certainly stopped being so after the systematic demeaning of the cultures of the Other used to justify colonial conquests and plantation slavery. This new threshold required in turn the European vision to be just as systematically imposed on the dominated peoples themselves. By the 1620s, Africans and Amerindians of the Antilles and the Atlantic coast of the American mainland had to be aware of their differential status on the European-imposed scale, just as Asian immigrants were to find out in the 1850s that European preconceptions of their failures and worth had accompanied them to the New World (Du Tertre 1667; Gage [1648] 1958; Trollope [1859] 1985).

All this is to say—and it is of extreme importance—that the phenomenon described in Haiti in rather sibylline terms as the "color question" is etched within the framework of an international hierarchy that was formalized well before Haitian independence. A female member of the Haitian bourgeoisie conveniently reaffirmed this age-old context when she told anthropologist Micheline Labelle "If they marry a *noir,* people will say that the children are horrible, and since color prejudice is international, if they are sent abroad to study they will have problems" (cited in Labelle 1976: 35).

Saint-Domingue, and then Haiti, thus inherited a differential evaluation of races, colors, religions, and cultures. This evaluation included an aesthetic in which blackness was found at the bottom of the scale. To pretend that this aesthetic has disappeared is ludicrous: photos of recent beauty contests or the sight of advertising posters confirm its continued existence. Admittedly, aesthetic evaluations vary according to the socio-economic class and phenotype of those who judge, and the results are sometimes surprising to foreigners (Labelle 1976, 1978). Generally speaking "white," for example, is *not* considered to be the most pleasing color. Social evaluations of phenotypes in Haiti are nonetheless generally *Western dominated* and, other things being equal, beyond a certain degree of increased melanin, these evaluations imply a denigration of blackness.

But here again, other things are rarely equal. Thus the reader who is unfamiliar with Haiti must be immediately cautioned lest he or she takes the preceding to imply that Haitian color prejudice is simply a toned-down version of Western racism. As Sidney Mintz (1984: 299) has lucidly written, "North American ideas about what 'color' someone is are far more hindrance than help in understanding Haiti." Nor am I certain that a European perception would be more useful.[2] To start with, Haitian "color" categories refer to many more aspects of phenotype than skin color alone, even when their etymology seems to indicate an exclusively epidermic referent. Epidermic shade remains crucial, but skin texture and depth of skin tone, hair color and appearance, and facial features also figure in any categorization. Thus two individuals who seem to be the same "color" can be classed in different categories because of other somatic criteria. Color thus functions as a dividing line, negatively delimiting a field of possible categories. In other words, it would be much easier for two Haitians to agree that X could *not* be considered *noir* because he is too "light," or that Y could *not* be considered *mulâtre* because he is too "dark," than to agree on the category (which is not always intermediate) in which to place X or Y. The color line that separates *clairs* (including subgroups such as *mulâtres, griffes, grimauds,* and *mulâtres bruns*) from the *noirs* (including the more or less dark epidermic shades and various types of hair) is the most important among a number of somatic boundaries that operate together. Color never operates alone, even in the perception of physical difference.

More importantly, color categories embrace characteristics that go far beyond the perceived phenotype into the field of social relations. These can include income, social origin, level of formal education, customary behavior, ties of kinship or marriage, and other characteristics. And different combinations of these social traits can move a person from one category to a more or less proximate one. Thus terms such as *mulâtre* and *noir* do not simply mean—and sometimes do not mean at all—"mulatto" or "black" in the American sense. The kind of social discrimination that operates in Haiti is not exclusively based on physical features, even when phenotype plays a role in the application and description of this discrimination. For example, up until very recently some people were discouraged from frequenting certain clubs because they were "too *noir*," although others, visibly darker, could enter. In short, Haitian color categories refer not only to skin color and other somatic features, but to a large range of sociocultural attributes that do not have a somatic referent.

The reshaping of these categories—a process that has been going on at least since independence—has been facilitated by the growth of beliefs and practices in which Western influence figures but does not go uncontested. If it is important to note that Haitian color prejudice relates to a Western-dominated hierarchy of races, colors, religions, and cultures, it is equally crucial to note that very few Haitians, even among the elites, ever accepted that hierarchy as a "true" depiction of their reality. In any case, the urban elites, the most Westernized part of the population, never gained such full control of the cultural terrain that they could impose a pre-packaged Western view on the rest of the population.

THE CULTURAL GUERRILLA WAR

We saw in chapter 2 the limits of the dualist view that treats Haitian society as if it consisted of two separate parts. I have also suggested that the physical to-and-fro of the peasantry from the hinterland to the urban trenches meant that it has come to occupy part of the urban social and cultural terrain. That terrain does not simply mirror the political scene. Nor is it a mere reflection of economic structures: while the economic and political divisions may be reminiscent of trench warfare, the cultural relations between the classes are more reminiscent of a guerrilla war. The peasantry is not the master of this space—or never for long—but it penetrates it deeply and harasses the enemy, while remaining ready to retreat at any point. It does not dictate the dominant cultural codes, but those who impose them must take its values into account. For example, there is no aspect of Haitian economic and political life that explains why the Jaegerhubers, a commercial family of German origin firmly ensconced within the bourgeoisie, should have invested a considerable amount of time at the beginning of this century in transcribing peasant songs. It is true that their interest in musical folklore had Wagnerian overtones, but their sympathetic view of the peasant tradition cannot be explained without reference to Haiti's cultural dynamics. The history of urban arts, of painting and music—as well as of religion, language, and the organization of kinship networks—all indicate the existence within civil society of another order of relationships alongside the dominant one. The peasantry cannot be said to be victorious in the cultural sphere, but it has an implicitly acknowledged presence there, to a degree as yet unmatched in the political and economic arenas.

Of course, even in this cultural domain the peasantry does not have the last word. Just as peasant practices filter into the city, the dominant culture's hostility to many of these practices filters back to the peasantry, subtly adding to its isolation by repeatedly stressing its inferiority.[3] Thus the cultural distance between town and countryside lies as much in the social assessment of practices and beliefs as in their actual distribution. A significant number of peasant practices that are publicly spurned by the elites are still nurtured privately among all urban classes. More important-ly, even when practices vary—as of course they do—they often take root in the same underlying values. The crux of the matter is that these underlying values are differently acknowledged, and carry a different symbolic weight in different class presentations.

Religion provides a good example of these similarities and differences. In the half-century of incubation that followed independence, what is commonly referred to as Vodoun by nonpractitioners emerged as the religion of the majority, a distinctly Haitian complex of philosophical tenets, religious beliefs, and ritual practices. But while the masses publicly cherished these practices and beliefs, which they never considered antithetic to Catholicism, the urbanites always professed an exclusive adherence to orthodox Christianity, even though, to different degrees, they shared religious beliefs rooted in the same African-dominated cosmology and took part in similar rituals. Elite distortion of Catholic (and today Protestant) theology and liturgy ended only when and where the influence of Vodoun on their "Christian" practice was publicly identifiable. Short of that, substantial tenets of the same philosophy and a number of the same basic beliefs are held by most Haitians.

Language offers another example. Most linguists have stopped calling Haiti bilingual. They speak instead of a diglossic situation, in which a bilingual minority imposes one language as the language of power. This analysis is a positive intellectual development but may still fall short of the truth. Two languages do indeed coexist in Haiti: French and Haitian. The Haitian (Creole) language probably arose during slavery and solidified during the first half-century of independence. All Haitians speak Haitian as their native language: only a few of the most educated urbanites are native bilingual. The majority of French speakers (less than 8 percent of the total population) reach varying degrees of competence through the school system. Thus the linguistic dichotomy does not appear at the level of communication, or even in an unqualified preference for French: any Haitian is capable of communicating anything to any other Haitian in Haitian, and the most francophile urbanites often prefer to use Haitian in situations where everyone is competent in French.[4] Rather, the dichotomy resides in the power attached to certain forms of communication, most of which include the use of French; in the fact that mere knowledge of French gives differential access to power; in the prestige attached to that language; and in the fact that this prestige is nationwide—even the peasantry believes in it to some extent. The political consequence is that the exclusive use of French in the nation's official discourse appears "natural." In point of fact, the elites have never bothered to make that exclusivity official: French became Haiti's official language during the U.S. occupation through a constitution that Franklin D. Roosevelt later claimed to have written personally. By then, French exclusivity in the spheres of power was threatened by English rather than by the Haitian language, and legitimization was seen by many as reinforcing not just French, but the entire French/Creole complex, set in contradistinction to English.

In its own way, the example of language hints at the complexity of Haitian cultural traditions and struggles, and at the cultural ambivalence of the Haitian elites. Because these elites inherited some of the ambiguities of the French colonists' sense of identity (see chapter 1), and because the peasantry consistently preserved its claim to the cultural arena, the dominant classes never succeeded in imposing Western cultural domination on the people. It is even more startling that they may never have entirely wished to do so. Haitian writers have rarely presented the West as a sociocultural ideal *in toto,* even though they clearly saw France, Germany, Holland, and the United States—more or less in that order—as imitable superiors in specific domains. But even those specific achievements did not imply the innate superiority of the "whites," inasmuch as many Haitian literati genuinely believed in the perfectibility of all human groups—the ultimate primacy of culture over nature. Within that framework, the recognition of Western achievements did not carry with it the need to reject all indigenous practices. Thus while the Haitian elites placed French literature on a pedestal, they reserved for themselves the right to speak the native language, to sing Creole songs, to write of the beauty of the peasant woman in verses patterned after what they perceived as the latest Parisian literary style. While they held foreign—especially French—diplomas in high esteem, they continuously decried the lack of natural and human warmth in the Western countries they visited. While they proudly adopted European manners, they also engaged proudly in many indigenous practices that they judged worthy of their time and attention. This in turn meant that the peasantry—and many customs or features that the elites' imagination associated with that peasantry, including "blackness"—were often ennobled in words, even if kept at safe distance in practice. It also meant that the Western-dominated hierarchy of races, colors, religions, and cultures was never swallowed whole, never accepted without modification.

Understandably, then, *mulâtrisme* as an ideology of *mulâtre* power, has always been on the defensive in Haiti, in part because it could always be accused of being a version of Western racism. Its most diehard proponents—who often looked, sounded, or acted more "Western" than other Haitians—rarely dared to claim exclusive social and political rights for any group of Haitians identified on the basis of "color," however defined. Light-skinned politicians and intellectuals consistently denied any trace of color prejudice. Even an immigrant like Joseph Saint-Rémy could write: "I belong to no caste, to no sect . . ." (Nicholls 1979: 94). In public, at least, they professed varying degrees of paternalistic "respect" for the black peasantry and many of its cultural traditions—Vodoun being for a long time the major exception. Early *mulâtre* claims to political control were therefore not based on assertions of inherited superiority but on the allegedly greater contribution made by their light-skinned ancestors in the forging of the Haitian nation.

The impossibility of publicly advocating color prejudice in Haiti in face-to-face debates was furthered by the history of Haiti itself—or by the elites' perception of that history. More for them perhaps than for the common folk, the Haitian revolution was and remains the final symbol of the regeneration of the entire "black race" from the abyss imposed by slavery (Nicholls 1979). The revolutionary war was a war against the "whites," and independence in 1804 a victory over colonialism, slavery, *and* white supremacy. Further, the relentless ostracism imposed on the black republic during the nineteenth century reinforced, among Haitian urbanites, a sense of racial identity that included *all* blacks. For instance, Pétion's *mulâtre*-dominated government did not abrogate Dessalines' law that gave near automatic citizenship to any black person landing on Haitian soil. Similarly, Pétion and Boyer both tried to help anti-slavery forces throughout the Americas as much as they could. Disagreements about the state notwithstanding, from the war of independence to the present the nation has always conceived of itself as a "black" community. This racial sense imposed severe limits on the expression of *mulâtre* ideology.

Demographics reinforced these limits, especially after 1843, when it became clear that power would have to be shared with a minority of dark-skinned individuals. The use of color rhetoric by black politicians since Toussaint Louverture had taught light-skinned leaders that it was politically dangerous to be either pro-white or anti-black in Haiti. If some light-skinned individuals did claim a privileged right to govern, they made it clear that this right proceeded in part from the blackness they shared with the rest of the population. Whether or not they were sincere is hard to tell, and probably beside the point. The important fact is that a combination of historical, cultural, and demographic factors made it impossible for them to claim political legitimacy if they excluded all positive references to blackness.

Given that there has never been a public discourse denigrating blackness in independent Haiti, some authors have concluded that color prejudice as such does not exist and that the "color question" is nothing more than "metaphysical sophistry" (e.g., Lamartinière 1976). I have already suggested that, contrary to such assertions, color is indeed salient in Haiti, if only because of the Western influence on sociocultural ratings, including aesthetic evaluations. The next three sections will show how color materializes in the play of familial and class alliances among the urban population.

THE BIOLOGICAL REPRODUCTION OF COLOR

Consider the demographic data for Saint-Domingue at the start of the slave uprising in 1791. How does it happen that there are so many people in Haiti who are still light enough to be considered *clairs* or *mulâtres?* The answer to this question unequivocally proves that color is salient when there are social choices.[5] For however much one plays with the figures, they do not agree with the statistical probabilities of demography or physical anthropology. The conclusion is obvious: it is just as impossible to explain the survival of light-skinned people in Haiti by genetic coincidence as it is to explain the survival of a black minority in the United States without reference to the (social) segregation of biological reproduction.

In 1789, Saint-Domingue had around 500,000 blacks, 27,500 free *gens de couleur,* and about 31,000 whites. Although in absolute terms the war of independence killed a greater number of blacks (Auguste and Auguste 1985), it affected the other two groups to a proportionately greater degree because they were so much smaller. The slaves' victories reduced the white presence to a negligible number and also sharply reduced the number of individuals of mixed descent, many of whom left the country for other islands or for the United States (particularly Louisiana, Maryland, and Pennsylvania). Thus Haiti became independent with a tiny white population (probably less than 1 percent) and a small mulatto minority (5 percent at most). Under these conditions, the laws of biological reproduction cannot explain the survival of this minority, which should have collapsed under the weight of a darker majority.

And that weight was substantial. Indeed, the epidermic line separating *clairs* and *noirs* itself shifted because of the preponderance of the darker tones: darker and darker people began to be included within the group of *clairs,* almost by default, so that a large number of individuals who are considered *mulâtres* today would have flunked the exam, on somatic grounds, at the end of the last century. But the *clair/noir* divide does not disappear under the weight of genetics; instead the main somatic boundary continues to shift. It is the elasticity and resilience of this boundary—the fact that it always allows for the isolation of a category of people called *clairs*—that bears witness to the social reality of color. It is the very survival of such categories and subcategories, all with increasingly fluid somatic referents, that shows the preeminence of social over biological reproduction.[6] The *clairs* of Haiti reproduced themselves essentially "from the inside" (that is, with no significant alliances with white outsiders), with the most *mulâtre* families (those that best combined light skin, valued facial and hair characteristics, *and* economic and social success) leading the way. In addition, the *mulâtre* sector of the Haitian elites has practiced an endogamous policy, marrying its sons to its daughters whenever possible. This choice can only be explained in terms of color prejudice, because class relations do not lend themselves to the same divisions. This is, moreover, the dilemma that (traditional) Marxist analysis of the *noirisme/mulâtrisme* duo refuses to confront. Either the color question is an immediate reflection of class relations—and then it would have no autonomy, for *the entire dominant class would be clair and all the clairs would be of the dominant class* (which is obviously false, and very close to the Denis-Duvalier 1938 thesis)—or color prejudice is relatively autonomous with regard to economic structures, and this autonomy must be taken into account.

THE SOCIAL REPRODUCTION OF COLOR

Color divisions do not simply replicate socioeconomic classes, or even income groups. In fact, the "color line" (the key boundary between *noirs* and *clairs*) and the boundary between poor and rich have both been moving since independence, each in its own direction. As mentioned before, somatic boundaries have moved to include darker and darker epidermic shades among the *clairs*. At the same time, fewer and fewer *clairs* are found among the underprivileged classes. Jean-Jacques Acau, the nineteenth-century leader of a private rural army that once controlled parts of the South and repeatedly challenged Port-au-Prince's central power, is credited with the famous saying "Nèg rich se milat; milat pòv se nèg" ("The rich black is a mulatto; the poor mulatto is a black").[7] But we must face the facts. Today there are many black-skinned individuals among the rich—or at least many more than before—but few light-skinned individuals among the very poor. We are far from the time when Candler (1842: 55) met, among the peasantry, a poor mulatto woman whose prejudice seemed to him more virulent than that of her urban counterparts.[8] Let me suggest that the movement of those two lines, color and income, is connected—and that it is through this dual movement that the reproduction of a social stratum perceived as *clair* fits within the reproduction of the dominant urban strata.

Jean Price-Mars, the dean of Haitian ethnology, provides the example that I shall use as a point of departure. Around 1870 in Cap-Haïtien, on the same street where Anténor Firmin, a young *black-skinned* intellectual, lived with his aunt, there also lived "a pretty young girl, a *mulâtresse brune,* Mlle. Marie Louise Salnave, also known as Rosa. [She was the daughter of the president who was executed in January 1870.] She lived with her mother, brothers, and sisters. . . . The two young people, Anténor and Rosa, fell in love and promised to marry. But on both sides of the two families, the parents, it seems, opposed the marriage" (Price-Mars n.d.: 119). The reasons were unclear, but wags hinted that the heart of the matter was that the Salnave family, which was light-skinned, believed that the union was a mismatch. At any rate, in 1876 Rosa Salnave married a *clair*. In 1878 Rosa's husband died. Three years later, she took Anténor Firmin as her second husband.

Price-Mars (n.d.: 119–127) refers to numerous alliances between *noir* and *mulâtre* families of Cap-Haïtien and to the imposing number of prominent *noirs* of the North in order to suggest that color prejudice was not at work in the region and therefore cannot explain Anténor's first rejection. I accept Price-Mars' description of these alliances, but I would like to suggest that they prove the opposite thesis. What these alliances suggest, and what Anténor's and Rosa's marriage indicates, is that even in Cap-Haïtien, not just any *noir* could marry a *mulâtre*.

Price-Mars' analysis falls short in the secondary role that it attributes to what I call "social direction," that is, the path that an individual is perceived to be taking up or down the social ladder. Assuming that social positions are never fully guaranteed in complex societies, that they must be gained or maintained and can always be lost, I would suggest that individuals are always in motion on that ladder, however minimally. Society judges this continuous movement positively or negatively, and "social direction" is the result of that judgment. It is a measure of the social distance between what is thought to be known of an individual's origin and what is thought to be known of his or her future. It is a value-loaded perception of a projected distance. Individual time matters a great deal in that light.

In the case of Salnave and Firmin, we can see how individual time mattered. To be sure, between 1870 and 1881 the actors' phenotypes had not changed: the individuals were the same, only older. But it is surprising that an ethnologist makes so little of the fact that this was a second marriage for Salnave. Her social direction was no longer on the ascent. On the other side of the somatic boundary—that is, on the Firmin side—there had been a rise in social standing and, more importantly, the promise of a future that might even end in the presidency. Price-Mars admits that between the young intellectual of 1870 and the man who married the *claire* daughter of a former president lay the difference of time and social promotion. In other words, by 1881 Firmin was one of the very few *noirs* who could enter what Price-Mars calls the clique "of patricians, who, because of their position of wealth, or what so appeared, occupied the summit of the social hierarchy" (Price-Mars n.d.: 126).

Price-Mars' references to cross-color marriages among the northern elites takes on their full meaning once couched in these terms. It was not that the North did not know color prejudice but that the aristocracy that had sprung from Christophe's secessionist kingdom had produced an extraordinary number of *noirs* who could marry *mulâtres* if their hearts so desired. I am prepared to concede that if this aristocracy had reproduced itself across the entire country, and if the promotion of urban blacks like Firmin had been more widespread, color prejudice would perhaps have disappeared. Socioeconomic status would have achieved the upper hand in what Lévi-Straussian anthropology pompously calls "wife exchange." But Christophe's kingdom did not extend across the entire country and the alliance it produced between the *noir* and *mulâtre* landed aristocracies did not operate on the national level, where the prejudice itself was regenerated. Moreover, the original northern alliance across the epidermic line was based on the accumulation of land. Yet we have seen that Pétion, Boyer, Hérard, and their successors, squeezed by the peasantry, abandoned land accumulation in favor of an exploitative system centered around the customhouses. The feudal dream in which a *noir* aristocracy would have equal footing with its *mulâtre* counterparts crumbled with this choice.

In other words, even though color has never functioned alone, it has had an independent social value, even in the North. It is a commodity in the game of inter- and intra-class alliances. It has an exchange value, which can be and is calculated, even if that value is much lower in the North than in the West (e.g., Jacmel) or the South (e.g., Jérémie). Color is always part of what Price-Mars (n.d.: 126) delicately refers to as the "particularities of the social condition" in Haiti. And as a particularity of an individual's social condition, color plays a role in the reproduction of the social groups to which the individual belongs.

Historian Jean Fouchard (1972) reminds us that a number of families in the Haitian elites have a *noir* branch and a *mulâtre* branch, while other families move from the *noir* to the *mulâtre* pole of intellectual and political factions, and vice versa. This is true, even though it is difficult to find *noir* branches among the families who have traditionally been at the very top of the economic ladder. But what no one has ever emphasized is the socioeconomic exchange governing these passages or alternations. Here, I would submit—as a working hypothesis that must be further developed—that the passage from the *noir* side to the *mulâtre* side is often coupled with socioeconomic promotion. Conversely, the passage from the *clair* side to the *noir* side is often an indication of demotion. Demotions and promotions crosscut one another, because the respective social directions of bride and groom usually cancel each other out, with the darker partner being, most often, the one on the rise. Thus the couple as such neither rises nor falls—it becomes. The results of the exchange are confirmed only one or two generations later.

I will take a classic case. A young woman who can be placed in the *clair* category works as a salesgirl in a store or as a secretary in public administration. Her limited education betrays her lower-middle-class origins, but she spends much more money on clothes than her darker colleagues. What she guarantees by her dress, her discretion, and the places she frequents is in the end a social investment—her color. She will probably not marry into the top layer of the *mulâtre* elite, because the *mulâtre* aristocracy is endogamous. But she will try to marry "up," to marry a businessman, a professional, a well-placed public servant, preferably also a *clair.* Chances are, however, that the desired *clairs* will tend to think twice about a legal union with her, since they are playing the same game. Hence it is most likely that the young lady will marry within the *noir* group. But not any *noir* will do. First, the groom will probably have one of the few phenotypes somatically valued in spite of dark complexion (e.g., *bon noir, noir fin, marabout*). More important, his social direction will be unambiguously upward.

In short, the light-skinned bride contributes epidermic capital while her darker husband brings a diploma, savings, or the promise of a successful future, together with a reasonably acceptable somatic package. Social direction being a projection into the future, the promise may never materialize. Further, even if the projection is correct, the results will not be immediately apparent. Once more, the couple as such does not rise, or barely. It will not be admitted into the *crème de la crème:* people will "forget" to invite them to certain birthday or tennis parties. But their children, already lighter than their father, will freely associate with those who match their status, family income, and perceived phenotype. Increasingly, they will gravitate around individuals a shade lighter than themselves. The children are the ones who will enter smaller and smaller circles inaccessible to both parents: they are the ones who have a chance of becoming *mulâtres* of a kind. And their own children—if they marry a *clair*—will become part of an endogamous circle, pushing the somatic boundaries a little further in the direction of darker shades, but in doing so continuing to guarantee the domination of color.

THE REPRODUCTION OF
COLOR AND CLASS

If we reverse the genders and place a male on the *clair* side of the exchange, we need make only small modifications to our scenario—he would need a higher level of formal education than his female counterpart, a professional diploma, a successful military career, or the label of "intellectual."[9] Numerous *p'tits mulâtres de province* have bartered their skin color for security. Not for their own security, perhaps (because they do not enter *ipso facto* into the most exclusive circles), but for the security of their children—or, to be more exact, for the security of their names.

For color prejudice weighed on the progeny very early. Jonathan Brown reports the case of a *mulâtresse* who rejected one of the best catches of Boyer's republic on the basis of his color. The young lady insisted, with arrogant frankness, that she herself cared little about the pigmentation of her suitor. "But to have children blacker than herself, *petits enfants griffes,* how horrible!" (Brown [1837] 1971, 2: 284). And as the main somatic divide moved to include darker skins among the *clairs,* this emphasis on the progeny increased.

And here is where the exchange is deceptive: it does not operate immediately but over the span of generations. In the to-and-fro of the exchange, many are the *clair* families that have a *noir* skeleton in the closet. And while these families have made it their duty to exhibit this skeleton if necessary to prove their blackness, in the meantime the reproduction of prejudice continues along on its merry way. Mothers know this—they who so strictly control those whom their sons and (especially) their daughters associate with. It is a matter of reducing the field in such a way that the exchange can involve only the trade-off between social promotion and phenotype, the other possibilities having been eliminated by restricted association. Numerous common expressions jovially but discreetly exchanged among close friends and relatives register the trade-off. The darker partner is said to be "putting some milk into his/her coffee," or simply "improving the race." The lighter one is said to be aware of his/her own game (in Haitian, "Se li ki konnen zafè li"). Yet the returns are not necessarily collected during the timespan of the marriage, but later on, even generations later. Thus the display of wealth and influence, or the schema of economic structures, never reflect color cleavages in the short run. At any given moment the exchange guarantees a discrepancy between the economic and political domains and socio-epidermic classifications. But the very fact that the exchange continues, and that most urbanites participate in it—within their own restricted pool—maintains the pernicious impression of "an aristocracy of the skin" that all the involved parties believe in. The phrase attributed to Acau can now be modified: a rich black *becomes* a mulatto, a poor mulatto *becomes* black.

COLOR AND POLITICS

The ambiguity inherent in the practices described above have made color prejudice a choice subject for dark politicians. While they could not easily point to institutionalized discriminatory practices in Haiti, such as those of the United States or South Africa, they had no need to prove the existence of an epidermal elite because everyone believed it existed. Predominantly *mulâtre* clubs, schools, neighborhoods, and political cliques existed, even though legally everyone had access to them and even though a small number of *noirs* were found there. Over time, this perception of an epidermal elite, whose income, education, and social status remained inaccessible to the majority and which treated that majority with arrogant indifference, created extraordinary resentment among urban *noirs,* particularly those of the middle classes. This resentment, which reached its height in 1946, reinforced the twentieth-century version of *noirisme.*

Ironically, the *noiriste* theory of power finds its direct origins in the political ideology espoused by many mulattoes from the 1780s to the 1830s. It boils down to an epidermic quota: the representatives of the largest color group should have "natural" access to power. This is an argument whose origins can be traced to certain pre-independence mulattoes, such as Vincent Ogé, but slavery and colonial rule limited its impact. After independence, Beaubrun Ardouin, writer, politician, and *mulâtre* ideologue, took up with renewed enthusiasm Ogé's argument that the mulattoes and their descendants had a natural right to rule Haiti by virtue of their origins—because the blacks came from Africa and the whites from Europe.

The *noiriste* theory of power is one more version of this argument of "natural" legitimacy. The crucial difference is that in the mouths of politicians perceived as darker than their opponents, in a context where color matters—even if in the rather labyrinthine manner described here—the argument could both refer and appeal to much larger segments of the citizenry. As such, *noirisme* has always been an extremely potent discourse in Haiti, and it is likely to remain so as long as the perception of an "aristocracy of the skin" remains. An embryonic *noirisme* was already visible in Louverture's polemical use of the "color question" against Rigaud in the late 1790s. *Noiriste* arguments appeared in 1843 in the fight against Boyer, then less subtly in the 1860s with the Parti National, whose slogan was, significantly, "The greatest good for the greatest number." There was no doubt in this context to whom the "greatest number" referred.

Whereas *noirisme* tends to make explicit references to skin color, *mulâtrisme* avoids them at all cost. After independence, light-skinned politicians systematically denied the existence of color prejudice. Once they had established the *mulâtre*-controlled form of "government by understudy," they removed most references to color from their political discourse. To be sure, they first tried, in vain, to associate Saint-Domingue mulattoes with the leadership of the Haitian revolution; but once that strategy failed, *mulâtrisme* capitalized on the illusion of competence. The theory was encapsulated by the middle of the nineteenth century in the slogan of Edmond Paul, a dark-skinned theoretician of the Parti Libéral: "Le pouvoir aux plus capables" ("Power to the most competent"). One can trace the roots of that slogan in the writings of many *mulâtres* in the immediate aftermath of independence.

The reference to competence gave a distinct advantage to the *clairs,* especially in the nineteenth century. Just as everyone knew to whom the "greatest number" referred, so they knew who claimed to be "most capable." As a group, the *clairs* had clear economic and educational advantages since before independence: they could indeed define what it meant to be "capable." But the reference to competence allowed them to claim power for themselves while deflecting accusations of discrimination. Competence was a commodity supposedly available to everyone, an objective toward which the *noirs* themselves aimed. In contradistinction, phenotypical resemblance to the majority was not an ideal, even for *noir* leaders. Indeed, a majority of the *noiriste* ideologues had light-skinned wives, light-skinned progeny, or at the very least progeny lighter than themselves.[10]

The competition between *noir* and *mulâtre* factions for control of the state apparatus never took on the appearance of an all-out color war. The "most capable," like the "greatest number" or other expressions of this type, functioned as a polite code behind which everyone recognized the "color question," without it being explicitly formulated and detailed. In fact, *noiriste* political factions never got rid of their own mulattoes. The most recent example of this is François Duvalier, but President Salomon also put the presence of "his" *mulâtres* in the state apparatus to good use (Gaillard 1984: 47, 142–146). *Mulâtre* political factions in turn almost always included black intellectuals and military men. Edmond Paul and Anténor Firmin, the most coherent theoreticians of the Parti Libéral (the *mulâtre* party *par excellence*) had black skins. Nord Alexis, a powerful general who sold his support to the highest bidding *mulâtristes,* was also black. Even in 1946, when the electoral battle clearly took on the aspect of a color struggle, the rivals of the *noiriste* candidate, Dumarsais Estimé, were all black skinned (Bonhomme 1957).

Contrary, therefore, to the interplay of family alliances, the appeal to color in the field of politics did not need a concrete somatic referent. Anténor Firmin asserted that, in the electoral campaign of 1879, *mulâtres* of Cap-Haïtien campaigned against him, a dark-skinned liberal allied to a *mulâtre* party, by arguing that he was "a *mulâtre* as light-skinned as a white" (Firmin, cited in Price-Mars n.d.: 117). Price-Mars doubted the veracity of this report, which reflects negatively on his native province, but one cannot doubt that similar tactics were used in the North, both in the nineteenth century and at other times, as well as in other places.[11] Light-skinned Sylvain Salnave sent his nephew into areas of the northern countryside where he himself was not known to campaign against the "yellow people." Early supporters of François Duvalier report that in 1957, Duvalier's opponent, Louis Déjoie, was described as being "very light-skinned," "almost white," in several areas of the Artibonite Valley, about 100 miles north of Port-au-Prince, where the masses of voters had never seen him. The game went on intermittently, the *mulâtres* making reference to their competence, which was more apparent than real, the *noirs* to their "natural" representativeness, which was just as much a matter of appearance.

But appearances mattered, if only because of the conflicting associations they engendered. The *mulâtres'* praise of the virtues of "competence" and "civilization," as well as their palpable somatic preference, linked them vaguely with a more sympathetic view of the West. Yet that linkage was denied by the *mulâtres* themselves whenever it seemed to displace the association between Haiti and blackness, or the fundamental values that permeated the cultural terrain. That, more than the personal shame of being taken for blatant racists, was what had kept the *mulâtres* on the defensive after independence. The U.S. occupation and the presidency of Elie Lescot removed this defensive attitude, sharpening the conflict and putting it in terms that convinced a majority of urbanites that Haiti's political and cultural future was at stake.

THE COLOR OF THE OCCUPATION

The United States' desire to create an American-style middle class in urban Haiti during the occupation remained unfulfilled. But the harassment of small landowners, the building of new roads, and the administrative and political centralization carried out by the Marines swelled the ranks of the peasants, artisans, students, and professionals who found their way to the coastal cities, and especially to Port-au-Prince. Between 1915 and 1945, an ever increasing number of newcomers rushed into the already limited space within which the ultimate battle for power was traditionally fought.

The *noirs* who surged into this urban arena did not always believe themselves destined to occupy its lowest rungs. Dark-skinned residents of Port-au-Prince were becoming increasingly qualified for public service, although their qualifications did not—as they had not for numerous *mulâtres* before them—go beyond the secondary school Baccalauréat. Since 1804, if not before, a minority of black businesspeople, intellectuals, professionals, and politicians had carved for themselves a niche in the structure of urban life. In the latter part of the century they were joined by the inheritors of the more open system of public education developed under Salomon. In the 1880s, Salomon, whose grandfather had been one of the few black magistrates of the Louverture regime, explicitly tried to give to a significant number of blacks what public education under Pétion had given to many light-skinned families—the hereditary privilege of academic competence. Competence doubtless varied from Grandpapa's primary school education to the prodigy grandson's European diploma, but its genealogical transmission occurred among a large segment of the population. Together, the descendants of the pre-1804 black professionals, the relatively recent elites created by Salomon, and the newcomers fleeing the decline of the provincial pyramids formed a new intellectual majority in the capital. The time was gone when economist Edmond Paul, himself a member of a dark elite family, could exclaim in all sincerity, "Le pouvoir aux plus capables," with the conviction that the "most capable" were also the lightest. Sometime before the end of the occupation, the reference to competence ceased to be to the exclusive advantage of the *mulâtre* minority.

But now that the "greatest number" also had their own "most capable," the *mulâtres,* who had been the previous winners in the war of rhetoric, suddenly changed the rules of the game. They abruptly revealed themselves to be less than conciliatory. They denied most of the newcomers the intellectual and political recognition they had been hoping for, the "elite" membership traditionally allowed to successful *noirs.* Naked color prejudice now supplanted the rule of the most capable, behind which it had been conveniently hidden.

Infractions of the law of the most capable preceded the occupation. The very existence of color prejudice and its mode of operation implied that, given equal levels of competence, the perception of "color," if not the exact degree of pigmentation, worked to the disadvantage of the *noir.* But U.S. racism added its institutional systematism to Haitian colorist favoritism. The Marines witnessed the successive installation of five *clair* presidents, three of whom were undeniably *mulâtres.* The U.S. "advisers," who in fact ran many government services, openly showed their preference for light-skinned officials, without considering the elaborate etiquette that the Haitian "aristocrats of the skin" had patiently refined for a century. The visibility of the *mulâtres* grew—as did their arrogance. These political precedents portended a battle of new dimensions, particularly since the occupation had affected the ideological landscape at least as profoundly as it had changed the rules of political competition.

THE *INDIGENISTE* MOVEMENT

I have already mentioned that in spite of color prejudice, Haitian national identity implied a positive identification with the black race. Martiniquan writer Aimé Césaire put it quite simply: it was in Haiti that *négritude* first appeared. However, this nationalist posture was always circumscribed by the intellectual and emotional attachment of the elites to the West, and to France in particular. These elites preferred Latin cultures and ways to Anglo-Saxon technocentrism and lack of polish: it was French literature that supplied them with their thematic and formal models. But they also valued what they saw as the achievements of northern Europe and the United States. In their view, there were no superior races, but there were superior cultures (Lewis 1983: 317). And since those cultures were European (or European derivatives), whiteness evoked a certain *savoir-faire* as well as a certain *savoir-vivre.*

The U.S. occupation, in different degrees and for different reasons, called each of these propositions into question. *Savoir-vivre* was the first to go. North Americans were not *sans-manière* ("without manners") in the sense that the elites would say this of the peasants, implying perfectibility. Instead they had crude manners, being by choice *de grossiers personnages.* *Savoir-faire* was more tenacious, but the occupation did not bring the spectacular changes in technology and material life for which many in the elites had been secretly hoping.

As the occupation forced a redefinition of whiteness, it also questioned its nemesis, blackness. The strong identification with blackness and the nationalist posture that cemented the ideological world of the elites could only be seen in the light of the slave revolution and independence. The nation stood for blackness because its black forefathers had fought for freedom *and* won over the best European army of the time. Indeed, this victory had been the sole empirical reference point of Haitian nationalist discourse. By the 1920s, however, the daily presence of the Marines had brought into question contemporary Haitians' claims that they shared their ancestors' courage and nobility (Danache 1950).

The pre-1915 Haitian elites had never held to any ideological proposition with fanatical conviction—except perhaps the association of the 1804 revolution with the regeneration of the black race. Ambiguity was their forte. But by undermining many tenets of the elites' vision of themselves and others, the occupation revealed inconsistencies inherent in that vision that they had conveniently ignored. More important, in questioning political independence—the proof of 1804—the occupation undermined the basis of the delicate edifice that these contradictory propositions constituted. The times called for a redefinition (Mintz 1984: 263–288), or at least for a reshaping, of the old categories within a more coherent whole. It is this reformulation that various intellectuals, loosely referred to by later writers as the *mouvement indigéniste,* tried to supply.

In 1928, the publication of Jean Price-Mars' book *Ainsi parla l'oncle* (Price-Mars 1983) launched the Haitian *indigéniste* movement. A series of attempts by *noir* and *clair* intellectuals to mount a wide-ranging reevaluation of the national culture followed Price-Mars' work. These writers criticized the elites' tendency to imitate the West and to ignore peasant culture. They emphasized the need to study the peasantry, to make an inventory of its practices, and to take into account the African roots of Haitian culture. The *indigénistes'* critique suggested that the elites' political failure stemmed in part from their contempt of Haitian popular culture, an argument at times quite explicit in Price-Mars' other writings (Antoine 1981; M.-R. Trouillot 1986b). But *indigénisme* as such had no political program and regrouped intellectuals of different political persuasions, including a few socialists.

This cultural nationalism can be distinguished therefore from *noirisme,* a strictly political ideology rooted in claims of "natural" legitimacy and calling for a color quota within the state apparatus. *Indigénisme* overlaps with *négritude,* but the scope of *négritude* is much wider. Whereas the range of *noirisme* is limited to relations of state power (and thus essentially to the urban arena), and *indigénisme* aims for the national arena, *négritude* theoretically aims for the world space in which the unequal evaluation of peoples, religions, and cultures originates.

These distinctions are important inasmuch as they continuously influenced political alignments among the elites. Since the nineteenth century, numerous *clairs* and other supporters of *mulâtre* political factions forcefully argued for the equality of all human races in the international arena while maintaining the colorist status quo in their own country (Firmin 1885; Price 1900; Nicholls 1979). By the same token, Jean Price-Mars, the founder of *indigénisme,* never endorsed *noiriste* politics; more, he publicly disassociated himself from *noirisme* during François Duvalier's regime, no small sign of intellectual integrity and personal courage (Antoine 1981).

Mass political symbolism, however, proceeds by association rather than by an intellectual exercise in classification. Haitian *mulâtrisme* had always been susceptible to the charge of duplicating white racism, even though, as we have seen, it was no mere derivative of Western values. It had survived the association with the West, in part because of another association equally potent among the elites: that of whiteness and *savoir-faire.* I have suggested that the practices of the U.S. occupiers raised questions about the Haitians' views of whiteness. The *indigéniste* movement provided new answers: no culture was superior, either in *savoir-faire* or *savoir-vivre.* Thus the most Westernized Haitians were not necessarily the best Haitians, nor the most useful to the country. These answers were not immediately "political." But in challenging the superiority of "white cultures" in the midst of the occupation, the *indigéniste* movement dealt a major blow to the rationale behind the claims to "competence."

THE 1946 DIFFERENCE

The *indigéniste* reevaluation of the cultural roots and tendencies of the nation opened the political field for the proponents of "legitimacy," the self-proclaimed advocates of the "greatest number." They could now insist on the associations implicit in the nineteenth-century world view, conveniently ignored by previous generations. And those associations themselves had become more powerful once *négritude* and *indigénisme* gave *noirisme* a new critical mass. If most of the *indigéniste* writers were not *noiristes,* most *noiristes* were *indigénistes* with an eye on the worldwide *négritude* movement. Thus, although *noirisme* itself was not in fact as popular in the political field as it now appears in retrospect, it had all the right cultural associations. By 1938, some *noiriste* intellectuals associated with the *Griots* group (which included a number of self-trained ethnologists and historians, among whom was François Duvalier) started to think of political strategies based upon these associations (Denis and Duvalier 1938). By 1945, President Lescot's growing unpopularity made it possible for most *noiriste* factions to call on such associations.

Lescot (1941–46) not only pursued the U.S. practice of systematically placing light-skinned individuals in the top echelons of the public service, but he also extended color favoritism to all levels of the administration without the slightest bow to the rule of perceived competence. In so doing, he repeatedly violated tradition. By 1945, for the first time in Haitian history, the distribution of power had become explicitly colorist. By then also—and again for the first time in Haitian history—a *mulâtre* regime was being accused of incompetence and judged guilty by a majority of urbanites. To add insult to injury, Lescot took many stands against the national culture, notably by facilitating an "anti-superstition campaign" that the Catholic church organized against Vodoun in 1941–42.

By 1945–46 these flagrant violations of political tradition and cultural tolerance, carried out in the midst of the intellectual reaction to the effects of the occupation, allowed a group of politicians to intermix *noirisme, indigénisme* and *négritude* in the perception of most urbanites. Anti-*mulâtre* resentment was at its height among the *noir* intellectuals and politicians, among students, and among the urban masses. At the same time, a majority of the population in the cities and towns was supportive of any attempt to restore national and cultural dignity, especially since the U.S. Marines had displayed to the Haitians, in their own country, the crassest dimensions of international racism. The most vocal among the *noiriste* intellectuals and politicians found themselves at the intersection of the three movements. Being from the masses, they said, they were its most "authentic" representatives, alone capable of ushering in the "new order" (Bonhomme 1946, 1957). Hadn't Lescot's government shown that a class of men born with silver spoons in their mouths would do anything to maintain their privileges? For the *authentiques,* the most vocal of the 1946 *noiristes,* cultural reevaluation and the regaining of national dignity, like the end of arbitrariness, required a change of "class" within the state apparatus.

Naiveté or Machiavellianism? Probably a little of both. The various associations put forward by the *authentiques* had been made implicitly by many urbanites since the nineteenth century, and it is possible that some of the 1946 leaders saw them as irrevocably intertwined. The fact remains that people who might not have supported the *authentiques* in other circumstances took their side in the battle against Lescot. The fusion of *noirisme, indigénisme,* and *négritude*—facilitated by the general indignation over Lescot's practices and the reevaluation of the nation in the light of the occupation—created an ideological tidal wave unprecedented in Haitian history, which imposed the presidency of Dumarsais Estimé.

Today it is easy to see that the *noiriste* retaliation against *mulâtre* power also hid a trap. But in re-reading contemporary accounts (e.g., Dorsinville 1972; Collectif Paroles 1976; Pierre 1987), we realize that in 1946, as would also be true in 1957, *noirisme* was perceived as the only viable political alternative by the vast majority of the middle classes. The very terms of urban political debate wold not allow the question of color to be set aside. As a privileged witness confirms:

> I told you: I was a *"noiriste."* And I will add that whoever in my social class in Haiti, after Lescot, under Lescot, whoever was not a *noiriste* would have been scum. . . . They forced upon us a culture of contempt. To this culture of contempt, we opposed our resistance and our hate. . . . (Dorsinville 1985: 21).

> All the ministers, all the important administrative posts, all the embassies were in the hands of *mulâtres,* the administrative offices of subcontracting companies were full of light-skinned girls. . . (Dorsinville 1972: 130–31).

> They ran the country as they would have run a plantation. And me, living there, the fruit of a certain culture, of a certain education, being conscious of my identity, I would not have been *noiriste? Merde!* (Dorsinville 1985: 21).

It must be understood how much this *merde* was shared among the middle classes, how it had profound repercussions for the thousands of intellectuals, artisans, small shopowners, well-to-do peasants, commodity *spéculateurs,* and vast segments of the lumpen masses. Moreover, this bitterness still resonates, because Duvalierism could not resolve either the color question or the more or less subtle forms of cultural and social domination. Nevertheless, in 1946 this general resentment against the *mulâtre* faction of the elites gave Estimé a political mandate of rare dimensions in Haitian history—as it would also give Duvalier, in 1957, the benefit of the doubt.

Estimé did little with his mandate. He enjoyed unlimited support in the first years of his presidency, but his popularity declined precipitously. His attempt to get re-elected facilitated the army's takeover. The same three-man junta that had ensured the transition from Lescot to Estimé announced new elections. Colonel Paul Magloire, once more the junta strongman, quickly became a presidential candidate. He won the 1950 elections—the first in which all adult males could vote directly for president—almost without electoral opposition.

The *authentiques* experienced Magloire's presidency (1950–56) as a frustrating interim. And, in many respects, this period was indeed a parenthesis, a reprieve in the denouement of the crisis. But for those who had lived through 1946, the frustration could be traced back to Estimé himself. The president had not been the *"mulâtre*-eater" his enemies had feared and his supporters had hoped. He had, of course, applied "color mathematics," giving an extraordinary number of *noirs* access to government positions. But he did not have a program that distinguished him from his predecessors (Collectif Paroles 1976), and the *authentiques* found his reforms limited (Bonhomme 1957: 13). Their frustration increased with Magloire, whom they saw as the very negation of the 1946 revolution, a reign of *"noirs* without color" at the service of the *mulâtre* bourgeoisie (Bonhomme 1957: 40). When the bourgeoisie itself seemed ready to abandon Magloire, when the church and commercial interests opposed his attempts to illegally prolong his term, it became necessary for the *authentiques* to find themselves a crown prince, an heir who would close the parentheses and carry on the uncompleted work of Estimé, who had since died in exile.

Only now have we begun to learn the appalling details of the maneuvering that permitted François Duvalier to surface as the Estimist representative in the 1957 elections.[12] The fact remains that this was Duvalier's most difficult campaign. Once he had won the support—or silence—of the most prominent Estimists, he inherited a political mantle and an apparatus that had solid support among lower level army officers and intellectuals. Above all, he inherited a vision of Haitian society which, vague and poorly defined as it was, presupposed continuity in change, the desire to complete an unfinished "revolution." If the reevaluation of the black race was legitimate, if the reevaluation of national culture and the restoration of national dignity was legitimate, then *noirisme* was legitimate. And if *noirisme* was legitimate, then Duvalier was legitimate. We now know that those syllogisms were profoundly incorrect; but once more, political symbolism proceeds by association; it feeds on analogies rather than on logic.

Victory was not easy, however. Duvalier's arguments were not remarkable, his personal image was rather dull. But though his campaign took time to get off the ground, by February 1957, he was considered a serious contender by those who had dismissed him a few months earlier. From then on, he campaigned seriously (Duvalier 1966b; Célestin 1958a, 1958b, 1959). By April he had mastered all the right analogies and had begun to take full advantage of his opponents' symbolic and tactical mistakes. More important, with the help of *noiriste* army officers, he virtually forced all the other dark-skinned candidates out of the race—a process of elimination that left him in a head-to-head contest with *mulâtre* Louis Déjoie on election day. Finally, the election itself was fraudulent: Duvalier won some districts with more votes than the actual number of residents.

Thus Duvalier ultimately owed his power to the army, which supervised the voting process and exercised a veto over the presidency. In fact, the army dominated the long transition from Magloire to Duvalier, shaped the climate for the presidential campaign, and paved the way for totalitarianism. I will return to the crucial role of this institution when I detail the context of the transition in the next chapter. The point is that, in spite of the fraud and the superficial character of the campaign, there is no evidence to indicate that Duvalier would not have won in regular elections. The dream of 1946 carried him, and it was a dream that embodied a century and a half of urban and rural frustration—frustration that the new middle classes that had arisen from the occupation, the self-proclaimed representatives of the masses in the state apparatus, decided to end once and for all.

Part 2
The Totalitarian Solution

5

The Transition to Duvalierism

The preceding chapters have used various lenses to examine the historical evolution of Haiti up to the 1956–57 presidential campaign. They portrayed the country's long-term problems as manifold manifestations of a chronic crisis that eventuated from the economic abuse of the peasantry and the ensuing gap between state and nation. They also showed how external dependency and local struggles in the political and cultural arenas limited both the vision and the concrete possibilities of the elites.

Part II stresses the Duvalierist answer to this recurring crisis: the creation and consolidation of a totalitarian regime. But the totalitarian solution was not the Duvaliers' alone, and the totalitarian temptation preceded François Duvalier's presidency. The worsening economic situation of the 1950s, the ideological chaos that typified an urban arena in which state fetishism had reached new peaks by 1946, and the propensity of the army to use blind force against peaceful civilians all helped open the road to totalitarian practices. To understand fully the context in which François Duvalier first institutionalized such practices, we need to go back to the years of Estimé and Magloire and look more closely at the transition from Magloire to Duvalier.

COSMETIC CHANGES

The fact that François Duvalier inherited a republic that was in a state of crisis has been obscured by three misconceptions. First, the totalitarian response with which Duvalier chose to confront the crisis so deepened that crisis that it came to be seen as a cause rather than a result. Meant as a resolution of the problem of the state, totalitarianism soon became the state problem. Second, right-wing opposition to François Duvalier, often led by *mulâtriste* factions of the elites, consciously entertained the illusion that *noirisme* inevitably led to authoritarian practices. The hypothesis is false. Estimé's government, which may have been one of the least authoritarian in recent Haitian history, was nonetheless the most *noiriste*. By the same token, the resurgence of *mulâtrisme* in the latter years of Jean-Claude Duvalier's term proves that totalitarian practices could exist without *noirisme*. Third, the deceptive prosperity of the successive regimes of Estimé and Magloire continues to distort the analysis of Duvalierism's stakes and options. Our first task in this chapter, therefore, is to go beyond this veil by showing that Haiti's economic system was already bankrupt during the two regimes that preceded the Duvaliers.

Few authors have noted the existence of an economic crisis in the 1950s; fewer still admit that the crisis preceded François Duvalier's coming to power.[1] The data, however, are there. A careful study of the economic indicators may one day show that the standard of living of some *urban* strata rose substantially during the terms of Estimé and Magloire. What is certain is that this economic well being—if this is what it was—did not extend to the entire population. The impression of progress is partially attributable to the systematization of governmental display during the Estimé and Magloire regimes, and is strengthened by the extent of the Duvalierist disaster, next to which all other failures pale in retrospect. Finally, foreign aid and the international situation following World War II briefly helped to conceal the country's deep fissures with a veneer of prosperity.

The greatest "realizations" of the decade of 1946–56 are in fact a direct result of the growth in foreign aid. Haiti became a country of projects for numerous international, governmental, and private organizations. The parade of acronyms began in 1946: UNESCO, WHO and other branches of the UN, IIAA (Institute of Inter-American Affairs), Point IV (Technical Assistance to Underdeveloped Countries), and other U.S.-dominated programs, as well as a number of health and economic "missions," burgeoned into a presence whose indispensability would become obvious only later. Between 1946 and 1956 the procession of missionaries seemed to be a sign of progress and was associated with new enterprises. To Estimé's display of achievements, Magloire added fanfare-laden openings:

the Minoterie (a state-run flour mill), Ciment d'Haïti (a cement factory), Reynolds (a bauxite mining operation run by the aluminum conglomerate), as well as the Albert Schweitzer Hospital (the only hospital in rural Haiti, and by far the best adapted, technically, to the country's needs). The Western economic recovery following the end of World War II reverberated in Haiti, and many foreigners and Haitians alike shared the impression of real and imminent progress.

However, apart from a (temporary) surplus in the balance of payments (Pierre-Charles 1967: 113), the most revealing indicators steadily pointed to continuing troubles. Even more, neither Estimé nor Magloire used the meager new funds for any reconstruction of the infrastructure.[2] This was the decade of government display, of picture-postcard projects. Estimé organized an international fair celebrating the Port-au-Prince Bicentennial, remodelled the business district, and built some housing for the urban underprivileged. Magloire in turn built Cité Magloire, a complex of relatively inexpensive dwellings that foreshadowed Duvalier's cosmetic undertakings—such as the housing projects of Cité Simone (named after his wife) and the rebuilding of the town of Cabaret (renamed Duvalier-Ville).

In fact, despite this opening fanfare, the interior of the country was in a state of decline, and the most serious problems grew worse. The years 1946–56 brought no change in Haitian dependence on agricultural exports. During the entire decade, more than 80 percent of economic activities remained concentrated in the agricultural sector, with slight annual fluctuations (in both directions). In 1951–52, for example, agriculture represented 87.4 percent of the gross national product, compared to 83.7 percent in 1946–47. The only notable change, a temporary one, was in the role of the artisans, whose share of the GNP grew enormously during fiscal year 1947–48, in large part because of activities associated with the Port-au-Prince Bicentennial.

But even as the size of the agricultural sector continued to grow, its productivity declined. If the Haiti of Estimé and Magloire did not industrialize, it was not because it was making advances in export agriculture. Port-au-Prince's new kiosks and plazas hid the debris of a country in which agricultural yields had slowly regressed to nineteenth-century levels. Coffee production for 1946–56 did not surpass the best years of Salomon's term, although the population had increased considerably. The diachronic picture put together by Pierre-Charles (1967: 97), treating the relationship between exports and population, bears witness to the enormity of the decline. The volume of coffee exported per capita in 1955 was about one-fourth that of 1843! Figures on cotton exports reveal a similar drop in relation to population: 12 ounces per capita in 1955, as opposed to 1.5 lbs. in 1843, 14 ounces in 1887, and 4.3 lbs. in 1935. And in spite of the temporary growth in the volume of some export crops, such as bananas and sisal, the decline continued. The total value of exports per capita for the years 1951–55 was lower than for the years 1924–28. This was not solely because local consumption had risen: the per capita domestic product had been declining continuously since the 1940s.

The reality that underlay both these figures and the veneer of urban renewal was an economic debacle of new proportions. Its impulse came from the maturing of the structural thresholds described earlier, as well as from the profound effects of the U.S. occupation. The crisis was compounded by an ecological degradation whose impact has hardly been acknowledged—in spite of Moral's depiction (1961). The straw that broke the camel's back was probably the demographic growth of the peasantry between 1930 and 1950, and its consequence for the relation between parasites and producers. The peasantry increased by a third during those twenty years (Moral 1961: 71–72). Ecological disaster and rural demographic growth each in turn strengthened the migratory flow toward the urban centers, and most particularly toward Port-au-Prince, whose population grew at the annual rate of 6 percent between 1950 and 1955. In the 1950s, nearly 50 percent of Port-au-Prince residents had been born somewhere else (Lundahl 1979: 629). The mean age of the entire population declined steadily between 1944 and 1955.

In other words, the first two crisis points described in Chapter 3 had matured; the third was not long in coming. The merchant-ruler alliance had drained the peasantry to such a degree that continued surplus extraction was forcing it below the subsistence level. Migration to the Dominican Republic, Cuba, and the provincial port cities bore witness to the rural world's impasse, even though the migrants were by no means the poorest or most desperate. The cities, overcrowded since the 1930s, were further overloaded by the dizzying growth of both traditional lumpen groups and of the new lumpen, created by the ongoing peasant debacle. Parasitism searched for individual ways out of the morass, but in such a system there was no exit apart from the state, the only viable arena of reproduction for the middle classes. This was the true lesson of the so-called Revolution of 1946, a lesson neglected even by the emerging left-wing parties tolerated by Estimé. By 1953–54, the country had reached the brink of the abyss. An incident, a hitch, a snag could turn Haiti upside down.

And unfortunately there was more than one. In 1953, the coffee harvest was poor, while the end of the Korean war signaled the end of the sisal boom. In 1954, Hurricane Hazel unexpectedly destroyed about 50 percent of the cacao crop and 40 percent of the coffee crop. Haiti could no longer benefit from the rise in coffee prices on the international market—a rise that had maintained, up until then, the illusion that Magloire was "doing something." Magloire's government tried to swim against the tide by reviving traditional nineteenth-century state mechanisms, such as borrowing and coffee taxes. In June 1953, the administration called for a new coffee tax; thereafter the government's share of f.o.b. coffee prices rose from 16 percent in 1953 to 24 percent in 1954 and then to 27 percent in 1955–56. The peasantry had once again been put in the stocks. Still, the budgetary deficit grew, as did the public debt, which reached $61 million in September 1957. François Duvalier was to inherit from Magloire an external debt that, *one month before his inauguration,* had reached "its highest level in Haitian economic history" (Pierre-Charles 1979: 151).

In late 1956, at the very height of the crisis, Magloire unveiled his plan to prolong his term illegally. The attempt was certainly not out of character. A cadet of the first graduating class of the new military school created by the Marines, Magloire had a taste for strong-arm tactics.[3] In his fourth year as president, when urban middle-class opposition to his regime was gaining ground, and when more voices were being raised against the violation of civil and political liberties, Magloire, with an eye to reelection, had shown his totalitarian inclinations. In one of the rare Creole sentences used in any of his public speeches, he informed the opposition in no uncertain terms of his decision to use extreme force: "Today, I am putting my iron pants back on to deal with the rascals" (Bonhomme 1957: 88). From then on he was called "Kanson Fè" (Iron Pants). People laughed at the nickname and wrote songs about it, some of which were played on the radio despite unofficial censorship. But the wisest already wondered if the democratic possibilities that had been opened up with Vincent, and especially with Estimé, were not about to be nipped in the bud.

Magloire's attempt to remain in power did not succeed—he was forced out by a strike in December 1956.[4] But the general's authoritarian practices did affect the campaign unofficially launched before his departure. First, his assault on civil liberties, made with the support of Colonel Marcaisse Prosper (chief of police of Port-au-Prince from 1945 to 1956), had already suggested the possibility of a totalitarian response to the crisis. Second, the climate created by the increased use of state and partisan violence further distracted attention from the crisis itself. The entire campaign would be dominated by personal attacks, both verbal and physical, made against a background of increased political repression.

DISCOUNT POLITICS

The early declaration of Senator Louis Déjoie, a *mulâtre* well known for his agro-industrial ventures, as presidential candidate infuriated the intellectuals and professionals from the new middle classes and unleashed the declarations of a series of candidates whose only purpose lay in opposing Déjoie. Déjoie's political rise was a class reflex to structural problems (Pierre-Charles 1979: 36). It embodied the hope held by certain sectors of the bourgeoisie of combining profit, power, and productivity in a new economic and political formula that was yet to be defined. But these sectors were embryonic, and in the context of 1956, where animosity toward Magloire and his *mulâtre* allies colored the political landscape, the result of Déjoie's announcement was a succession of venomous and superficial debates. Déjoie's early start was read as a sign of desperate eagerness, and his candidacy was perceived solely in terms of full-fledged return to *mulâtrisme*. It may have been that, of course, but it was also much more. Nevertheless, the "color question" returned to the top of the political agenda. Worse, the question of the next president's "color"— avoided in 1946 and 1950 simply because all the candidates were dark-skinned—had once again become worth asking.

Duvalier, who emerged as the ideal candidate of the *noiriste* camp after much underhanded wheeling and dealing among political friends of the late Estimé, became Déjoie's most important opponent and the one most likely to benefit from the "nationalist" ardor of the new middle classes. Two other dark-skinned candidates occupied the political foreground. Clément Jumelle, former minister of finance under Magloire, had the support of some technocrats, but the corruption of the degenerate regime remained a stain that he could not remove. Daniel Fignolé was the uncontested leader of most of the urban lumpen, especially in Port-au-Prince, but faced serious competition from Duvalier outside of this particular area.

Neither these men nor the slew of minor candidates with short-lived hopes addressed the issue of the crisis. Déjoie may have wanted to, but the very terms of the debate offered no opportunity for a serious discussion of the country's problems. Speeches, news reports, and editorials (Bonhomme 1957; Célestin 1958a, 1958b, 1959, 1960) all show the absence of any program to have been the outstanding characteristic of the campaign. That was more than unfortunate because the 1957 election was the first in Haiti's history that could have involved the entire country: the technical prerequisites for carrying out national electoral campaigns had been met; the president was to be directly elected by the voters; and women were voting for the first time. But the campaign lacked any real issues. Déjoie did not even have a bourgeois program, only bourgeois allegiances. Jumelle did not have a technocratic plan, only a technical education. Fignolé did not have a populist project, only populist intentions. And François Duvalier did not have a *noiriste* agenda, only a rhetoric. Partisan politics, as encoded by the urban classes, was to remain an end in itself.

Thus class alternatives were not clearly represented in the 1956–57 campaign, as some analysts suggest (e.g., Pierre-Charles 1973, 1979).[5] In 1956, as before, a presidential candidacy was an individual undertaking, as it remains today in the Duvaliers' wake. Further, in 1956–57, the candidates' personalities dominated political discussion more than ever before, and perhaps more than today, in part because universal suffrage had just changed the rules of the electoral game.

The absence of a political discourse with concrete references was partially attributable to the peasantry's age-old isolation from the arena of power. But the political vacuum stemmed also from the bourgeoisie's own handicaps. The merchants' dependence on Europe and the United States, the cultural inroads of the peasantry, the intellectual strength of the middle classes, and the defensive attitude of the *mulâtres* had always prevented the local bourgeoisie from establishing its hegemony on the political scene. Though the import-export merchants had been the main beneficiaries of the system, they had never been either able or willing to control the Executive directly. To be sure, they had financed one or another warlord, but they had had little control over Executive decisions once the general of their choice was in power. The Legislature, traditionally controlled by *mulâtres* (who were often tied to the merchants), remained the major institutional arm of the bourgeoisie in the political arena, although not always an effective one. Still, theoretically at least, until 1946 it elected the president; and given the small number of individuals involved, the merchants could always try to buy individual votes. In short, the Haitian bourgeoisie had never before needed to formulate, either on its own or through an intervening group of intellectuals, a political discourse that would appeal to the majority of the citizenry.

This point is important at a time when well-intentioned observers reduce Haiti's problems to a matter of procedures of access to political power. In its humblest expression, this position suggests that once a president is selected through "free" elections, Haiti will be on the road to democracy. Such observers do not understand that democracy, as conceived in this electoralist discourse, demands a class hegemony, and probably a bourgeois one at that. Yet a major feature of the 1956–57 period was the crisis of hegemony of the traditional power groups (Pierre-Charles 1979: 39). This crisis of hegemony was manifested in 1956, as it is today, by *the impossibility for the Haitian bourgeoisie of formulating a political discourse,* even through an intervening class. That had been true since the end of the nineteenth century, after the demise of the Parti Libéral during Salomon's regime; and this crisis of hegemony partly explains the rapid succession of governments at the turn of the century. But the U.S. occupation had patched up the holes and permitted the traditional elites to hold onto political center stage without fighting for this position. The emptiness first showed in 1946. In 1957, with the advent of universal suffrage, it reached new dimensions. Control of the Legislature no longer guaranteed the outcome of presidential elections. This was not realized during the 1950 election simply because there was no campaign as such—Magloire was the winner from the start. Further, only males voted in 1950. But the circumstances of the 1956–57 campaign required the bourgeoisie to fight openly—hence, perhaps, the class "reflex" of Déjoie's early announcement.

But it is here that one can speak of an ideological handicap: the bourgeoisie was unable to fight in the open. The total powerlessness of the Chamber of Deputies and the Senate in 1956–57 marked the end of the nineteenth-century legislative tradition. Déjoie's candidacy thus represented a desperate gesture, a wish rather than a true political project. It was this ideological vacuum, created by the age-old isolation of the peasantry and the political decline of the bourgeoisie, that gave the *noiriste* elements from the middle classes their chance: not that they could campaign any better on the issues, but they were able to evoke all the right associations. The most famous speech of this campaign was made by François Duvalier and its leit-motif was a phrase that captured the moment: "They have gone mad."

For Duvalier, the mad ones were the traditional power groups behind the throne; but in retrospect, the entire political society ran amok in 1956–57. The political campaign offered the sad spectacle of a country on the brink of an abyss, for the first time enjoying the possibility of an open debate on structural issues, yet systematically refusing to confront these issues.[6] Only a few journalists realized the size of the political debts that were maturing and tried to raise the level of the discussion. But the debate offered only an alternative of personnel for the state's highest office. The dice were loaded. The peasantry, the only valid stakeholder, the only actor whose intervention could have changed the terms of the discourse, remained a far-away reference point, engulfed in rhetorical discussion of the "masses," the "vital forces," the "hinterland," the "people." The lumpen had a field day: they sold out to the highest bidder, or responded to vague promises of salvation through the state. This was gutter politics, politics of the lowest caliber: no standards, no ideals, no restraint. Control of the Executive was not merely the main issue; it was the only issue. What a sad use of freedom of speech in a country with a repressive tradition!

Freedom of speech, for what it was worth, did not last. Where Magloire had hesitated, his two former classmates, Léon Cantave and Antonio "Thompson" Kébreau (nicknamed "Thompson" after the submachine gun he had such a propensity to order used) had fewer reservations. Cantave and Kébreau succeeded each other as commander-in-chief after Magloire's departure. Between January and May 1957, Cantave increased the role of the army in political decisions and further limited civil liberties. Between May and September 1957, at the price of a still unknown number of corpses, Kébreau installed the totalitarian order. Five provisional governments succeeded each other after Magloire, but the civilian ones among them—all cut short by military coups—were mere proxies. The army ran the show.

THE GIFT OF THE MARINES

The totalitarian response to the crisis was the brainchild of the army trained by the Marines, and particularly of the cadets of the graduating class of 1930–31, which included Magloire, Cantave, and Kébreau. These three officers imposed the law of the bayonet to an extent hitherto unknown in Haitian history. The last years of Magloire presaged the era of François Duvalier. All the practices that Haitian journalists were to baptize *kansonférisme* ("Iron pants politics") emerged during those years. In 1954, Marcaisse Prosper's policemen invaded the offices of the newspaper *L'Alliance Démocratique* and arrested Daniel Fignolé and a number of his supporters. Several legislators rushed to the embassies for asylum. The wave of arrests continued, and 1955–56 was one of the most painful in the history of the Haitian press. The rules governing the use of state violence were changing. The brutal murder of the Ludovic Désinor family, attacked at home during the night by criminals said to be working for the government, and the increased physical violence against women indicated that the traditional constraints on state violence were disappearing. Magloire systematically repressed the parties on the left that had been tolerated by Estimé until 1948. Martial law and the dissolution of the legislative chambers finalized the stripping off of the democratic mask.

But Magloire as an individual was associated with *mulâtrisme* and that association has always placed limits on the use of state violence in Haiti. Thus he could not use to the fullest the repressive potential of the army. That potential was extraordinary, however, in part because the army was the only national institution to escape Kaplan's law of diminishing returns, which afflicted, for instance, the press, the clergy, and the Legislature. The political turmoil increased the army's capacity to deal with the population without intermediaries and to do so in its own terms. The *kansonférisme* sketched out by Magloire was easily confirmed by Cantave and systematized by Kébreau.

On January 26, 1957, Cantave bared his teeth. Any person who offended any state representative, in speech or writing, was henceforth subject to arrest. Military terror set in between January and May 1957. From February 22 to 26, the army committed a series of murders that still remain unpunished. During the civilian regime of Franck Sylvain (February 7 to April 2)—one more in a long list of temporary "understudies"—military arbitrariness affected even citizens residing abroad—for instance, passports were not delivered to those who might come back and upset the apple cart. A columnist of *Haïti Miroir,* recalling Magloire's banishing of left-wing writer René Dépestre, wrote: "Franck Sylvain's government has done nothing new. . . . It has followed in the footsteps of *kansonférisme.*"

That the successive civilian governments played into the hands of the army was also due to the fact that the totalitarian temptation was winning out in all camps, except perhaps that of Jumelle. The workings of the kind of state control referred to as "totalitarian," says Poulantzas (1971: 121), are correlated "with a lack of direct expression of the class struggle in the institutions of political power." Yet what distinguished the campaign of 1956–57 in Haitian political history was precisely a combination unique in its monstrosity: a structural crisis, a high degree of partisan feeling, and a new political ardor created by universal suffrage, all coupled with the total absence of debate on the most important issues related to the crisis.[7] State fetishism was at its height in all camps and classes, and the temptation to pursue a totalitarian project on the heels of this fetishism did not therefore depend solely on the maliciousness of a particular clique.[8] Although Cantave's army set the limits of private violence, Fignolé threatened the "bourgeois" with the terror of the lumpen masses. Supporters of Déjoie armed themselves and organized a private mini-militia for the senator.

But Duvalierist terror came into its own during the campaign, in part because of the support of the influential *noiristes* within the army. Soon after the installation of one more provisional civilian government, the participating Duvalierist representatives used a technicality to pull out in an uproar. Duvalierist terror immediately struck both the civilian government and the supporters of the other candidates in various towns and provincial cities—in Barrdères, Jérémie, Grande Rivière du Nord, Quartier Morin, Port-Margot, Gonaïves, and Saint-Marc, to name only a few. The civilian provisional government—a coalition controlled by Déjoie—fought back with its own brand of terror, controlling radio programs and trying to transform judges into "lackeys of the Executive" (Pierre Antoine cited in Célestin 1958a: 313). But it was May 25 that showed whose brand of totalitarianism would triumph, and Cantave emerged the winner.

On May 25, 1957, Haiti was on the brink of civil war. Déjoie's supporters, who controlled the civilian government but who were afraid of Cantave (whom they suspected of working for Duvalier), tried to create a split in the army. Their soldiers attacked the Casernes Dessalines barracks, but after half a day of farcical battle, with neither strategy nor glory on either side, they once more accepted Cantave's authority. Déjoie never recovered from this failed attempt, which gave François Duvalier the opportunity of taking his second most decisive step toward the presidency: the elimination of Daniel Fignolé. The victorious Cantave resigned "in the interest of the nation," only to be replaced by Kébreau. With Kébreau's approval, Duvalier persuaded Jumelle to join him in offering Fignolé the interim presidency in order to quiet down the Port-au-Prince masses. Fignolé accepted, only to be removed nineteen days later by pro-Duvalier officers. The farcical war had ended, and it was Duvalier's side of the army that emerged victorious. For all practical purposes, Papa Doc had become the only dark-skinned opponent of *mulâtre* Louis Déjoie.

From May 25 to October 22, 1957, the army, temporarily reunited under Kébreau, systematically established the basis for a totalitarian Executive. The Military Council of Government (the new junta, led by Kébreau) completed the work Cantave had begun. It took power on June 14 and proceeded to launch a series of decrees designed to strengthen its power. On June 15, 1957, it promulgated the "Decree Against the Lockout" which forbade merchants the right to strike. Massacres of Fignolé's supporters occurred on June 15 and 16. A state of siege followed—with retroactive ambitions! Citizens were arrested for political crimes committed before the new measures had been promulgated.

Two institutions still blocked the road to totalitarianism: the press and the judiciary. They became the Military Council's next targets, and fell rather quickly, not only because the army flexed all its muscles, but also because the crisis and accompanying political degeneration confirmed the weakness of most national institutions. The timidity of many journalists and judges was not necessarily due to a lack of individual courage. The *esprit de corps* itself was dead. No one had the sense of belonging to an institution with clean rules and responsibilities, if only because everyone had (or was suspected of having) partisan loyalties that would override any attachment to a journalistic or judicial body. The army's rapid action quickly washed away the already wobbly forces of these two civilian institutions.

On July 3, 1957, a decree from the Military Council put an end to civil justice: "Even crimes and misdemeanors against persons and property do not escape Military Jurisdiction if the Authority deems it necessary. The Military Authority is endowed with the right to search the homes of citizens DAY AND NIGHT.... In a word, it may take any measure necessary to restore LAW AND ORDER...." (cited in Célestin 1959: 97–98; emphasis in the original). And to add insult to injury, the decree forcibly retired all the judges of both the Court of Appeals and the Supreme Court.

The army's second target was the press, or rather the freedom of expression that many citizens—not all of whom were professional journalists—exercised in the press. We have already seen that Magloire and Cantave severely limited freedom of expression. Kébreau's army undertook to obliterate it. The decree of August 26, 1957, was the expression of the Duvalierist state, *although Duvalier was not yet in office.* The decree limited the hours that could be devoted to electoral debate or advertising, and thus to political discourse—because in this situation the two overlapped. It banned "drawings, prints, paintings, writings, *or any other mode of expression of thought* aimed at undermining the authority of one or more Members of the State's Constituted Corps" (emphasis mine). And it announced that the "Military Authority will arrest *on the spot* anyone who has perpetrated any of these infractions" (Célestin 1959: 147).

Totalitarianism was spelling out its principles, but few thinking heads took heed. The Association of Haitian Journalists protested timidly, but also asked its members to "guard against stepping out of line." *Haïti Miroir,* up until then a champion of public liberties, vacillated—the decree, said one of its editors, could restrain certain abuses by the press, although its provisions were too strict. The press did not understand that freedom of speech is one of the few domains in which *any* retreat is a defeat. Since Magloire had had no real opponent in 1950, the 1956–57 campaign was Haiti's first opportunity to consolidate universal suffrage and to enlarge the scope of political discourse. But the press responded to Kébreau in terms dictated by the army, because the stakes of the campaign masked the country's own stakes. On August 30, 1957, an editorial in *Haïti Miroir* was already tolling the death knell of democracy. Haitian democracy, said the journalist, "has died almost without having lived."

State discourse confirmed the death knell. On September 2, 1957, twenty days before Duvalier's "election," the army outlawed wearing khaki "or any other cloth of that shade" throughout the entire country, under the pretext that people who dressed in light brown were committing crimes all over the place. The decree concluded: "The Haitian army does not guarantee the life of anyone who, without authorization, transgresses this measure." Soldiers received orders to open fire on anyone wearing light brown who was suspected of being a civilian.

Violence saturated the Haitian political climate during 1956–57, and not only because the military wanted it this way. The army became the privileged instrument of that violence, the institution which systematically thought out and implemented the totalitarian order. The third debt had matured, and an army trained by the Marines, the time-bomb bequeathed by the occupation, was ready to make of it a blood reckoning. What a lovely gift from the Marines!

AUTHORITY, VIOLENCE, AND NEUTRALIZATION

The Duvalierist victory at the ballot box on September 22, 1957, was therefore a victory devised and shared in by the army. It was a victory of those best prepared and most willing to use violence: the army, which supported Duvalier wholeheartedly after May 1957, and the top Duvalierist civilians, who would later take the reins of state violence over from the army. Again, this does not mean that Duvalier would necessarily have lost the election had he not used violence. We do not know. On the other hand, what we do know is that this violence, which seemed inherent in the Duvalierist campaign, was also inherent in Duvalierist power after September 1957.

The originality of Duvalierist violence predates the election itself.

Duvalier's civilian supporters turned out to be effective in their use of violence during the campaign in part because of the complicity that they enjoyed from the ranks of Cantave's and Kébreau's army. But the superiority of their violence also stemmed from its geographic and demographic scope, from the rapidity of its execution, and from the originality of its methods. This efficiency suggests that a minority of Duvalierists, including army officers, was ready, as of 1957, to violate systematically the traditional rules governing political violence. Duvalierism's paramilitary apparatus, which was soon to give birth to the *tonton-makout* and then to the civil militia, was already at work during the campaign.[9] The hired thugs who threatened or attacked the Déjoieistes foreshadowed the unofficial henchmen of the future regime. According to one eyewitness: "[They] call themselves 'detectives,' or auxiliaries of the latter, and advertise their political affiliation without embarrassment: DUVALIERIST" (Célestin 1959: 98). The attack on Déjoie's Women's Political Bureau on August 7, 1957, showed that belonging to the female sex was no longer a protection against political violence (Célestin 1959: 130–31). Indiscriminate bombings of residential areas also showed the contempt for victims of chance. This would become one of the markers of the regime.

Yet the most original characteristic of Duvalierist violence, even before the taking of power, was the *extent of its social base.* We know that it was directed from Port-au-Prince by people belonging to the middle classes. But in Saint-Marc, in Gonaïves, in Arcahaie, the social base included peasants and probably a large part of the lumpen. In Port-au-Prince as well, where violence was the most systematic, the majority of Duvalierist forces were recruited from among the new urban parasites—not only the middle class professionals who formed the Duvalierist high command, but also artisans and small shop owners. This important characteristic of the Duvalierist striking force before the elections was to reappear after Duvalier's inauguration in October 1957, with the additional weight that access to public monies gave it. Duvalierist totalitarianism did not involve simply a willingness to use force, but also a strategy of economic redistribution that permitted it to recruit, at a low price, the individuals who executed it. To understand this strategy, which relied upon the demographic power of the urban parasites, we must return briefly to the economic situation.

Well before Duvalier, the growth of parasitic groups and the decline of agricultural productivity had led the state to take an ever increasing surplus from the peasantry. The most recent wave of increases, as we have seen, began in June 1953. It continued during the whole of Magloire's regime and during the first twelve years of François Duvalier's regime. Coffee taxes, the main source of government revenues, rose from 16 percent of the f.o.b. price in 1953 to 27 percent in 1956–57 and 37 percent in 1969. But Duvalier distinguished himself from Magloire and all who preceded him by the way in which this steadily growing surplus was redistributed. Three key points of the new redistributive system deserve note: (1) redistribution directly affected an ever larger number of parasites; (2) individual gains were, however, lower; and (3) as a result, government leaders could buy a larger number of sympathizers with less money.

After 1957, redistribution of state funds by François Duvalier's regime affected more people than under either Magloire or Estimé. Direct political patronage, participation in governmental projects or in the military and paramilitary forces—every sign of political allegiance to the regime had economic consequences for the person who showed that allegiance. And since the net monetary value of the compensation was not necessarily correlated with the social origins of the individual being compensated, the system gave the impression of being accessible to everyone. A minor self-employed artisan could be rewarded as much as a renowned journalist. Women could benefit tremendously and, if they were married, independently of their husbands. The state was perhaps "medieval," as Pierre-Charles says, but the surplus did not go from the peasantry to the king by way of local lords. Rather, the surplus was taken directly by the chief of state and redistributed from there to the barons of the regime, who in turn gave part to their valets. Of course, when state funds were insufficient, the fact of allegiance gave any valet the right to extract more as he saw fit. He became a baron of a kind, as did the hundreds of artisans, small shop owners, and peasants who became the uncontested lords of their neighborhoods or villages. It was the individual fidelity of these men and women that provided the famous *tonton-makout* (literally, "Uncle with a basket," so named after a bogeyman in a folk tale) with its critical mass. The person so promoted had to continue proving his allegiance to those at the center of political power, the *sine qua non* of his maintenance of local power. But his allegiance in turn strengthened the government, because it proved to others that everyone was capable of rising, of growing wealthier, of doing well, if he or she decided to pay the price of this success with both life and honor. In short, the shrewdness of Duvalierist redistribution (à la François) was that everyone could hope to profit some day.

For the majority of claimants, however, success was no more than a possibility. The average amount that any individual received from political activity declined greatly. If François Duvalier's regime paid an extraordinary number of partisans, the average cost of each was much less than in previous years. The operation was possible because of a weeding-out process at the summit of the political pyramid. The treatment of the army is a perfect example of this (Delince 1979). If the loyalty of three sublieutenants cost the same as the allegiance of one general, François Duvalier bought two sub-lieutenants, fired the third, and retired the general. Accounts of Duvalierist terror reported after Jean-Claude Duvalier's departure abound with examples of "useless" crimes, of extreme abuses that the regime's hired men committed for a pittance. And in fact the majority of the people targeted as being Duvalier's henchmen and killed by the mob in 1986 and 1988 were miserable wretches whose average incomes hardly exceeded what some elite families spend for four servants. But therein lay the shrewdness: the state apparatus could support an extraordinary number of cheap allegiances at the bottom of the pyramid and *at the same time* provide ever increasing incomes for the shrinking minority that reached the upper echelons.

The elimination of thousands of professionals, middle-level bureaucrats, and army officers by means of imprisonment, torture, and forced (or encouraged) emigration effectively reduced the number of pretenders to political leadership. It also changed the traditional balance of power between parasites in the state and parasites kept far from power. Contrary to what one might think, it was not the most prominent *tonton-makout* who maintained the regime of François Duvalier, but the high number of actual or potential *makout* of second rank whom the government bought at a very low price. The ferocious competition at the bottom of the ladder, which evokes the image of a basket of crabs, neutralized the potential for mass revolt.

The formula was risky, but it produced results because of its daring nature. François Duvalier systematically repeated it in other domains, with so much success that it warrants further discussion. To borrow a term from Pierre-Charles, I will call this the "auto-neutralization" tactic because it led potential opponents to render one another ineffective and thus to defuse from within, so to speak, the combined threat they constituted for Duvalier. It was a variant of the old divide-and-rule method, and rested heavily on individual expectations within a group to isolate its potential leaders; it was possible only because of the parasitic nature of the urban strata. As applied by François Duvalier, the "auto-neutralization" tactic consisted of increasing a group's access to political, economic, and ideological resources just enough so that the number of individuals in the group that aimed for new privileges became large enough to block the emergence of mass opposition. Average individual gains were low, but the number of claimants for crumbs who remained convinced of their chance was always sufficient to hinder the group solidarity necessary for effective action. François Duvalier used this method with the army and the indigenous clergy, to cite only two major cases. The example of the army is important enough for us to explore it further.

NEUTRALIZING THE ARMY

Soon after the elections it became clear to General Kébreau that Duvalier would not share power. It was equally clear to Duvalier that he had to get rid of Kébreau and seize direct control of the army, the only "strong" institution in the crisis and therefore the one from which an effective response to his own growing quest for power might come. But Duvalier did not start with the powerful Kébreau. Rather, he first transferred Kébreau's main assistant, Lt.-Col. Franck Beauvoir, out of the country.[10] Shortly thereafter he ordered Kébreau to transfer the eighteen officers he thought were most loyal to the general away from Port-au-Prince. Kébreau refused, but in losing Beauvoir he had lost his most powerful assistant and his link to many junior officers. Duvalier thus dismissed Kébreau rather easily, with the help of Colonel Flambert, an officer at the National Palace who was also Kébreau's personal enemy, and a slew of under-officers who thus assured themselves immediate promotion. Flambert became chief of staff, with a general's stars (Pierre 1987: 139–48).

In spite of its relative strength, the army was affected by the events of

1956–58. It had lost Magloire and the officers who followed Magloire into exile. If it still escaped the law of diminishing returns, it nevertheless carried scars of the partisan dissent which had led to the caricature of combat on May 25, 1957. Its Achilles' heel was partisan politics and Duvalier knew this. He thus submitted the army to an increasing "politicization," forcing officers to compete for favors from the chief of state. The favorites of the day served as a buffer between the disgruntled and the center of power. Thus nine months after his nomination, Flambert was dismissed, along with fifty other high-ranking officers. At the same time, a new and imposing group of under-officers (mostly *noirs* and of modest middle-class origins) was promoted to the middle ranks. This coup was perhaps even more daring than Kébreau's dismissal, because this time Duvalier rid himself of the officers who were the most representative of the military leadership produced by the occupation: sons of professional and intellectual *noir* families, *mulâtres* from small towns—in short, the jewels of the middle classes, traditional allies of the bourgeoisie, the potential Magloires and Kébreaus of the future. But to cover up the massive promotion of *noirs* of modest origins, Duvalier named a *mulâtre* chief of staff (Franck Merceron) and a *mulâtre* assistant chief of staff (Paul Laraque, an intellectual from the South). It goes without saying that Merceron and Laraque did not last very long. In 1961 they too went into exile. The process that began with Kébreau's departure ended in June 1962 with the exile of Chief of Staff Jean-René Boucicaut. By 1963, according to a former officer, "The chief of staff had completely lost his residual responsibilities. A prisoner of the system of allegiance to the chief of state, he had been made into an accomplice of presidential arbitrariness" (Delince 1979: 211).

Analysts have spent much time on the transferrals, dismissals, and early retirements that punctuated the Duvalierist takeover of the army. But it is important to realize that these early retirements were possible because of the promotions that went hand in hand with them. The post-occupation Haitian army had never seen so many rapid promotions as in the first years of François Duvalier's term. These promotions never filled the vacuum created at the top, but they satisfied, albeit momentarily, a sufficient number of potential protesters to end the possibility of collusion against the regime from the bottom. Indeed, there was no military plot against François Duvalier's presidency of which he was unaware. The decapitation of the army, which had remained one of the strong institutions in the country, bears witness to the effectiveness of the auto-neutralization policy.

That policy was applied with more or less success to different institutions and social groups, but it was especially among those urban groups traditionally involved in political struggles that it was most effective. In fact, the Duvalierist strategy caught those groups and classes off guard. It undermined them from the inside, forcing one against the other. Numerous intellectuals and professionals of the traditional middle classes were tempted by "apolitical" but well-paying positions in public service. These middle-class newcomers—the very people who had made the Duvalierist victory possible—saw in these changes the realization of Estimist promises, while many among the lumpen associated individual promotions with the revenge of the underprivileged promised by Fignolé. Duvalier counted on the state's role in the reproduction of the urban classes not engaged in commerce, and he won.

Because the rules were changing, responses were slow in coming, even from the Bord de Mer. Traditionally, merchants had rarely interfered with the details of day-to-day politics, focusing instead on the overall picture. The auto-neutralization tactic required their near total silence in the political domain. But they quickly adapted to the silence, particularly because *their share of the profits did not diminish*. For in spite of *noiriste* propaganda, François Duvalier was quite polite to the *mulâtre*-dominated Bord de Mer. The official distribution of the f.o.b. coffee price bears witness to these commercial profits: the peasant-producer share dropped from 67 percent in 1951–52 to 41 percent in 1966–67, whereas the share for merchants and *spéculateurs* rose. The Duvalierist state may have frightened individual merchants, but it did not tamper with the structures of the Merchants' Republic.

THE FORMALIZATION OF THE CRISIS

At this juncture, however, only a far-reaching remodelling could save the country. Magloire-style temporary solutions could no longer heal the wounds. But the remodelling did not come: Duvalierism had no program other than power for power's sake, and any challenge to the *status quo* might signal its demise. Moreover, a structural remodelling would mean directly confronting the local merchants as a class—which *noirisme* had always avoided in spite of its vituperative discourse against the "light-skinned bourgeois." Similarly, remodelling implied a qualitative change in relations between Haiti and the United States, which Duvalier feared, given the fragility of the equilibrium on which his power rested.

Yet the crisis persisted and required some sort of response. It was at this point that François Duvalier opted for a solution that surprised both his right- and left-wing opponents, the Haitian diaspora, and French, U.S., and Vatican political leaders (to cite only the most astonished). Since power for power's sake was the sole aim of his reign, and since the crisis cast doubt upon the traditional formulas of power, Duvalier adapted power to the crisis. He transformed all the symptoms of the Haitian malaise, beginning with arbitrariness, into innate aspects of sociopolitical life, systematizing all the ad hoc responses of previous rulers. It was as if the nineteenth century had come back with a twist, inverted by Duvalier's systematization. What had been a problem now became a response; what had been a response suddenly became a problem. What had been temporary entered into the structural long term. In a word, François Duvalier's regime *formalized the crisis.*

The formalization of the crisis began as an attack on the declining national institutions that had been kept off balance since the U.S. occupation. Civilian institutions—including the ideological apparatus (churches, schools, universities, the media, professional associations, sports clubs, and all sorts of social clubs, down to the Boy Scouts) were undermined, closed down, or reduced to impotence. From 1958–59 onward, Duvalier managed to bury what was left of the independent press—already muzzled by Cantave and Kébreau. Journalists of *Haïti Miroir, L'Indépendance,* and *La Phalange* were jailed or tortured. The decade of the 1960s saw a forced silencing of the Haitian press that was to last until 1986. The years 1960–62 also marked a turning point in the history of the Catholic church, one of the institutions hardest hit by the Duvalierist state. The successive expulsion of three bishops created a vacuum at the top of the Catholic pyramid. The expulsion of the Jesuits in 1964 and of the Order of the Holy Ghost Fathers five years later eliminated two religious orders already isolated by the auto-neutralization of the clergy. The years 1959–61 also witnessed the attack by the Executive on the Legislature and the Judiciary. Teachers and students were also attacked, in 1960 and 1961, after a strike that only ended when Duvalier bought out some of the leaders.

The auto-neutralization tactic implied that the Executive prevented institutions from reproducing autonomously by striking at the top of their hierarchies and by blocking their internal mechanisms of reproduction. But Duvalier did not leave unfilled the vacuum thus created unfilled. He not only filled it with new personnel, but very often with new institutions or with parallel forms of organization. For instance, the closing of the Grand Séminaire prevented the training of new Catholic priests, and the expulsion of influential clergymen (white, for the most part) created a further gap, but Duvalier also named two Haitian priests, who came from the lower middle classes, to posts as government ministers. This not only created a precedent in the relations between church and state, but it also raised the expectations of other Haitian clergymen, who therefore abstained from commenting publicly on Duvalier's moves against the church. Later, in 1966, he compelled the Vatican to "nationalize" the clergy with the nomination of five Haitian bishops. Similarly with the press: the regime was not satisfied with silencing the independent press. It proceeded to create its own media, bombarding the public with radio programs extolling the virtues of "The Leader" on a newly created station, "The Voice of the Duvalierist Revolution."

Nor did Duvalier leave unfilled the vacuum created by the decapitation of the army. He closed the Military Academy to block the institutional renewal of the hierarchy, but compensated for this by promoting soldiers from within the ranks. In 1959 he appealed to the U.S. Marines to provide special training for soldiers loyal to him. In 1962 he founded a parallel institution, a civil militia called the Corps des Volontaires de la Sécurité Nationale, or VSN (Duvalier 1969: 315–18).

Duvalier also revealed his skills at manipulating institutions by centralizing the university system in 1960 under the umbrella of l'Université d'Etat d'Haïti (Duvalier 1969: 73–78). Then, in 1963, he moved against the unions, the last institutions to fall prey to Duvalierist aims. The Executive had now effected a qualitative transformation of the state apparatus, one that Duvalier was ready to make official: in 1964, with all national institutions submissive to the centralizing Executive, he declared himself President-for-Life.

It was this capacity of Duvalierism to transform the aberrant into the normal, the exceptional into the official, always keeping its enemies in disequilibrium, that I have called the formalization of the crisis. The Haitian state had always revolved around the Executive; with François Duvalier, the Executive *became* the state. The Haitian state had always helped to enrich its rulers. With François Duvalier, the enrichment of these rulers became the very principle of governmental accounting. The Haitian state had always been violent. With François Duvalier, the legitimacy of daily violence became the very principle governing the relations between state and nation.

The formalization of the crisis meant the spread and normalization of slush funds—so called "nonfiscal" accounts directly controlled by the Executive—a nineteenth-century invention that had been revived by the U.S. occupation. The Haitian Executive had traditionally had access to special accounts and controlled "autonomous" centers of profit. Duvalier multiplied the number and scope of these institutions by strengthening old ones (e.g., a monopolistic tobacco company created by the Americans) and by creating new ones (e.g., an insurance company), all of which became sinecures for directors, petty bureaucrats, and officials, as well as sources of income for the government that were increasingly independent of the ministry of finance.

In short, the series of measures often attributed to Papa Doc's dementia was in fact deliberately aimed at integrating the economic, social, and political contradictions inherent in the crisis into daily life. Attentive to history and the passage of time, the Duvalierists waited for time to supply the veneer of legitimacy that would allow the Executive to absorb the state entirely, and the state-Executive to absorb the nation. Sometimes emphasizing violence, sometimes using the auto-neutralization tactic, Duvalierism worked its way into normality, making possible both the Presidency-for-Life and, in 1971, at François Duvalier's death, the establishment of a hereditary republic.

Duvalierism played on time, and time, unfortunately, seemed to be abundant. The relative growth of profits kept exporters and commodity speculators away from day-to-day politics. Importers benefited from the frantic spending of the *nouveaux riches*. Washington's double standard—which evaluates a third world regime in terms of degrees of Soviet influence—gave Duvalier ballast in spite of Kennedy's recriminations.

Duvalier successfully maneuvered all parties, playing one force off against the other, practicing the art of auto-neutralization in all domains so that by the mid-1960s the formalization of the crisis was a *fait accompli*. This in turn implied the permanence of the regime, confirmed daily by violence, and the continuing degradation of the country's institutions.

Lyndon Johnson's administration, and later the Vatican and France, approved the dictator's "original" solution, first tacitly, then more and more openly (Duvalier 1969). Ethnocentrism and racism combined with economic and political imperialism—as well as with the memory of Haitian arrogance—to justify the indifference of the West. Auto-neutralization, and the possibility for the middle classes of establishing themselves in Africa (the Congo and Senegal), in Europe, and especially in North America (Canada and the United States) underburdened the political arena, adding to the state's margin for maneuver. And as the field emptied, as everyday responses fell in line with the Executive's formulas, François Duvalier chalked up points. Ratifying the division inherited from the structures of Pétion and Boyer, he made the criminal decision that the maneuvers of Kébreau had already pointed to: he pitted state against nation.

6
State Against Nation

Once pitted against the nation, the state could not remain unchanged. This chapter examines the interconnected transformations to which the state was subjected at the hands of the Duvaliers. It focuses on some of the already described aspects of the Duvalierist apparatus—terror, graft, and centralization—and shows how they modified traditional mechanisms of power. These transformations, together with the auto-neutralization tactic, led to new forms of state intrusion into the organization of everyday life. The accumulation of such changes eventually led to a qualitative change: *the remaking of the traditional authoritarian state into a totalitarian apparatus.*[1] Under the Duvaliers, the state forced civil society to abide by the political rules it defined. In so doing, it transformed substantial components of civil society in ways newly and wholly dictated by the political sphere.

Let me be clear on one point. The argument of this chapter so emphasizes the systematic nature of Duvalierist practices that it will become impossible to avoid the issue of *intent*—that is, the extent to which Duvalierist leaders systematically planned such an enduring system of control. It is impossible that all the formulas of power underlying the Duvalierist state could have been hatched in advance in the brains of one man, or even in those of a group of men. Certainly, there is no evidence of a clearly defined period of elaboration preceding the implementation of most Duvalierist practices. On the contrary, the history of the Duvalierist institutions reveals moments of experimentation, of retreat, and of dilemma. Indeed, the strength of the Duvalierist state is at least as much a confirmation of the weakness of Haitian civil society as it is testimony to Duvalierist acumen. Yet it is equally improbable that the Duvalierist state held together without any planning whatsoever, that its leaders never stepped back from day-to-day events in order to weigh the terms of the relationship between state and nation. We will look at the most calculated formulas of Duvalierist resilience in the next chapter. However, the argument here does not turn on the degree of conscious planning. The aim is to understand the logic of the Duvalierist state even more fully than did those who ruled it from 1957 to 1986.

NOT JUST ANY DICTATORSHIP

It is frequently said that the essential characteristic of the Haitian state during the past thirty years has been its "dictatorial" nature. For many, both Haitians and foreigners, the very name Duvalier has become a codeword for dictatorship. However justified, this reaction does not get us very far. To begin with, "dictatorship" has no super-historical essence that recurs in all, or even in most, "dictatorial" situations. Caligula's "dictatorship" was not the same as Péron's; and neither the latter nor that of Mussolini can be reduced to those of, say, Marcos or Trujillo. The concept of "dictatorship" cannot be operationalized. It does not enable us to dissect the state apparatus, to go beyond a repetition of facts that document the abuse of power. In minimalist terms, "dictatorship" refers to any form of state power wherein the Executive branch enjoys a degree of primacy beyond the balance traditionally accepted in liberal democracies. At the most, it refers to the constant threat of physical violence by the holders of state power, in excess of the limits defined by an established constitution.

Besides being inherently vague, the notion of "dictatorship" has no comparative value. In Haiti, as in many peripheral societies, dictatorship— defined as some point along a loose continuum of absolutist power—is the traditional form of government. The Haitian state has always been authoritarian: from Dessalines to the two Duvaliers, Haiti has known nothing but dictators. Thus what must be sought are the distinguishing characteristics of the Duvalier dictatorship. For we cannot treat this dictatorship as if it were just the extreme end of a range. From 1804 to our time, the balance of forces among the different components of Haitian society has changed— which suggests different rules in the use of, and limits to, state power.

Second, since at least February 1986, a vast majority of Haitians have recognized publicly that the dictatorship that collapsed with the departure of Jean-Claude Duvalier was something unprecedented even in their own history, as they perceive it. They may be wrong; but the burden would be on the nonparticipant observer to objectify this perception and to demonstrate not just that they are wrong, but how and why they have chosen to be wrong.

I start on modest grounds, in agreement with most Haitians, that within a dictatorial continuum—marked by breaking points or shifts—something changed qualitatively with the Duvaliers. During the past quarter of a century, Haiti's social fabric was not torn apart by just any autocratic system, but by a particular dictatorship, the concrete manifestation of a particular form of state power. Since Haiti has known nothing but dictators, the Duvalier dictatorship will of course be strikingly similar to many preceding governments. But this dictatorship was nonetheless uncommon, and our analysis will reveal striking differences.

Though vague, the two notions of dictatorship mentioned above provide us with two points of reference: the use of violence (stressed by the maximalist definition) and the centralization of power (stressed by the minimalist definition). If the Haitian state did change qualitatively under the Duvaliers, then we ought to be able to observe the consequences of that change, in terms of the use of force by the state and in the position of the Executive within it. Did the Executive enjoy primacy in the Duvalierist state in a fashion that was *qualitatively* different from that which it had enjoyed traditionally? Was physical violence, potential or real, used in a *qualitatively* different way by those who held state power?

Put thus, it becomes immediately apparent that the differences that distinguished the regimes of the two Duvaliers from those that preceded them were not merely quantitative. Sometime around 1961–65, the accumulation of these differences and the extent of their growth transformed differences of degree into structural innovations. The state had broken through the culturally specific limits of authoritarianism. We will begin with the use of violence because it exemplifies the nature of these changes.

VIOLENCE AND TRADITION

The exercise of state power is *always* violent; the state *always* claims a monopoly on force. In liberal democracies the limits to such violence, the conditions under which it may be used, and the division of the monopoly among branches of the state apparatus are fixed by law.[2] In most dependent countries of Africa, Asia, Latin America, and the Caribbean, the state has traditionally been authoritarian, but this does not mean that the dictators can do whatever they like. Rather, in these countries state violence is subject to social codes, always unwritten, often not explicit, but whose influence can be recognized in the particulars of history. Simply put, a society recognizes when the state has gone beyond the culturally specific limits on the use of violence by its dictators.

Thus it seems inadequate and even somewhat misleading to suggest that Duvalierism was characterized merely by the extreme use of state violence. Rather, Duvalierism distinguished itself by a *new kind* of state violence, one that systematically violated the codes governing the use of force by the state. I will offer two simple examples to support this point. In Haiti, the state's use of violence always touched on innocents, but it did so "by accident," so to speak: the cultural code limited physical abuse to individuals who seemed to threaten the dictatorship of the day directly. Since at least the time of Christophe, unfortunate people have died or been beaten for nothing more than being in the wrong place at the wrong time. The difference lies not only in the fact that the Duvalierist state touched *more* innocents than any of its predecessors but in the additional perversion of the very notion of innocence. The state no longer excused the victims of circumstances: all those who died had by definition been in the wrong. As far as I know, the history of the past thirty years does not reveal a single case in which a *makout* was punished for excessive violence, even against another *makout*. It is this change in the definition of the terms concerning the use of force that allows us to speak of a qualitative difference.

The second example is similar. The traditional code governing the dictatorial state has always protected women against the direct exercise of political violence. Pétion, who took part in the conspiracy to murder Dessalines, sent a note to the Emperor's widow in which he tried to justify the crime and also guaranteed her the political protection of the state. From the emerging days of the state to the rise of Duvalierism, women, like children, were by definition political "innocents," even though there were exceptions to that rule.[3] Yet what characterizes Duvalierist violence is not the fact that it also touched women, and not even the fact that it touched many more women than preceding regimes; it is, rather, the *complete* disappearance of the protection traditionally conferred by femininity. Everyone knew—and François Duvalier wanted it known—that women could fall victim to state violence. The unusual became the principle.

Duvalierist state violence thus involved, first of all, a large number of activities that were in striking disregard of the traditional code. To sum up the most important of these:

(1) The Duvalierists used force against a large number of individuals beyond the socially accepted range for victims of state violence. Children and the elderly were no longer protected by their age. Whole families disappeared or were forced to flee when it was known that one member was (or was considered to be) in conflict with the government.

(2) Duvalierist violence eliminated the gender distinction that, until then, had ensured preferential treatment for women. Under the Duvaliers, women were sometimes treated the same as men, often worse. Many women were attacked because a husband or male relative was out of reach—in exile or in a foreign embassy. The Duvalierist preference for the sexual "conquest" of females associated with the political opposition, from torture-rape to acquaintance-rape to marriage, infused the politicization of gender with violence. Womanhood, which had traditionally afforded partial protection from the state, now became a disadvantage.

(3) Duvalierist violence broke the tradition that accorded partial protection to certain high-level civil servants, and especially to members of the ideological institutions—schools and churches. Traditionally, the state had shown a degree of respect for rank and status in civil society. Above and beyond a certain social status, a person was considered out of direct reach of the violence of the day: the government simply provided enough room—and time—for its most "respectable" opponents to rush to the embassies of their choice. Again, that was not always the case; but it was the understanding. Duvalierist violence took away that respectability by forcing the "notables"—judges, clergymen, physicians, prominent writers, village elders, and other pillars of civil society—to participate in the repression, either as its victims or as accomplices of the state.

(4) The Duvalierists used violence against groups that could not be defined in political terms. A neighborhood, an entire town, a soccer team, or a group of individuals sharing a surname though otherwise unrelated could become the target of state violence.[4] Duvalierist violence struck spatially defined social entities (cities, villages, communities) or civil organizations (religious congregations, schools, social clubs), irrespective of any individual member's hostility to the government.

Two series of crimes, among many others, show these multiple transgressions of the traditional code. When a dozen youths from Jérémie launched a guerrilla struggle against François Duvalier in the summer of 1964, the entire town was threatened by state violence. The elites paid for the actions of those youths with dozens of their own lives. Infants were raped and killed for offenses against the state committed by cousins twice removed, or even by former neighbors (Chassagne 1977). The events following the attempted murder of then 12-year-old Jean-Claude Duvalier, in 1963, provide another case. Jean-Claude and his sister Simone were shot at on their way to school, most probably by François Duvalier's former *makout* chief, Clément Barbot. They escaped unharmed. François Duvalier suspected the army's best marksman, U.S.-trained Lt. François Benoit. Hordes of *makout* went to Benoit's house and gunned down every living being in or around the dwelling: family members, domestics, a visiting child from another family who just happened to be there, even the family dog. Benoit himself had been tipped off and escaped to the Dominican embassy. At least one passerby was gunned down because his *first name* was Benoit.

In indiscriminately attacking groups that were not defined in political terms, and individuals who were thought to be (and in many cases obviously were) political innocents, Duvalierist violence broke down traditional solidarities within civil society. Whereas before Duvalier an individual was protected by a claim that his or her relationship with a targeted suspect was "just" familial, friendly, religious, or social—that is, nonpolitical—Duvalierist violence recognized as legitimate targets *all* individuals who had a relationship with a political suspect, regardless of the nature of that relationship. It thus succeeded in casting a pall over most relationships. Fathers repudiated sons, sometimes publicly. Neighbors denounced neighbors. Cabinet Minister Luckner Cambronne summarized the Duvalierist desire to submit all traditional solidarities to the principles of the state: "A good Duvalierist must be ready to sacrifice his own mother."

THE LOGIC OF THE ABSURD

Because it violated the cultural codes through which civil society mediated the exercise of state power, Duvalierist violence appeared limitless. And because it seemed limitless, it has been called irrational. That term is inappropriate. Duvalierist violence certainly knew no limits with respect to the codes that had traditionally restrained authoritarian regimes in Haiti, but it was far from illogical. Its logic lay precisely in the fact that it seemed limitless. The disappearance of traditional restrictions had a symbolic value far beyond the immediate usefulness of eliminating genuine opponents. Violence became potentially "total," a daily sign of the omnipotence of a state that obeyed no logic besides its own. But because it reminded everyone of the state's omnipotence, that violence became a daily deterrent that kept potential agitators at bay—an even more effective means of protecting the state than the traditional violence it replaced.

Indeed, the use of force by the Duvalierists was rarely punitive, especially after 1965—hence its seeming senselessness. A tally of its casualties would count more scapegoats, more victims of sheer arbitrariness, of accidents of birth, or of presence at inopportune times and places than opponents who represented any real menace to the regime. But the very frequency of these accidents, the fact that they could befall anyone at any moment, engendered what local observers justly called "a climate of terror." The victims were so many sacrificial offerings, confirming the permanence of power, a reminder to the people of their smallness in regard to the state, a reminder to the executioners of the omnipotence of their chief.

Duvalierist violence was totalitarian both because it was limitless and because it was preventative in both principle and practice. It fits Eqbal Ahmad's model (1980) of the neofascist state in the third world. The aim was not just the physical intervention of the state into the sphere of political conflict, a characteristic of all Haitian dictatorships. Rather, it was the complete emptying of this sphere on behalf of the state. Duvalierist violence sought to bring political struggle to an end for want of participants in a political sphere totally filled by the state—and in this, it was new to Haitians. The effectiveness of this generalized violence had enormous consequences for Haitians' perceptions of the political practices and informal codes by which they were governed. Repeated recourse to unlimited violence gave rise to a new political morality, which in turn became a condition of the continued existence of the monstrosity that had borne it.

First, the maintenance of this state of generalized violence necessitated the continuous renewal of the regime's repressive forces. The principal organizers came from the parasitic strata attached to the dominant alliance: professionals, artisans, petty bureaucrats. But the ranks of the *tonton-makout,* as well as those of the civil militia, included members of all social classes. The active participation of a wide range of the population won at least a minimum of social acceptance for the totalitarian code of state violence. Few people may have been ready to proclaim their willingness to commit any crime on behalf of the regime, but there were enough to act as if they were—and enough to replace them when they themselves disappeared. Neither of the Duvaliers had trouble staffing their repressive apparatuses, even though the most horrendous felonies may have been committed by a rather small number of individuals.[5]

CHIEF AND NATION:
THE TOTALITARIAN EXECUTIVE

The Duvalerist Executive can be viewed as a series of reductions in which the first term swallows the second: State = Nation; Executive = State; Chief of State = Executive. François Duvalier invented none of these equations. As we have seen, the tendency to submit the nation to the state dates at least from the time of Boyer. The tendency to reduce the state to a militarized Executive dates from the time of Louverture and was systematized under Dessalines. It continued despite Pétion's republican façade, and was officially codified at the end of Boyer's regime. Similarly, the temptation to reduce the Executive to the person of the chief of state dates from Dessalines' empire, Christophe's kingdom, and Pétion's dictatorship, all of which set the tone for a tradition of centralized power.

But until the reemergence of the structural crisis and the 1956–57 conjuncture, no political faction had managed to make all the terms in the three equations of equal value. Dessalines thought of himself as the only noble in his empire, but he died in part because those who shared control of the state refused to allow the entire machinery to be reduced to its chief, even as they began to reduce the newborn nation to a reflection of state power. Soulouque certainly reduced the state to the Executive (especially during Haiti's second empire), but the commercial bourgeoisie relied upon the institutions of civil society, thus involuntarily making itself the nation's shield against the regime. Above all, until the U.S. occupation the mass of urban parasites was not sufficiently strong to enable the Executive to employ it as a club against the peasantry. Indeed, throughout the nineteenth century, the opposite was often true: political leaders used segments of the peasantry as a club against the urbanites. In that century the peasantry retained room to maneuver within its own stronghold.

The totalitarian difference is that François Duvalier closed the circle, achieving equal value for all these terms. If the nation could be reduced to the state, if the state could be reduced to the Executive, if the Executive was only the chief of state, then the chief of state was the nation. This Mephistophelean wager was possible because of the nation's exhaustion. It necessitated violence without limit, but it also implied the reshaping of the networks of power.

The Duvalierist Executive was distinguished by its replacement of the pyramidal structure of the traditional dictatorship with a centrifugal structure in which those who held power enjoyed it only on the basis of a direct link to the chief of state. This redistribution of power from the omnipotent center (the chief of state) duplicated the organization of violence in at least one important way: it admitted of no intermediate echelon. Every *makout* spoke in Duvalier's name; every *milisyen,* or member of the civil militia, was a Duvalier (Hurbon 1979).

This formula, in which the chief of state served as the sole reference point or center, was the cornerstone of the Duvalierist state. The supreme chief was the only actor. One spoke either in his name or against him. François Duvalier himself enunciated this principle in a speech on June 14, 1964: "Dr. Duvalier is neither Dessalines, Soulouque, nor General Salomon, though he considers himself their student. He has the intention of governing as a master, an authentic autocrat. This means, I repeat, that he wishes to see no one in his way except himself."

Popular perception quickly registered Duvalierism's intolerance of hierarchies: whoever was "too high" had to fall. And indeed, the Duvalierist state proceeded systematically to destroy the short-lived nobilities it created. The emergence of any heterogeneous organization, the institutionalization of any practice with a semblance of autonomy, within or around the Executive, was always in potential conflict with Duvalierism, even when political loyalty was not in question. The deliberate dissolution of hierarchies within the ministries and the army was meant to destroy any independent power base, whether or not the individual allegiance of the higher ranks was guaranteed. The rule applied even to Simone Duvalier—François' wife—when she seemed to have created a pyramid of power independent of her son Jean-Claude's authority in the 1980s. No one could be closer to the chief of state than the chief of state himself.

The breaking down of hierarchies within the Executive went hand in hand with the Executive's efforts to subjugate other branches of government, as well as most national institutions. The age-old weakness of the Legislature and the Judiciary made them easy prey for the expansionist Executive. By 1961, the Executive-state was attempting to establish direct control of all the state ideological apparatuses and the related institutions that linked the state to civil society: churches, trade unions, schools, recreational and social clubs, the press, and professional associations. Indeed, the Duvalierist state never displayed its totalitarian nature as clearly as in its effort to swallow up the multitude of so-called private initiatives and activities that, in Gramsci's view, are the pillars of civil society.

Of course, Laënnec Hurbon is right to remind us that Duvalierism's strength resided not in the outright annihilation of the traditional institutions and apparatuses but in their domestication (Hurbon 1979: 86). However, his choice of words is unfortunate. These institutions did not remain "as they were" after they had been tamed. The very fact of their domestication, which rendered these apparatuses "spectacularly effective" (Hurbon 1979: 86) on behalf of the regime, took away the relative autonomy they had traditionally enjoyed in relation to the authoritarian state, thereby modifying both their function and their nature. Each and every one became an appendage of the Executive; and since the Executive was nothing but the chief of state, national institutions were, at least in principle, nothing but an extension of his reach.

The Duvalierist state could not tolerate the existence of any institution outside of the Executive itself. Thus it shattered the internal hierarchy within each of the country's institutions, as well as the traditional balance of power among them. The army and the clergy offer the most telling demonstration of this. Duvalierism broke down the traditional military hierarchy to the point where the ranking system lost much of its usual significance. The authority of a major, or even a simple lieutenant, who was a *makout* far exceeded that of a colonel who did not enjoy this direct link to the chief of state. A minister, a priest, or a member of the Legislature might be less able to help a qualified candidate enter the university or the civil service than a chauffeur or a sergeant—if the chauffeur or sergeant spoke (or was thought to speak) in the name of the chief of state.

THE REIGN OF INEFFICIENCY

The totalitarian structure of the Duvalierist state and the need for a direct link to the chief of state as a guarantee of power implied the rejection of all forms of parallel organization, and consequently of any division of labor within the state organization. It is the centrality of the chief of state more than the (admittedly real) lack of qualified managers that explains the utter incompetence of the Duvalierist administration. In this respect, too, it is necessary to reject easy explanations, as well as the illusions entertained by foreign "experts" and by the "professionals" of the Haitian diaspora.

The Duvalierist regime has been described as the reign of incompetency, where all power lay with mediocre individuals. And it is certainly true that Duvalierist violence forced so many professionals and technicians to go into exile that the majority of white collar Haitians are now outside the country: we hear again and again how scandalous it is that there are more Haitian doctors in Montreal that in all of Haiti. That noted, however, we must be aware of the political and psychological need for expatriates from the petty bourgeoisie to transfer all the guilt they feel for their absence onto the two Duvaliers. Now that the Duvaliers are gone, the moment of truth is approaching with frightening speed for those who have enjoyed the pleasures of exile on the banks of the Seine, the St. Lawrence, or the Hudson. For the flight of technically and professionally qualified Haitians was due not only to the dictatorship, but also to the attraction of the capitalist metropolises.

Furthermore, it is not at all certain that the professional exodus between 1958 and 1970 substantially reduced the competence of those who held power or the top civil service posts, if we measure that competence against the standard of previous regimes. There certainly was an absolute decline of skill in the first twenty years of the Duvalier dynasty, but as we have seen, there was a relative growth in administrative competence in the first half of this century. Furthermore, Jean-Claude Duvalier's regime, which had a number of degree-holding officials—including one minister imposed by the United States—showed that the presence of qualified personnel did nothing to redress the incompetence of the bureaucracy.

The members of François Duvalier's cabinets were generally drawn from the same pool of talents as were those of Magloire and Estimé, and many of those who have served in Duvalierist cabinets, especially in recent years, need not envy their predecessors if their competence is measured in traditional terms. Moreover, the return of many sons and daughters of the petty bourgeoisie and especially of the bourgeoisie during the last decade of Duvalierism, along with the invasion of foreign aid workers of every description attached to neocolonized ministries, filled many potential gaps. In short, the problems of the Duvalierist state did not lie in the pool of skills on which it could draw, even if the dictatorship reduced that pool.

Beyond theoretical competence, effective administration implies a division of labor, that is, an organization that utilizes the individual capacities of civil servants on behalf of some recognized goal. Whether one likes it or not, effectiveness means hierarchy and division of responsibility. This in turn implies mediating links, as well as some distribution of decision-making down the chain of command. The actualization of "competence" thus requires a heterogeneous (though not necessarily unequal) distribution of power. The Leninist model of "democratic centralism" notwithstanding, at a certain level of complexity and efficiency it becomes impossible for all points to remain equidistant from the center.

In the Duvalierist distribution of power, the identification of the chief of state with the Executive, and the swallowing of the state by the Executive, required a centrifugal form of organization. *Makout* power—that is, power without mediation—was the sole guarantee of the chief of state's omnipotence. Duvalierism could not abandon this organization of state power without ceasing to exist. Yet for the reasons just mentioned, this very formula ensured inefficiency. Even when an administrative superior clearly held more power than all of his immediate subordinates—and that was not often the case—the basis of that power was neither his role nor his title, much less his competence, but his subordinates' perception of the strength of his ties to the center. A *makout* minister could control his department and even obtain results that others termed "spectacular," but he obtained such results *as a makout*. At the lowest levels of the administration, efforts to achieve a measure of efficiency necessarily conflicted with the centrifugal distribution of power and its intolerance of formal hierarchies. Conflicts on the job, once they became apparent to a superior, were resolved according to the real distribution of power. Somewhere, closer to the center, someone had to decide against efficiency.

The Duvalierist state thus had to tolerate inefficiency, irrespective of the intentions or competence of individual members of the administration. Inefficiency (not incompetence) became the structural precondition for the maintenance of the Duvaliers' power. The complete disappearance of efficiency as a measure of the functioning of the bureaucracy in turn ensured the chronic orgy of corruption that typified the two regimes.

AN EMPTY SWIMMING POOL

No Haitian chief of state has ever lived on his salary; every regime has enriched at least a few of the ministers and senators who served it. Similarly, Haitian governments have operated on the assumption that even a middle-level position within the state apparatus will be used for personal ends. Hence nomination to a government position has always tended to be a double favor on the part of the Executive. The Executive furnished a job (with a regular salary), along with the opportunity to collect the spoils attached to the post. The limits to corruption varied with the government of the day, but in response to factors that did not question the principle itself. The more centralized the Executive, the more corruption tended to be obvious, as during the regimes of Domingue or Soulouque. The more "efficient" a regime appeared to be, the less the urban outcry about corruption.

The appearance of efficiency depended as much on the rhetoric of the regime, on the size of the surplus exacted from the peasantry, and the vagaries of the international market for coffee as on the managerial capabilities of those who controlled the coffers of the state. Government use of monies for the benefit of the nation (e.g., the construction of schools, bridges, health clinics, and roads) was always a happy accident. Still, the desire to appear—if not to be—efficient in the eyes of varying constituencies laid an ethical veneer over some government practices.

What characterized the Duvalierist state was thus not so much the admittedly high degree of administrative corruption that prevailed within it, but the total disappearance of this ethical veneer. Corruption became the very foundation of the administrative machine, its only *raison d'être*. One entered the state apparatus *only* to benefit from it, for there was no pretense about doing anything else. Corruption became politically effective as never before; it guaranteed the unconditional endorsement of the regime's supporters.

The collapse of the ethical façade was in part due to the constant eruption of arbitrariness and violence within the administrative machine; but it was also linked to the declining political returns from any claim to efficiency. As we have seen, the highly centralized distribution of power cancelled out the already limited search for administrative efficiency. That in itself reflects a political choice. From the Duvalierist point of view, power was more easily maintained through extreme centralization than through the use of state funds for minor projects of dubious political benefit. Since the totalitarian state had engulfed the nation, the bureaucracy no longer needed to pretend to serve the interests of that nation. It *was* the nation and its well-being was therefore that of the nation. This equation was implied in the claims of representativeness that *noir* middle-class intellectuals had made in 1946. But Estimé's regime had still courted constituencies perceived along traditional lines: regions, localities, members of particular professions or income groups. The Duvalierist tactic of auto-neutralization initiated a new tendency in Haitian state politics, that of pleasing some members of all of the traditional constituencies without pleasing any constituency in toto—except, perhaps, the merchants.

From that viewpoint, even the appearance of efficiency was useless. To be sure, the Duvalier regimes also built their share of bridges, slums, and health clinics; but their flashy inaugurations were addressed to an audience conceived in different terms from those of Magloire or Estimé. The spectacle had other ends; it was less to show off the long-term achievements of the government to local audiences than to exhibit the Government itself. We can take as an example the case of the town of Duvalier-Ville (Cabaret), where the entire achievement consisted in the inauguration of an unfinished project. Soon after the inauguration the town was literally left to rot. Similarly, the Duvalierists built a public school and a huge swimming pool in Simone Duvalier's home town of Léogane. The school remained unstaffed and the swimming pool was hardly ever filled. Magloire would never have permitted that—not because he was worried about the population's physical fitness, but because a swimming pool without water would have hurt his image of efficiency.

As efficiency became less useful politically and as the ethical façade it helped to maintain crumbled, the political returns on corruption increased. The erection of Duvalier-Ville was in many ways reminiscent of Estimé's border town of Belladère, but it was also very different. In the short run, it was meant to be a spectacle of government achievement, though a spectacle conceived in different terms from those of the 1940s. In the long run, however, Duvalier-Ville was not built to ensure the support of the bedazzled inhabitants, but the enduring allegiance of those, in and out of Duvalier-Ville, who profited from the bribes and embezzlement accompanying its construction. After the day of inauguration, it had no other purpose. That is why no one took an interest in the project once it was declared finished. That is also why no one paid attention to Léogane's empty swimming pool: most of the monies allocated for that project probably went to build heated pools in the private residences of some of the barons of the regime.

THE POLARIZATION OF THE NATION

This analysis of corruption points to a key facet of Duvalierist power: the dismantlement of traditional constituencies. This phenomenon was related to the tactic of auto-neutralization, as well as to the breakdown of traditional solidarities by Duvalierist violence. Here, I will analyze the political polarization that arose on the ruins of these constituencies as yet another proof of the state's seizure of civil society.

The formalization of the crisis implied the institutionalization of the split between political and civil society: the chief of state swallowed up the entire executive branch, the Executive engulfed the state, and the state engulfed the nation. Each process, and the many steps involved in each, occurred in part because of the weakness of national institutions and the lack of vision of the so-called political elites. Auto-neutralization played a key role in that respect, masking the polarization of the society at the same time that it reinforced it. But polarization there was, and the political opposition played into the Duvalierists' hands by encouraging it. By the mid-1960s, only two options remained: one was either a Duvalierist or an anti-Duvalierist—that is, in the last analysis, a *makout* or a *"kamoken."*

The totalitarian state reached this extreme degree of polarization by travelling a twisted path. The Duvalierists were, of course, the first to suggest that whoever was not for the regime was therefore against it. But the silence of many nonpartisans confirmed—*ex post facto,* as it were—the *kamoken* credentials of those who had been so singled out by the regime. The survivors explained their withdrawal by pointing to the "lack of prudence" of those who fell victim to the arbitrariness of the regime. This polarizing tactic is typical of totalitarian regimes and movements. Hitler and Mussolini used it; it is part of the political arsenal of racist and religious movements with fascistic leanings. The mass reaction to the tactics is equally well known: a vicious cycle of fearful indifference, as the dominoes fall one by one. We can recall the words attributed to Pastor Niemoeller: "When they came after the Jews, I said nothing, because I was not a Jew; when they came after the Communists, I said nothing, because I was not a Communist; and when they came for me, there was no one left to speak out." Haitian reaction to political polarization was equally barren, if less eloquent.

No doubt Haitians in particular will object that posing the principle so crudely oversimplifies the various responses to Duvalierist power. But the dual process of polarization and neutralization was a key characteristic of the Duvalierist state. Haiti was, for all intents, divided into two parts: the "authorities," as they were sometimes called, and the others. Those who became the "others" acknowledged this fact only after they found themselves isolated as *kamoken*. Every individual was constantly forced to define his or her position vis-à-vis the regime, to situate himself or herself in terms of the fundamental divide between those who ruled and those who were ruled: Duvalierist or anti-Duvalierist, *makout* or *kamoken*. In the course of daily life anyone could claim a relationship, even fictitious, to the sole center and source of power in order to ensure a place on the side of the survivors. But in so doing, each thereby confirmed the existence of the polarity.

To make the point more concrete, I will take an example that may seem ridiculous, but whose very vapidity suggests how profoundly Duvalierism rent the social fabric of Haitian society. A thief is surprised robbing a house, and a crowd chases him. He runs away shouting "Long live Duvalier!" Whether his pursuers stop or continue matters little. In any case, they hesitate. They evaluate the implicit claim.[6] The example is commonplace, and its immediate political consequences almost nil. But the point remains that even a thief caught in the act would try to situate himself in relation to the Duvalierist/anti-Duvalierist divide, thus accentuating its impact.

A list of similar cases would go on forever. Thousands of everyday disputes, from a parent's argument about a child's school grades to a brawl at a nightclub over a dancing partner, afforded one or another of the contending parties the opportunity to claim ties (often fictitious) to the chief of state. "Don't you know who I am?"—a frequently used rhetorical question that hitherto had referred to social and economic status came on such occasions to mean, "Don't you know my political ties?" Or else a claimant would silence his or her opponents by intimating that the latter were *pale mal* ("speaking evil")—that their discourse reflected opposition to the authorities—regardless of what was actually said. Many urban Haitians became experts at such bizarre exercises in political hermeneutics, in which the capacity for instant interpretation meant the difference between winning and losing an otherwise apolitical argument. They found hidden meanings in innocent sentences in order to place their opponents in the "other" camp, among the *kamoken*. This was often enough to end the debate.

In short, whether polarization was the brainchild of Duvalierist strategists or a practical effect of the Duvalierist approach to power, it worked in favor of the regime and did so in part because the "others" contributed to its maintenance. But here again, we must note the Duvalierist ability to institutionalize the absurd. Under Jean-Claude, an editorialist for the government newspaper *Le Nouveau Monde* wrote bluntly that the very concept of an "independent" press was antithetical to the existence of the regime. Neutrality was impermissible as a public position and the Duvalierist state systematically eliminated it, forcing individuals and organizations into one camp or the other (sometimes into one camp *and* then the other).

Sadly enough, the political opposition—and the exiled opposition in particular—fell blindly into the Duvalierist trap, intensifying the polarization and thus repairing gaps that might otherwise have threatened the chief of state's authority, especially that of Jean-Claude. According to an article in a short-lived periodical published in Montreal, to be defined as a *makout* it was enough to be "objectively in open or disguised conflict with the Haitian people by [virtue of] one's class position" (*Makandal* 1971). No doubt real *makout* enjoyed a definition that gave them more allies than they ever needed! From the comfort of Brooklyn row houses, of cafés in the Quartier Latin, of tenured positions in Quebec, Haitian exiles called on intellectuals who remained in the country to "define their position" toward the regime in unambiguous terms, to situate themselves according to the fundamental divide. A "Maoist" interpretation of artistic practices called for songwriters, poets, and novelists to limit themselves to political statements. The hysteria reached its zenith in editorials in the 1970s that condemned any trip to Haiti as an implicit endorsement of Jean-Claude Duvalier's government and summoned "outside" intellectuals (those living abroad) to take a stand not only vis-à-vis the regime but also vis-à-vis any "inside" intellectuals thought to be Duvalier supporters because they were able to survive in Haiti.

That a few years later many of these "inside" intellectuals who had looked suspicious to the exiled opposition were in exile themselves (or murdered by the regime) did nothing to change the opposition's acceptance of the Duvalierist polarization. Once those individuals had fallen, they were transformed from "collaborators" into heroes—by the same analysts. Indeed, some of the new exiles joined the chorus themselves. The relative freedom of speech enjoyed outside of Haiti's borders allowed individuals to locate themselves in the *kamoken* camp more easily. Taking a public stance in New York or Montreal cost little and enabled the individual to cloak himself or herself in the mantle of consistency. The majority of Haitians who remained in the country had to define themselves in relation to the authorities *every day*—and sometimes redefine themselves when their very lives were at stake. But the principle remained the same on both sides. For the thief in flight, for the driver involved in an automobile accident, as for the exiled editorialist and the *makout* exacting a pledge of allegiance from an administrative subordinate, the political center remained the final point of reference, in relation to which everyone had to take a stand. The individual's position with respect to the political divide defined his or her place in national life. There were *makout* priests and *kamoken* priests, *makout* doctors and *kamoken* doctors, *makout* and *kamoken* schools, soccer teams, and surnames.

THE POLARIZATION
OF THE ECONOMY AND SOCIETY

In retrospect, the political polarization may have mattered less than the economic and social polarization that it helped to mask. The urban focus on the political divide and the exiles' grandiose pledges of resistance did little to alter the total indifference of the urban parasites and the profiteers of the alliance to the needs of the hinterland. Yet for the majority of Haitians, especially the peasants, the social and economic cost of the Duvalierists' policies was enormous.

The statistics produced by the Haitian government, or by such international institutions as the United Nations, the World Bank, and the Organization of American States, give only a superficial overview of Haiti's economic problems, but they at least offer a point of departure. The average Haitian's life expectancy at birth is between 47 and 54 years of age (United Nations 1980; World Bank 1984). Recent calculations suggest that the infant mortality rate is between 126 and 180 per 1,000 children. Of those children who survive, 87 percent are malnourished (World Bank 1984; United Nations 1983). In 1984, Haiti had 1 doctor for each 8,200 inhabitants and 0.77 hospital beds for each 1,000 inhabitants. The regime of Jean-Claude Duvalier spent $3.44 per inhabitant per year on health, and $3.70 on education (Latin America Bureau 1985). To these numbers we must add one of the lowest per capita gross national products in the world: $232 in 1977, $300 in 1981 (United Nations 1982; Thoumi 1983; World Bank 1984).

The actual legacy of Duvalierism is worse than even these numbers suggest. First, the figures are provided by cooperating foreign agencies influenced by U.S. governments that were sympathetic to the Duvaliers, and minor variations—viewed as signs of "progress"—often helped to justify U.S. aid to the regime. More importantly, such national averages—low as they are—still hide extreme inequalities. For example, whether accurate or generous, the figure of 1 doctor per 8,200 inhabitants is deceptive: it implies that access to medical care is distributed more or less evenly among the population. In fact, the distribution is extremely uneven. In 1979, for instance, the northern parish of Acul (pop. 60,940) had a single hospital-clinic complex, a "gift" from a local legislator. Yet the government's own media acknowledged that the complex was no more useful than Léogane's empty swimming pool. A reporter for Radio Nationale stated: "There is no resident doctor. The clinic is run by a nurse and visited regularly by a nun from the Catholic Sisters" (Radio Nationale 1979: 22). In such cases, can we speak of 1 doctor per 8,200 inhabitants, or none for 60,000? The reality is unrelated to the numbers. Some people in the parish probably enjoyed better access to health care than a number of residents of the capital city of Port-au-Prince, where many private clinics failed for lack of paying clients. Indeed, a few in Acul may have been only a plane ride away from the best possible care available—in Florida or Puerto Rico. At the same time, most residents received absolutely no treatment for diseases now easily controlled in most other countries.

Statistical averages mask the extreme polarization that was being created between a well-to-do minority, amazingly wealthy, and the bulk of the population. The despair of the urban poor and the peasantry comes from their sense that this polarization is growing. In the early 1980s, less than half of 1 percent of Haiti's estimated 5.3 million people enjoyed about 43 percent of the national income. This figure itself hides as much as it reveals for there is extreme variation even among the richest members of this minority. Many residents of Port-au-Prince and its adjoining suburbs can point to families whose known yearly expenditures suggest incomes well above U.S. $100,000. Few simpletons were taken in by the Duvalierists' anti-bourgeois slogans. The flow of expensive cars, of marble floors and gold bathroom fixtures *increased* under the Duvaliers and the merchant bourgeoisie did well under the two regimes.

The peasants' despair and the bitterness evident among the urban poor result from their perception that the growth of these inequalities is even beyond the control of those who hold power. Popular expectations rose slightly after the fall of Jean-Claude Duvalier, but the flight of those who occupy the next to lowest level of the socioeconomic pyramid resumed with renewed vigor one year later. By formalizing the crisis, the Duvalierist state in effect embraced and sharpened all the inequalities that it had inherited. They became the basis on which the state operated, and continued to reproduce themselves on a greater scale than even François or Jean-Claude Duvalier had intended.

THE SPATIAL POLARIZATION

The polarization of the country's spatial organization has also deepened. The trend toward the centralization of wealth in Port-au-Prince began long before François Duvalier's access to the presidency, but it too accelerated after 1957, and particularly during Jean-Claude Duvalier's rule. Today more than half of the well-to-do families live in Port-au-Prince. With its dirty slums and ostentatious suburbs, Port-au-Prince is a monstrous capital imprisoned in its own contradictions. In it live or work the most powerful and most desperate Haitians. It houses 20 percent of the national population, but swallows up 80 percent of state expenditures. Its demographic growth rate far exceeds that of the nation, and its size is about fifteen times that of Cap-Haïtien, the second largest city. The processes of economic, political, and demographic centralization reach their peak within its perimeters, exacerbating what a geographer has called an "urban macrocephaly" achieved at the cost of the provincial towns (Godard, in C.E.G.E.T. 1985).

In contrast, the regional centers are decaying. With a combined total of 57 percent of the population, the provincial towns wither, patches of dust guarded by the middle-aged: the old have left for the cemeteries, the young are packing for a better future elsewhere. Those who remain do so without will or intent. Too young to die but too old to think of leaving, they watch without hope over the deserted porches. No one can even recall past splendors. The city of Les Cayes, on the southwest peninsula, reflects perhaps more than any other the consequences of the flattening-out of the provincial pyramids. This is hardly surprising: "In one generation, the South lost close to 10 percent of its population, which moved toward the West, above all to Port-au-Prince" (Locher, in C.E.G.E.T. 1985).

The demographic and social history of the provincial towns remains to be written, but they probably furnished a majority of the newcomers to Port-au-Prince, as well as a substantial proportion of those who recently emigrated abroad.[7] Similarly, it seems likely that many of the current residents of the provincial towns recently came from the immediate hinterland. Be that as it may, the spatial polarization has certainly affected relations between these towns and their hinterlands. The Duvalierist state sapped the traditional power of the provincial notables, if only because henceforth local power had to be confirmed in Port-au-Prince. Cap-Haïtien and its dependencies resisted that centralized control most strongly, but the recent history of many former enclaves testifies to the weakness of the regional centers. The most vivid metaphor for this new spatial organization is the layout of the new national roads system, which skips villages and regional market towns in the name of speed and "modernization." In terms of space and time, interior towns have grown more distant from their administrative dependencies, and local economic exchange has declined, while the coastal towns of the South and Cap-Haïtien have moved within Port-au-Prince's reach.

CONCLUSION

We can now return to the question of intent. The combined results of the various processes of polarization described in this chapter could not have been hatched in advance in the minds of those who planned the Duvalierist takeover, or of those who solidified Duvalierist power between 1957 and 1964. But one must insist that the two Duvaliers and their immediate supporters *chose* to formalize an existing crisis. To keep themselves in power, they *chose* to maintain that formalization by re-shaping institutions and constituencies, and by combining violence and auto-neutralization. The process of polarization, and especially political polarization, were the result of this choice, not of the structures that the Duvalierists inherited. The Duvalierist formulas of power were not simply legacies of the past, but living proof of the use of such legacies for private purposes. The Duvalierist state was not a *product* of the crisis, but a *response* to it, and a highly political response at that. It implied an awareness of the division between state and nation and a will to enlarge this gap, while at the same time concealing it.

7

The Continuities of Duvalierism

There is no better proof of the systematic character of the Duvalierist enterprise than its unusual resilience: it survived François Duvalier himself. This chapter examines the most deliberate steps taken by the Duvalierists to consolidate power. It offers supplemental evidence of the connection between Duvalierism and Haitian social structure, and illustrates further that the totalitarian response cannot be reduced to a patchwork of random responses.[1] In the next sections, I will examine further some Duvalierist strategies of survival. They can be arranged in two groups:

(1) The creation of an ever increasing base of consent that, without ever according the regime total respite (which would have required a true "consensus"), nonetheless gave it a kind of permanent reprieve.

(2) The strategic alliance with the local bourgeoisie and with U.S. imperialism, particularly through the proliferation of subcontracting industries.

This separation is more didactic than analytic. In practice, the implementation of the Duvalierist strategies was an intertwined process. The effectiveness of any single scheme depended on a complex package from which the mechanisms described in preceding chapters cannot be dissociated, particularly the auto-neutralization tactic and the use of state-sponsored violence. We need to reemphasize, however, that terror alone was not enough to maintain the successive Duvalier regimes or to guarantee the transmission of power from François to Jean-Claude. The use of state violence, systematic as it was, remains an inadequate explanation of the survival of Duvalierism, if only because no regime can perpetuate itself for so long solely by the use of terror. In Haiti's case, the ruthless killings of Dessalines (1805), Salnave (1869), or Guillaume Sam (1915)—to mention three notorious examples—show that the use of violence can also be part of the opposition's arsenal. François Duvalier died of natural causes, and in office—a rare enough event in Haitian history. Both he and his son lasted longer than most Haitian chiefs of state, and Duvalierism holds the record for the longest single-party rule in Haitian history.[2]

Further, none of the armed attempts against the two Duvaliers gained the massive and spontaneous support that their initiators had counted on. None of the many armed invasions from 1958 to 1983 managed to enlarge, on the ground, the ranks of the attackers. Finally, even before the massacres that accompanied the failed elections of November 1987, the events that occurred after Jean-Claude Duvalier's departure proved that Duvalierism as a system could survive the family whose name it bears. In short, although the survival of Duvalierism cannot be explained without understanding the use of force, violence simply does not answer the basic question of Duvalierist resilience.

GENERATING CONSENT

The difficulty of analyzing the resilience of any dictatorship is in part theoretical. Only a few scholars have tried to conceptualize state violence and repression (Fontaine et al. 1983; Hoffmann 1984). The liberal tradition, which conveniently ignores the state monopoly of violence, sets coercion and consent as antithetical phenomena and predisposes us to see any state that uses force as fundamentally illegitimate. In that tradition, consent appears only as a verbal acceptance that by definition precludes the use of force.

But from a more dialectical point of view, coercion and consent can be seen as organically inseparable, part of a continuum inherent in the fabric of political power. In this perspective, consent cannot be viewed as a totally passive acceptance. It is active in two ways: those in power have to seek it; and those being ruled have to participate by accepting it. The generation of consent takes place in that encounter and the real question is the nature and the modalities of this dual participation. Second, consent is not limited to verbal acceptance, let alone verbal support. It cannot be measured by statements of the kind: "I don't care if ———," "I agree with ———," or "I disagree with ———." It is measured neither by polls of public opinion or at the polls of electoral precincts. Finally, consent cannot be reduced to class interests, even though it effectively ties class-specific interests, practices and discourses to the national arena. It nationalizes certain class practices, and in so doing gives the rulers of the day room to maneuver, even though they may not enjoy verbal support or consensus.

Consent and consensus are thus related, but they are not the same. Consensus is akin to the Gramscian idea of "hegemony," to the extent that it implies overwhelming agreement preceding the immediate political discourse. It refers to a political legitimacy obtained at the level of the deep structure, the sort of legitimacy enjoyed by many chiefs of state and most forms of government in Western participatory democracies.

In Haiti, political consensus never permeated the entire society, both because of the age-old isolation of the peasantry and because of the merchant bourgeoisie's inability to become hegemonic. Further, the imperfect urban agreement that was worked out during the nineteenth century broke down during the U.S. occupation. By 1946 the growing debate on the balance of power among urban factions led to new questions about the adequacy and legitimacy of government. The issue of the form of rule, taken for granted since the 1820s (despite Soulouque and Salomon) was reopened—albeit without peasant participation and without definite answers. We have seen how chaos in the political arena influenced the climate of the 1956–57 campaign and facilitated Duvalier's accession.

But once gained, power needed to be maintained; and this required, in part, the generation of consent. The Duvalier regime achieved this through a number of strategies. Two of these—the broadening of the *noiriste* discourse within a nationalist framework and the identification of the chief of state with the nation—aimed at verbal consent and I will return to these later. Two other strategies were aimed primarily at practical acceptance, especially among the lower classes. They were: (1) the expansion of the role of the state as a mechanism of redistribution; (2) the use of the civil militia as an organization of consent.

I have dealt with the ways in which redistribution completed the auto-neutralization tactic under the Duvaliers. I will simply add here that these schemes generated much more than the vocal allegiance of a few individuals. This politicization of the state's economic monopoly was both more intense and more subtle than the one envisioned by Beaubrun Ardouin. The Duvalierists did not always require an oath of allegiance. Rather, they were willing to make concessions on this issue. To obtain a lower level public job, an individual had to prove that he or she was not *against* the regime, not necessarily that he or she was *for* it. The key word was to not *pale mal* ("speak badly," or "speak evil"), as the Haitian expression went; and many people who tacitly disagreed with the regime tried not to "speak badly."

Not speaking badly also gave potential access to the unofficial network of redistribution, run by members of the presidential family and the most important power brokers. This network reached not only political cronies, but relatives, godchildren, classmates, soccer teams, music bands, carnival groups, and neighborhood or village organizations whose members were not necessarily vocal partisans of the regime. But the patrons, of course, could not be completely disassociated from the government. So even when their protégés did not have to give anything in return, not even political allegiance, the patronage system—like the civil state apparatus or the military—acted as an institution of rule. It became one of the many arms through which the state reached into the civil society in the name of *this* particular government. It produced practical consent in a manner relatively independent from expressed political positions.

A CONSENTING ARMY OF VOLUNTEERS

Nowhere was practical consent more ingeniously secured than in the creation of the civil militia. Immediately after seizing power, Papa Doc enlarged the band of goons and thugs who had served him so well during the campaign. They became part of an independent coercive force acting as a semi-secret police, the *cagoulars,* operating at night, hiding their faces behind *cagoules* (or ski-masks). Incidentally, both the name and the methods were a direct reference to European fascist organizations of the 1930s. By 1958–59, members of that secret police had replaced their masks with dark glasses and operated increasingly in public view, even though the regime denied their existence. They came to be referred to by the people as *tonton-makout* and became the living symbols of Duvalierist coercion.

This secret police was made up primarily of middle-class urban dwellers and a few landowners. Nurses, schoolteachers, clergymen, military officers, doctors, and shop owners filled its higher ranks. It remained largely a middle-class organization until the fall of Jean-Claude Duvalier, despite the increased participation of richer peasants and members of the commercial elite. But in 1962, François Duvalier created a civil militia, the Volontaires de la Sécurité Nationale (VSN). He explicitly presented the VSN as an officialization of the dreaded *tonton-makout.* The leaders of the VSN were indeed *tonton-makout* in the original sense—that is, members of the secret police, thugs and proven criminals. But if a few VSNs had actually been *tonton-makout,* not all *tonton-makout* became VSNs. Some of them remained undercover. Many refused to enroll or to wear the VSN uniform simply because the militia was a lower class organization. More importantly, not all VSNs were *tonton-makout* in the original sense. In fact, the Haitian language distinguishes between a *tonton-makout,* a member of the secret police, and a *milisyen,* a member of the civil militia. The first term suggests verbal acceptance of the regime and active participation in the repressive apparatus; the second suggests only membership in the militia.

But the regime itself did its best to equate *tonton-makout* and *milisyen,* even though for more than ten years the primary task of most *milisyen,* who until the late 1970s were largely unarmed, was to wear a uniform. This uniform—blue denim shirt, pants, and hat, with a red kerchief—evoked the traditional costume of the Vodoun god Zaka (the peasant god of agriculture), the colors of the Haitian national flag before Duvalier, and the peasant armies of nineteenth-century Haiti, crushed by the Marines during the U.S. occupation. And while the middle-class members of the secret police arrested and tortured opponents of the regime, the peasant-dressed members of the militia, peasants themselves or members of the urban lower classes, marched to the sound of military music in the streets of the capital city, intimidating by their very presence the bourgeoisie and the middle classes.

The confusion engendered by the regime helped it in many ways. First, it reinforced coercion, not only in the cities but also in the deeper hinterland. Whether or not a member of the militia used physical force against a community, each male *milisyen* or female *milisyèn* returning home from one of the many urban parades was the local proof of state power and could act as such. The very presence of this individual suggested to the community how far the arms of the state could reach. Second, the confusion partly shielded the *tonton-makout,* the men and women who did the real work. Third, the existence of so many *milisyen* also suggested that the government enjoyed a much greater verbal consent than it in fact did. Most people knew friends or neighbors whose presence in the militia did not imply ideological allegiance to the regime. But most people still saw the general fact of membership as a sign of such allegiance.

The civil militia was in more than one way the organization through which the Duvalier regime reached into civil society in both verbal and practical terms. Partly because of the dichotomy between towns and countryside, Haiti had not previously known a countrywide grassroots organization of any sort, except perhaps the informal networks of its market system. There was no national educational system. In fact, up until the 1980s, rural schools were under the Department of Agriculture. There was no national religious network. The Catholic church had a countrywide hierarchy, but priests alone could not provide it with a permanent presence in the hinterland. The practice of Vodoun, in turn, curtailed a national hierarchy for that religion. Thus the civil militia was one of the few organizations with a nationwide membership, especially after Papa Doc had shut down all the other associations with a potentially large membership, including the Boy Scouts. The militia respected the local hierarchy to the extent that it tended to recruit major Vodoun priests, village big men, rich peasants, or landowners as commanders. But it did not duplicate the strict hierarchy of the army. The militia was the only organization you could join by talking to your next door neighbor and thus become a member of an organization that was recognized throughout the country. And you could do so irrespective of location, class, age, or gender. Women were allowed. (Significantly, its top commander was a woman, a nurse by training.) Older people were allowed. More important, poor people were allowed. And many among the urban and rural poor joined that institution not just because it was a "genuine [economic] elevation" (Chamberlain 1987: 16), but also because for the first time they were becoming citizens— acknowledged members of the nation.

It is against this background of practical consent, constantly regenerated, that one must look at the Duvalierist discourse and its attempts to induce ideological acceptance.

HAITIANS, MY BROTHERS

Foreign journalists and scholars in search of exotic buffoons have enjoyed painting François Duvalier as an incoherent madman, a black Ubu, a tropical Caligula who would spout any amount of nonsense at any time. Many Haitian opponents, at home and abroad, have also treated Duvalierism with condescension. This mocking attitude comes partly from the national shame that Duvalierist practices have inflicted on Haitian pride. But that condescension also concealed a strategic counterattack by the Haitian bourgeoisie, a counterattack that survived the departure of the Duvaliers. There are segments of the Haitian elites, including many right-wing politicians, who want to reduce Duvalierism to an epiphenomenon, some unfortunate accident that can be explained in terms of the individual characteristics of the Duvaliers, *père* and *fils*. The stratagem is to make the Duvalierist discourse seem so incoherent that the problems it pointed to (but did not nothing to resolve) appear remote, swept under the rug by the emphasis on François' paranoia and Jean-Claude's stupidity.[3]

It is both foolish and dangerous to treat the Duvalierist discourse with such arrogance. At best, such an approach is tantamount to saying that the Duvaliers tricked the Haitian masses, especially the urban masses—which, of course, explains nothing. At worst, this arrogance is a cheap and easy way to sanction the Haitian dominant classes for whom it has been crucial—especially since February 1986—to make the whole phenomenon of Duvalierism look like a monstrous accident, now finished. Here we will take the symbolic aspect of Duvalierism seriously, not to attempt a study of Duvalierist doctrine, but to insist on the ways in which the Duvalierists effectively manipulated the *noiriste* discourse to assure themselves a minimum of consent on the part of diverse segments of the population. This systematic manipulation reveals the extent of the Duvalierists' awareness of the gap between state and nation.

As a political principle, *noirisme* was established on the basis of a double ideological coup: (1) racial consciousness is the only basis for national cohesion; (2) the black petty bourgeoisie—the middle classes—is the natural representative of the masses (Jean-Luc 1972: 93).

The first proposition is false (first coup). The second is not only false but can hardly be deduced from the first (second coup). Hence, *noirisme* is a mask veiling the political goals of a fraction of the middle classes, a buffer between dark-skinned politicians and the masses they claim to represent.

Schooled in the political struggles of the 1940s, Duvalierists hinted at the possibility of a third manipulation that would close the circle. They claimed more loudly than the Estimists that the black petty bourgeoisie— dubbed *classes moyennes* ("middle classes") in Haitian political parlance—was the sole political representative of the masses, and *therefore* the only class that could lead in the nation's cultural and moral regeneration. This is a circular proposition because it goes from the cultural to the political to return to the cultural. But what Duvalierism won thereby is the practical adherence of those who did not believe in its political formulas (or in *noirisme*), but who did see the need for a reformulation of the social and cultural stakes. Thus strengthened, Duvalierism could remove its *noiriste* mask before certain groups without embarrassment, to replace it with a more general nationalism. In short, Duvalierism used *noirisme* as a catalyst, and drew from it its own momentum while taking care to enlarge its bases.

Having guaranteed himself the support of the *authentiques,* but being absolutely certain as well that the *authentisme* of 1946 was "out of touch" with the electoral context of the 1950s (Dorsinville 1985: 20), Duvalier the candidate set out very early in a deliberate search for the ideological ambiguity that would allow him to speak to the nation as a "brother" without ever defining the terms of this brotherhood. Electoral, and later governmental, propaganda transformed him from *noiriste* leader into multicolored Messiah. Moreover, unlike Estimé, he did not hesitate to dissociate himself from *noirisme* when he felt it necessary—for example, in numerous speeches given in towns across the South, where he presented himself as an apostle of national unity (Duvalier 1966b). The theme of unity gave a thrust to the rhetoric of color, but the initial *noiriste* base guaranteed the allegiance of a central nucleus of supporters. Those who publicly approved Duvalier before and after 1957 and those who remained silent all had their own reasons for doing so; but once combined, all these reasons allowed the discourse to regularly redress its inherent inconsistencies. Those who openly attacked François Duvalier had trouble following him through the minefield of cultural contradictions because he managed so well to hide the socioeconomic stakes behind the imagery of political symbolism. Today, more than thirty years later, it is easy to forget that the nickname "Papa Doc" was first used by Duvalier himself; as an ethnohistorian and a country doctor, he knew that it evoked positive echoes in Haitian political symbolism.[4] By the same token, although many intellectuals smiled at the Doc's oratorical leitmotif—the famous "Haitians, my brothers" which began almost all of his speeches—the choice was equally shrewd. The "brotherhood" varied with those addressed; but the very vagueness of the language allowed flexible identification by those believing themselves to be addressed. The late Karl Lévêque (1971: 26), a perceptive Haitian sociologist, has written:

> In the Messianic set of themes [of Duvalierism], individuals are addressed as subjects. They feel "acknowledged" in matters that touch them most intimately—resentment of all the anguish, pain, and humiliation suffered because of their poverty and their color. . . . Duvalier truly delivered a speech [*une parole*] in which a part of the masses . . . and especially a part of the poor and humiliated petty bourgeoisie, saw themselves—a speech to which they could sign their own names.

Armed with the verisimilitude of his discourse and relying on the enlarged base given by the manipulation of cultural problems to fit the *noiriste* melting pot, Duvalier as president achieved another ideological coup: the identification of the leader with the nation.

MY ONLY ENEMIES ARE THOSE OF THE NATION

Discord within the nation had been obvious since at least Lescot and Estimé. The Duvalierist solution exacerbated this discord and brought about the polarizations described earlier. But instead of denying the discord, the individuals in power proclaimed loudly that it was a problem they had inherited, remained silent about the fact that they were intensifying it, and presented the Duvalierist state, and the leader who incarnated it, as the sole and necessary solution. Even as it increased the polarization of the nation by formalizing the crisis, the Duvalierist state claimed to be the guarantor of the (already compromised) national unity. We find in this formula the typical Duvalierist strategy of inverting questions and answers—and here as elsewhere the strategy bore fruit.

The strategy was probably born in the random to-and-fro of political rhetoric. Its thematic premises preceded the taking of power. François Duvalier declared his candidacy to be "in the spirit of National Unity" because "my only enemies are those of the nation" (Duvalier 1966b: 17). Moreover, the theme of unity and reconciliation had peppered the Duvalierist discourse since the end of the 1930s (Denis and Duvalier 1938; Duvalier 1966b, 1967). But it was from the moment that power was assured—and especially once he was in the Palace—that Duvalier insisted, more than ever, on national unity and the role of the state in building this unity. The new emphasis had been outlined in Duvalier's last campaign speech, delivered at a time when the results of the "election" were already certain:

> Twenty-five years ago, the conception of public interest isolated the state in its neutrality. With 1946 a new order appeared. It shifted the role of the state: it extended beyond juridical activity and imposed on the state a larger responsibility in the utilization of human and material resources.

The theme of national unity and the emphasis on the role of the state returned with the president-elect's first press conference after the election. His inauguration speech insisted on the responsibility of the new head of state "to reconcile the nation with itself," a slogan that would continue to resonate nearly twenty years later (Duvalier 1966b: 230–35; Lévèque 1971: 22; *Le Petit Samedi Soir* 25–31 October 1975: 15). The packaging of the Duvalier regime as the instrument of reconciliation was completed in the columns of the pro-government press (e.g., *Le Nouveau Monde, Panorama*) and especially with the publication of François Duvalier's complete works and of a shortened edition, the infamous *Bréviaire d'une révolution* (Duvalier 1967), modeled after Mao's little red book.

The successive publication of *Oeuvres Essentielles* (Duvalier 1966a, 1966b) and the *Bréviaire* (1967) was seen as a display of megalomania. Perhaps it was; but the gesture was not without judgment. It was less a matter of presenting Papa Doc's eternal thought to the illiterate masses than of showing a certain urban public how to read the regime. The short sentences, slogans, and leitmotifs of the *Bréviaire,* as well as the catechistic formulas that punctuated the Duvalierist discourse, had only one goal: to portray, in deliberately crude and ambiguous strokes, a Duvalier of choice, the man who was indispensable to national unity.

National unity itself remained vague, but little did that matter. Therein lay its usefulness. For the right, national unity was any alliance that would block Communism, and the government took great pains to tell the bourgeoisie and the United States that Duvalier was their last bulwark against socialism (Pierre-Charles 1973, 1979). To the *noiristes,* national unity meant the "color" balance within the state apparatus, the "equilibrium," as they called it. To the cultural nationalists, Duvalier promised the "regeneration" of the nation. Lévèque (1971) has shown the constant use, in Duvalierist discourse, of terms that suggested a setting right of the nation, terms such as "regeneration," "redemption," "reparation," and "reconstruction." And especially after 1968, the grand word of "reconciliation" was heard everywhere because there was also the need to wipe away spilled blood—particularly bourgeois blood.

Demagoguery, one could say. Perhaps. But remember that even some sectors of the Haitian left gave Duvalier the benefit of the doubt up until the beginning of the 1960s, thus increasing the credit that the government would use to establish its antisubversive legitimacy. At that time, of course, few could have guessed the extremes to which the government would go. But that is precisely the point. The Duvalierist discourse did not aim to convince everyone at the same time. It did not even aim to convince everyone of the same primary truths. The dupery was in shouting out that there was a Haitian illness, that this illness could be cured by the state, and that the state could only be Duvalier's. The three propositions did not follow. Nor did the same people hold them to be true to the same extent. But the Duvalierist address worked as a finite text because at any single moment different segments of the population paid serious attention to one or another of the three propositions. The nation was the state. The state was Duvalier. The nation was ill and thus had to come to terms with itself in the very person of the leader who embodied it.

Duvalier, with cynical care, took up all the slogans of his past speeches and writings that emphasized this identification of the chief of state with the nation and had them written in neon lights at city entrances and in public places: "I Am the Haitian Flag, One and Indivisible." "My Only Enemies Are Those of the Nation." "To Wish to Destroy Duvalier Is to Wish to Destroy Haiti." Propaganda techniques reminiscent of Mussolini's Italy or Hitler's Germany (Nicholls 1979: 232–33) presented Duvalier as the incarnation of the founders of the nation, if not of God himself. Dr. Jacques Fourcand's *Catechism of the Revolution,* parts of which were taught in some schools, included a Duvalierist version of the Lord's Prayer:

> Our Doc, who art in the National Palace for life, hallowed be Thy name by generations present and future, Thy will be done in Port-au-Prince and in the provinces. . . . (Cited in Nicholls 1979: 233)

Similarly, schoolchildren were required to recite, everyday, the pledge of allegiance to the Haitian flag, whose colors had been changed to red and black by the Duvalierists in order to reproduce a flag used during Dessalines' regime.[5] Gradually, the political vocabulary changed. The French term *apatride* ("stateless person"), used by the government press as a general label for opponents, identified the president with the homeland by putting the enemies of the chief of state and those of the nation in the same bag. *Apatrides* and *kamoken* (whose executions were sometimes public and whose corpses were exhibited) were "antinationals"—again a term with profound negative echoes in Haitian political parlance. The *makout,* the civil militia member, the "integral" Duvalierist were all identified with the nation. They represented the chief of state; and the chief was the nation. Duvalier himself put this identification into words:

> Haitians, my brothers . . . if in your heart of hearts you have felt that *I was you and you were me* . . . may I not proclaim in this solemn moment that I have won over my people. (Duvalier 1969: 314; emphasis added)

THE MORAL DEFENSIVE

The ideological victory was not as clear-cut as the discourse implied. The Duvalierist discourse, even when set forth from a position of power, was effective only when combined with practical consent, violence and auto-neutralization. That combination was uneven, with each of these legs playing different roles at different times, and the discourse was rarely the most important part for long. Duvalierism in power never arrived at a consensus; it never became hegemonic. Its power remained an embattled one, incarnated in a government that was always perceived as falling, or was always questioned or threatened by one or another vocal force. Its continuous harassment by an opposition that distinguished itself by its noisy stubbornness is the simplest proof that Duvalierism never got halfway towards unanimity.

Beyond the political discourse of opponents of diverse persuasions, the Duvalierist ideological machine also came up against the disapproving silence of the masses. This silence was not so much political disapproval per se as a moral reprobation deeply rooted in Haitian culture and triggered by the inhumane demands of the totalitarian state. I noted earlier that Duvalierist practice led to the emergence of a new political morality. It does honor to the profound humanism of Haitian culture that, despite the new political codes, the nation never gave the totalitarian state the ethnical legitimacy that François Duvalier expected. Popular "common sense" solved the moral dilemma created by Duvalierist politics by distinguishing sharply between those individuals who were willingly involved in politics (and the practices associated with them) and normal human beings. Even those who admitted that the Duvalierist way was the only way to remain in power rebutted that very same assertion by shifting to a more moral ground to suggest that politics was "a business for scum" (in Haitian, *vye mounn, vakabon*). On the one hand, then, the acceptance of the new political morality opened the way to consent, but on the other the abandonment of the entire political arena to "scum" who could live out this new morality on a daily basis prevented a consensus. In short, the totalitarian discourse never broke through the humanitarian principles by which Haitians judge human behavior. The debate on the political or cultural necessity of Duvalierism aside, everyone agreed that what was being done was not "good." "Se pa bagay mounn fè mounn"—these are not the sort of things that people do to people. At the height of its power, therefore, Duvalierism was hampered by the combined ambivalence of the various reactions it caused. Although diverse groups within the population adopted or claimed certain aspects of the program, and although individuals with differing tendencies had sympathy for certain aspects of the discourse, most had complaints about other aspects that were just as basic.

The verbal excesses of overly zealous collaborators, especially during the 1960s, the brutal practices of the *tonton-makout* and François Duvalier's idiosyncratic arrogance all helped to keep alive this silent reprobation. The author of the Duvalierist *Catechism,* a well-known physician and former director of the Haitian Red Cross, threatened to create "an Himalaya of corpses" to protect the regime. An influential minister of government suggested that a staunch Duvalierist should be ready to kill his own mother. These are things that one does not say without major sociocultural costs in a country where the notion of "respect" is the philosophical gauge of human relations. Thus what François Duvalier won in the perception of the state, he lost in the perception of his government. The ethnologist lost ground to the dictator. In this sense, Duvalierism was just "not the way to do things." Thus, in spite of his open support for the regime, the average Duvalierist remained, until the end, a shameful individual. Duvalierism at the pinnacle of power never stopped being morally on the defensive.

Out of necessity, out of preference, and because of their talent for cerebral acrobatics, those traditional intellectuals allied to the regime— many of whom were by hobby or training ethnologists, historians, or literati of one kind or another—took on the impossible task of making Duvalierism morally aesthetic. François Duvalier spent relatively large amounts of government funds in order to maintain a mass of propagandists, journalists, and essayists whose main purpose was to organize a moral defense by exposing the "human" side of Duvalierism. The preface to Duvalier's collected works emphasized the "extreme sensitivity, the ability to feel . . . the basic generosity . . . of the chief," a man who saw politics as his "sacerdotal mission" (De Catalogne 1966: 19– 36).

This discourse raised little enthusiasm in the 1960s but the ambiguities it implied bought time for the regime. And time was always an advantage to the totalitarian state, based as it was on the acceptance of the unusual. Duvalier made brilliant use of his successive reprieves. At the beginning of the 1960s, the provisional consent of the urban middle classes and of the well-to-do sectors of the rural population allowed him to establish the totalitarian apparatus. After the installation of the Presidency for Life, time borrowed through the use of violence, auto-neutralization, the impact of the militia in rural areas, and sheer political propaganda gave him the opportunity to reconcile himself with those who, at the very beginning, had believed him to be a wild card or a potential enemy—the local and foreign holders of capital.

Indeed, beyond the ideological and political manipulation described so far, the Duvalier regime's possibility for continued renewal rested on the generous guarantees and enormous advantages it promised, and gave, to the Haitian bourgeoisie and to U.S. politicians and capitalists.

CONTINUITY AND CHANGE

With the perspective gained from the passage of time, the two Duvalier regimes appear as two sides of the same coin. There are, of course, dissimilarities, but most of them are superficial.[6] The greatest difference between the two regimes lay in the deepening of relations between the state and holders of capital at home and abroad, and in the increased support of the U.S. government. It was not, however, a difference in principle. On the contrary, the blueprint for the economic policies executed under Jean-Claude Duvalier, which constitute the core of what Haitians have dubbed *Jean-Claudisme,* can be found in the speeches of François. In the late 1960s, Papa Doc augured the second, "less explosive," phase of Duvalierism. He projected a vision of what may be described as a totalitarianism with a human face, one that rested on increased economic dependence, particularly on a subcontracting assembly industry heavily tied to the United States.

The economic basis of *Jean-Claudisme* was indeed a banal wager on the attraction that Haiti's cheap labor force represents for U.S. capital. The best summary of that vision comes from François Duvalier himself when he told then U.S. Vice-President Nelson Rockefeller during Rockefeller's 1969 visit to Haiti: "Haiti could be a great reservoir of manual labor for Americans establishing re-export industries because it is closer, more reliable and easier [sic] than Hong Kong." The flow of U.S. tourists was seen as an additional exchange that would reinforce movement between the two countries. Duvalier added, in the same speech: "Haiti could be a great land of relaxation for the American middle class—it is close, beautiful, and politically stable" (Duvalier, in Pierre 1971: 49, 41).

The program was certainly not new. It repeated the fruitless experiments attempted in the 1950s with Washington's support in Puerto Rico and Jamaica, major segments of which have now been integrated into the Caribbean Basin Initiative.[7] In Haiti itself, light assembly industries, acting as subcontractors for U.S. firms, first appeared in the 1950s. Their role in the national economy was already noticeable during Magloire's regime, and it developed in spurts during the beginning of François Duvalier's term. The important point is that Papa Doc personally championed the Duvalierist reliance on cheap labor—a reliance that implied closer dependence on the United States and a political climate much less turbulent than that of the mid-1960s. In short, the formulas that best explained the survival of the second Duvalier, notably the systematic search for the explicit endorsement of the local bourgeoisie and the U.S. government, had been on the drawing board before the death of Papa Doc.

The first Duvalier regime was nevertheless incapable of instituting the formulas that came to typify *Jean-Claudisme.* That failure was not for lack of conviction. Rather, the obstacles were both too many and too severe. First, even though the increased reliance on cheap labor envisioned the development of light industry, subcontracting to U.S.-based firms, it required some basic infrastructural amenities such as transportation and energy sources. Second, it required the participation of the Haitian bourgeoisie, which would provide local capital and basic services, including personnel and local representatives to deal with the state bureaucracy. Third, it required open support from Washington without which few U.S. corporations or entrepreneurs would risk investing in Haiti.

For various reasons, the first Duvalier regime could not meet these technical, ideological, and political requirements. Even after 1969, François Duvalier still aroused a residue of distrust among the Haitian bourgeoisie and the U.S. politicians he courted. Other obstacles, especially the technical ones, had little do to with the personality or the past of the aging dictator. Still, the fact that they were solved at about the time of his death amplified the perceived differences between the two regimes.

In 1971, the Péligre hydroelectric plant began operating in a more or less adequate manner, under the management of a new body, L'Electricité d'Haïti. The event was overshadowed by François Duvalier's death and the accession of Jean-Claude to the presidency, but it symbolized a turning point in the history of the Duvalierist state, because it allowed Duvalierism to enter its second phase. A year later, there were 150 U.S. firms in Haiti (Groupe de Recherches Nouvelle Optique 1972: 4), mostly newcomers, and the number almost doubled between 1971 and 1977, to decline slightly at the very end of the decade. Per capita energy consumption more than doubled between 1970 and 1981, not only because of Péligre but also because of the development of thermal plants around Port-au-Prince, where the industries were concentrated.[8]

Statistics fell in line with reality. During Jean-Claude's regime, coffee officially became the second largest national export for the first time since independence. The categorization is deceptive, of course, because the "light industry" label aggregates, somewhat misleadingly, diverse commodities. Thus coffee remains in fact the primary export commodity. Indeed, if all agricultural exports were grouped together, they would still make up the largest category, especially after the early 1980s when coffee regained some of its importance because of a rise in prices. But the changes in the statistics did reflect a real transformation. Manufacturing output grew more than 10 percent a year at the end of the 1970s, and the net value of assembly industry exports, approximately one-fourth of all exports, grew by about 30 percent a year—a favorable rate compared to the poorest countries of Latin America (C.E.P.A.L. 1982: 322–27). Today, Haiti operates in the world-economy as a supplier of garments, dolls, magnetic tapes, and electronic equipment. Until recently, it was the major exporter of softballs and baseballs, though Haitians play neither sport.

WASHINGTON'S BLESSING

In 1964, while François Duvalier was crushing Haiti's national institutions, the arrival of B.E.L. Timmons II in Port-au-Prince as U.S. ambassador marked a turning point in Washington's attitude toward Duvalierism. Despite nationalist boasting and personal difficulties with the Kennedy administration, François Duvalier's government had always given the United States the most tangible sign of its submission: unconditional support for U.S. capital. Between 1957 and 1961 the Reynolds Mining Company, which has a monopoly on Haitian bauxite mining, paid only 7 percent of its local income in taxes to the Haitian state.[9] The exports most tightly controlled by U.S. firms (e.g., sisal, sugar cane, copper, bauxite) generally increased in Papa Doc's early years. But François Duvalier and John Kennedy did not particularly like each other, in part perhaps because of some early attempts by Duvalier to court Fidel Castro.

Duvalier's total disregard for international opinion, amplified by the repulsive practices of the *tonton-makout,* also interfered with the image the Kennedy administration sought to project in Latin America and the Caribbean.

The coming to power of Lyndon Johnson signalled the changes symbolized by Timmons' arrival. Even before Kennedy's death, Duvalier had managed to convince the U.S. administration that a totalitarian response was the only guarantee against the rise of the left.[10] In 1962, he had used U.S. anticommunist paranoia to further his plans: he had convinced the United States to finance the François Duvalier International Airport in exchange for the Haitian vote at Punta del Este to expel Cuba from the Organization of American States. As Duvalier increasingly played the anticommunist card after Kennedy's death, relations between his regime and the United States improved steadily. Still, Washington was somewhat embarrassed by the apparently gratuitous violence of the regime, and although U.S. support included military aid, it fell short of openly encouraging U.S. investors to risk their fortunes in Haiti.[11] The decade neared its end with the Haitian government looking for ways to mollify its great northern neighbor.

At that time, the Parti Unifié des Communistes Haïtiens (Unified Party of Haitian Communists, or PUCH) unwittingly gave Duvalier the opportunity to obtain this support. At the end of the 1960s, PUCH began a clandestine infiltration of the country by militants and an attempt at urban guerrilla welfare that ended in total failure in 1969. This time, Duvalier had the chance to prove, with Haitian blood, his reputation as an unflinching anticommunist. Between 1967 and 1970, the government physically eliminated, imprisoned, or forced into exile hundreds of progressive intellectuals, writers, professors, journalists, and union and peasant leaders. The vast majority of these people had no contact with the PUCH, or with any other political organization.[12] In ideological terms, most of the victims were barely what U.S. nomenclature would describe as left of center. But that was all it took. Exploiting the legal precedent of an anticommunist decree promulgated by Estimé in 1948, Duvalier used the proven existence of a few armed communists to push the Legislature into voting a legal monstrosity, the Anti-Communist Law of April 1969. Every "profession of communist belief, verbal or written, public or private" was declared a crime against national security and made its perpetrator into an "outlaw eligible for the death penalty meted out by a permanent Military Court" (Trouillot and Pascal-Trouillot 1978: 446–47).

The tangible evidence of a communist menace and the 1968–69 political transition in Washington provided the perfect occasion for the U.S. government to make public a change of position which it had already showed in deeds. The period from the election of Richard Nixon as president of the United States to the crowning of Jean-Claude Duvalier as President for Life of Haiti saw the formalization of the alliance between the two governments. The massacres of communists and the stifling of all those who spoke, even timidly, of economic redistribution, constituted the symbolic fulfillment of the deal on the Haitian side. In 1971, Washington's blessing of Jean-Claude Duvalier's access to the presidency sealed the pact. U.S. vessels patrolled the sea around Haiti to ensure that the inauguration proceeded undisturbed.

THE *JEAN-CLAUDISTE* BOURGEOISIE

Washington's blessing, increasingly evident during the latter part of the 1960s, also helped the Duvaliers to meet the political obstacle that the Haitian bourgeoisie's aversion to Papa Doc had meant for the development of the subcontracting formula. For most of his life, Duvalier the elder had attacked with ideological vehemence the light-skinned elite, traditionally linked with commerce; the local bourgeoisie, particularly the *mulâtres* and foreign-born merchants of the Bord de Mer, lived in fear of him. The president had established a reputation as a *mulâtre*-eater during the "Vespers of Jérémie." It was to alleviate those fears that, in 1966, Duvalier publicly pronounced the end of "the explosive phase of Duvalierism" and published the first volume of *Oeuvres essentielles,* whose purpose was to emphasize the program of national unity.

The appeal to the bourgeoisie had mixed results. Only a few *mulâtres* allied themselves with the president, who married one of his daughters to one of them—thus foreshadowing by a decade the marriage of his son Jean-Claude to Michèle Bennett. But the large merchants hesitated, especially when some of them were literally kidnapped and held for ransom by the regime in order to rescue the practically empty state coffers.

Thus until the end of the 1960s, the cream of the local bourgeoisie, mistrustful of the *noiriste* ideologue, stubbornly refused to dance to the Duvalierist tune.

We can easily understand the difficulties of the Bord de Mer. Inherently antinationalist, with no turf of its own to protect, it was concerned with the structures that shaped the nation only insofar as it could profit from them. It paid little attention to production or to the producers as such. Admittedly, some bourgeois did invest in agroindustry, and Louis Déjoie's political gambit may have aimed at employing these new formulas. But Déjoie left the political scene during the skirmish of May 1957 without having provided a program that the bourgeoisie, or the agroindustrial sector within it, could claim as its own. Afterward, the Bord de Mer entered a period of retrenchment; production was not its strong point.

The crisis was also one of hegemony, and thus had very pronounced ideological and cultural features that Duvalier used to further his political goals. In this respect particularly, the Bord de Mer was behind the times. For a century it had governed through understudies. It had never learned to "talk country," even jokingly. It has never even paid serious attention to—much less understood—the stirrings of cultural nationalism that had moved many subgroups of the urban classes since the beginning of the nineteenth century. The nationalist discourse had gained a great deal of ground as a consequence of the U.S. occupation, without the Bord de Mer realizing what the rise of the middle classes implied politically, busy as it was counting its change. Although the reaction of the *authentiques* surprised most bourgeois, the Bord de Mer believed it would regain its influence, especially after Magloire took over from Estimé. After all, Magloire's regime was a classic case of government by understudy—the last of the type, to be sure, but nobody knew that in 1956.

In the beginning of the 1960s the Bord de Mer was thus confronted with an adversary whose very existence was confusing to the merchants. Here was a president resolved to change the operative principles of political power underlying what most merchants had come to view as "their" republic. The merchants were used to verbose and intimidating presidents, especially among the *noirs*—Soulouque and Salomon, for example. But those presidents had challenged merchant power over the particular composition of a regime, never over the degree of involvement of the state within civil society, and never over the margin of maneuver the state conceded to the merchant class as a whole. The difference with Duvalier was that he claimed to *be* the republic, and he acted as if he believed it. He had no objection to the merchants prospering; he did not even mind if they maintained their domination over the economy. But he insisted on the right to dictate the economic and social price that the merchants would pay for this domination, and he saw to it that the state's share of the spoils increased so as to fit current political realities. If the bourgeoisie truly valued its economic domination, it would have to pay up. Either that or it would have to learn silence and to allow an even more thorough fleecing of the rural and urban producers by the government. Similarly, if it valued its social domination, it would, at the very least, have to learn to share control of the social system with the *nouveaux riches* from the black middle classes. Gone were the days when Soulouque's chief of police, a tailor by trade, would settle for being low man on the totem pole. The successive chiefs and overlords of the secret police under both Duvaliers wanted to gain entry to the most select clubs of the Port-au-Prince bourgeoisie. Government ministers of middle-class origins proudly sent their children to the most exclusive schools, even if they were among the few *noirs* to attend them. In short, Duvalierism did not call into question the Holy Alliance of rulers and merchants of the nineteenth century, but it wanted to renegotiate its terms to benefit the tiny minority of the black petty bourgeoisie that claimed the right to eternal rule. Not surprisingly, the Bord de Mer took some time to understand this change.

The merchants first reacted to François Duvalier's regime in nineteenth-century terms, objecting to what they perceived as Duvalierist arrogance. They conveniently ignored the fact that the regime was not challenging their structural role in the distribution of the peasant surplus. In fact, Duvalier strengthened the merchants' position vis-à-vis the peasantry, and the Bord de Mer should have been delighted. Its share of commodity prices continued to grow and it benefited from the exorbitant spending of the *nouveaux riches*. The *tonton-makout*'s purchases supported the importers of luxuries and permitted them to survive the difficult 1960s. But the ideological chaos of the bourgeoisie, the development of totalitarian violence, and especially the *noiriste* discourse from which Duvalierism drew its original impetus clouded the political calculations of an economic elite accustomed to simpler accounting procedures. Cloaked in its patrician attitude, the bourgeoisie reacted to the Duvalierists in the *mulâtriste* terms of the nineteenth-century Parti Libéral: it would not come to terms with "those people."

It was at this point that international capital came once more to the aid of Duvalierism, in the form of Clinton Knox and Nelson Rockefeller. Rockefeller's visit in 1969 gave a boost to Duvalierism's shaky fortunes and lent it, in the eyes of the local bourgeoisie, the moral legitimacy that the Haitian nation had refused it. If a U.S. millionaire, the embodiment of capital and the second most prominent citizen of his country, accepted Duvalier, the local agents of capital had no choice but to go along. In addition, Rockefeller's visit led to the nomination of Clinton Knox, which revived the Republican tradition of putting black ambassadors on display in Haiti. In the last few months before François Duvalier's death, Knox became one of the most influential individuals in Haiti, outside of the immediate Duvalier family. He personally engineered, with Luckner Cambronne (the very same minister who was "ready to kill his own mother") and others on the Haitian side, the transmission of power to Jean-Claude Duvalier. Finally, in the local context, the presence of a dark-skinned black American in the corridors of the National Palace also suggested that Washington fully endorsed the logic of color quotas. As positive signals from the United States escalated, the Haitian bourgeoisie, never known for original thinking, responded to the advances of the "new" regime. By 1972, it was, for all intents and purposes, *Jean-Claudiste.*

Its support was not free. The light industry (plus tourism) solution offered the bourgeoisie the possibility of diversifying its investments and increasing its income without increasing its risks. Haitian entrepreneurs had always accepted a subsidiary role vis-à-vis foreign capital, and Duvalierism offered them the possibility of two subsidiary functions rather than one. On the one hand, merchants could still operate as intermediaries for Western countries in the export of agricultural commodities and the importation of manufactured goods. On the other, the most entrepreneurial ones could, from then on, invest a minor portion of their profits in the assembly industry, as junior partners of foreign investors. Rich landowners and political supporters who had accumulated fortunes by depleting the Treasury could do likewise. The modest requirements in fixed capital, the short-term returns, the minimal degree of economic planning, and the low risk of assembly industries were agreeable to Haitian entrepreneurs, who were always ready to close up shop and always mistrustful of long-term investments. Moreover, the local share of these investments remained small. François Duvalier's original appeal was made to U.S. capital, which would continue to be by far the largest contributor to the financing of the assembly industry. The Haitian bourgeoisie, a minor partner, thus profited from the protection of the U.S. investors and was therefore doubly shielded from political disturbances. Further, the totalitarian state guaranteed that wages would rise only superficially, if at all. Finally, the children and allies of this bourgeoisie could also share in factory management with U.S. citizens and with officials of the regime. The chance to play a safe subsidiary role outside of commerce was something the Haitian bourgeoisie had dreamed about without ever having been able to effect for itself. Happily surprised by the second phase of the regime, the bourgeoisie supported Duvalierism with all its heart, thus giving it a second wind, especially after François Duvalier's death relieved it of a minor embarrassment.

The Duvalierists in turn demanded a social protocol from their former adversaries: the right to be treated as equals. The bourgeoisie, now won over, readily obliged: it would "rub shoulders" with those self-same individuals it had once disdainfully referred to as "those country people." Only to a certain point, of course. The *haute bourgeoisie* remained endogamous—it would not marry presidents, although it might play with them. And to seal the alliance symbolically, Jean-Claude Duvalier would have to settle for Michèle Bennett, the divorcée daughter of a *spéculateur,* whom he married in May 1980. Contrary to commentaries in the international press, the bride was not considered bourgeois by most Haitians before the marriage. She was only light-skinned—not even a *mulâtresse;* and her relatives had gained prominence in the import-export trade only *after their political alliance with the regime,* when their activities were completely exempted from customs duties and taxes.

Thus there were sociocultural limits to the gains made by the tenants of the *Jean-Claudiste* state apparatus, even if their new status had become a permanent inconvenience in the social domination of the traditional elite. But, in spite of the ridicule with which some *mulâtre* patricians and *noir* intellectuals greeted this multimillion-dollar wedding—incongruous incarnation as it was of national unity—that ritual said exactly what it was meant to say: Duvalierism had come full circle.

BREAD, SWEAT, AND TEARS

The government repeatedly proclaimed the success of the "less explosive" phase of the Duvalierist project. Jean-Claude Duvalier enjoyed saying that he was leading the country through an "economic revolution," just as his father had led it through a "political revolution." In fact, it was the nation that paid the cost of this second phase of Duvalierism, as it had paid the first. *Jean-Claudisme* was to the polarization of incomes and standards of living what François' regime had been to the polarization of political life. The *makout/apatride* dichotomy was now coupled with another split, just as basic, between the haves and have-nots. Official statistics could not completely mask the disastrous effects of the assembly industry on the Haitian economy. I have already cited some of the figures; I will cite others later on. But first it is important to set out the principles that explain the disaster. First, assembly production never reached a level where it could spur an economic recovery. Second, the design itself was faulty, if only because it bypassed the problems of rural Haiti.

The light industry strategy never brought the returns expected by those who stubbornly imposed it on the Haitian people. Neither the number of factories nor the number of jobs were large enough. Subcontracting assembly plants did provide employment to many people in the Port-au-Prince area, between 40,000 and 60,000 depending on the estimates. However, this was not enough to make a substantial change in the national employment picture. Factories succeeded each other, making the job market unstable even when the net number of jobs remained relatively steady. Further, given labor conditions, the absence of unions, and the excessive demands of the employers (from sudden shifts in schedules to sexual harassment), few Haitians held their jobs long enough, even in the more stable firms, to benefit significantly from their employment. Finally, in spite of the very low cost of labor, many potential investors looked suspiciously at Haiti's infrastructure and at its political stability. Hence, far from increasing steadily, as was expected, industrial production wavered through the 1970s and 1980s.

The light industry strategy was destined to misfire primarily because it ignored the impasse posed by the relations of production in the agrarian world. The crisis inherited by François Duvalier and exacerbated by his regime and that of his son had its roots in the contradictions of a peasant country ruled by an unholy alliance of merchants and political profiteers, an alliance cemented by the state. By ignoring the problems of the rural world and the difficult relationship between it and the urban classes, the light industry strategy in the end complicated them. Thus, for example, the creation of the Delmas industrial park on the outskirts of the capital intensified economic and spatial polarization by increasing the gap between Port-au-Prince and the rest of the country. While electric production expanded rapidly, the new averages concealed enormous variation. In 1979, the Port-au-Prince metropolitan area consumed 93 percent of the electricity produced in the country (Kermel-Torres in C.E.G.E.T. 1985). To make matters worse, rates for private residences rose by 53 percent between 1971 and 1981 (ibid). In other words, although the official statistics registered a massive improvement, the gulf between the electrical consumption of the haves and the have-nots was doubly exacerbated; indeed, the gap was much greater than in the days before Péligre. Although the area around Port-au-Prince had long enjoyed a more or less "modern" energy capacity, after Péligre it became *more difficult* for the great majority of citizens to afford electricity. The number of subscribers declined, both in proportion to the total population and perhaps in absolute terms as well. The rise in residential rates eliminated the poorest households from the demand market and forced subscribers of modest means to subsidize indirectly the subcontracting industry through the government agency that sold them the electricity they consumed.

We could tell similar stories for the construction or transportation sectors. The result in all cases was the same: the assembly industry accentuated economic and spatial polarization without benefiting the nation. The new momentum that it brought to this polarization process was so obvious by the early 1980s that even international organizations, such as the World Bank—which fully support the subcontracting strategy—began to suggest that factories be scattered throughout the various departments. The government never bothered to accommodate this suggestion, and in any case the proposal itself was shaky. First, it was bound to run into technical and political difficulties that could not be overcome without more profound reforms. More important, the redistribution of factories to the four corners of the country would not eliminate the most fundamental problems created by the assembly industry itself.

The light industry/subcontracting strategy also proved to be both a fiscal and a commercial disaster. The profits generated by its exports were substantially reduced by the need to import basic materials and by tax evasion. The subcontracting formula therefore contributed to the growth of Haiti's trade deficit, which rose from $12.4 million in 1970 to $68.4 million in 1975 and $183 million in 1980. Graham and Edwards (1984: 75), who cite these figures, ascribe them to the increased price of imported oil. That explanation falls short of assessing the role of light industry in energy consumption. For example, the massive increase in traffic on the Jean-Jacques Dessalines artery, the main road leading from the Port-au-Prince slums to the Delmas industrial center, benefits mostly the car importers and diesel fuel wholesalers. At any rate, the import-export price index for the years 1969 to 1985, the index of the terms of exchange, and the schedule of imports in constant prices for that same period suggest that differences between import and export prices alone do not account for the growth in the trade deficit (IHSI 1986: 66–67; 70–71). By 1985, that deficit exceeded $125 million (Hooper 1987b: 33).

The deficit stemmed in part from a tremendous rise in import values, itself partly caused by increased corruption. The local gourde is of no use in foreign exchange and Haiti uses the U.S. dollar for international transactions. The gourde has long been tied to the dollar, at the fixed rate of 5 gourdes to $1 and U.S. currency is also used interchangeably with the gourde in local transactions. Export values, U.S. government aid, and the huge remittances from Haitians living abroad—about $125 million a year (Chamberlain 1987: 21; Hooper 1987b: 33)—have maintained the free circulation of the dollar and a relative correspondence between official and actual rates of exchange. The difficulties faced by the U.S. dollar and the U.S. trade deficit of the 1980s thus hit Haiti hard. But Haiti's problems were exacerbated by escalating corruption. Members of the presidential family and prominent Duvalierists increasingly dipped into U.S. aid money, often without bothering to engage in any intermediate transaction to cover the embezzlement. Larger amounts of U.S. dollars found their way into the Duvaliers' personal foreign accounts without ever entering the local economy. The unofficial rate of exchange started to reflect the rarity of the dollar. By 1983, the Haitian gourde had registered a 13 percent decline on the underground market. By 1985, it was almost impossible to convert gourdes into dollars without a 10 to 15 percent surcharge. Duvalierists and merchants, who had greater access to U.S. currency, became impromptu bankers, concentrating the available dollars in fewer and fewer hands.[13]

The scarcity of foreign currency also testified to the failure of the new assembly plants to provide the basis for a new export policy. By the end of fiscal year 1984–85, the value of exports was barely five times higher than in 1969–70, while the value of imports had risen more than tenfold (IHSI 1986: 99). And again, prices alone only tell part of the story. Exports of the main agricultural products—essential oils, cacao, and coffee—were erratic and not necessarily because of fluctuations in international prices (IHSI 1986: 58–63). Sisal production for export virtually disappeared, and Haiti lost its position as a leading exporter of many essential oils. Some analysts point to the peasants' increasing lack of interest in the production of those crops as at least one explanation behind the export figures (Girault 1981; Girault, Kermel-Torres, Lebigre in C.E.G.E.T. 1985). Crushed by taxes and by oligopolies in the commercialization of export crops, the Haitian peasant was becoming an economic maroon, avoiding all production that benefited the urban middlemen.

Coffee, Haiti's main export crop since independence, tells that story better than any other peasant-produced commodity. At the end of Jean-Claude Duvalier's regime, export production was about equal to what it had been when the president took office, although after many booms and busts: 16,160 tons in 1969–70; 26,790 in 1975–76; 13,580 in 1980–81; 23,670 in 1982–83; 18,200 in 1984–85 (IHSI 1986: 62). These fluctuations do not bear any direct correlation to prices. Thus even though prices increased slightly between 1982 and 1985, the value of coffee exports went down to $3.34 million in the fourth quarter of 1985, the second lowest quarter in the last ten years. The growth of local consumption may account for some of the decrease in exports, but equally likely is the peasants' voluntary, if not systematic, withdrawal of labor as a gesture of resistance. With the continuous support of international organizations, Jean-Claude Duvalier's government had tried to bypass the rural world in the hope that the subcontracting industries would reverse the trade deficit. In practice, that strategy had the opposite effect: it contributed to an increase in the commercial imbalance.

The commercial disaster was compounded by a fiscal debacle of hitherto unseen proportions. Subcontracting affected the country's balance of payments, and the Haitian deficit quintupled between 1975 and 1981 (World Bank 1984). Even the World Bank admitted that the assembly industry had made "almost no fiscal contribution" to the national economy (Hooper 1987b: 37). Moreover, in a system where, by tradition, state revenues depend almost entirely on customs duties, the development of light industry increased the proportion of imports that escaped customs control, and the opportunities for corruption in customs administration increased. We will probably never know the number of luxury goods that escaped taxation under the pretext that they were necessary to the functioning of the Delmas industrial park. In any case, according to the always generous official statistics, the value of merchandise that was not taxed by the Haitian government increased tenfold in the first six years of Jean-Claude's regime, going from $11.4 million in 1970 to $112.2 million in 1976. These figures continued to grow and the government turned increasingly to internal taxes to make up for revenues lost at the customhouses. From 1980 to 1984, total government revenues increased from $134.4 million to $189.9 million. In those same years, custom revenues declined from $65 million to less than $57 million, even though import quantities and values continued to rise. The increase in government income was therefore due solely to an increase in internal revenues, which jumped from $69.3 million in 1980 to $132.9 million in 1984 (IHSI 1985, 1986).

Lest one interprets these figures as suggesting a partial redistribution of the economic burden, let us remember that internal taxation, in the Haitian context, does not primarily refer to revenues gathered from graduated income or business taxes. They chiefly include all the fees, excise taxes, and duties not collected at the customhouses, mostly consumption taxes of one kind or another. Further, the proliferation of fees, tariffs, and related off-budget-accounts also increased the proportion of state funds embezzled by high officials. Members of the presidential family each had their *own* "internal revenues," that is, a particular set of duties or fees, collected by the state, that went directly to them for their private use. Many high officials had a similar right to collect tribute of one kind or another under the guise of some new fiscal requirement. For instance, one of the many departure fees that Haitians paid to leave the country reportedly went directly to the president's mother and provided her with about $3,000 a day! Jean-Claude Duvalier is said to have accumulated more than $500 million during his years in office, in addition to the funds wasted on lavish personal spending.

Beyond levies such as the airport fees, which affected mainly the middle classes, the fiscal shift to internal sources of revenue meant a much greater squeeze on the peasants and the urban lower classes. It was the peasant, weighed down by export and local market taxes, and the poor urban dweller, burdened by consumer fees, who paid most of the cost of the Duvaliers' "economic revolution." They were the main targets in the state's attempt to make up for the deficits created by the light industry strategy and the greed of the Duvalier family and its immediate allies. Rural tax collectors were not idle. Taxes on common consumer goods, used by peasants and the urban poor alike, provided an increasing share of government revenues—for instance, taxes on flour, sugar, petroleum, tobacco, and matches provided as much as 25 percent of government revenues in 1985 (Hooper 1986: 10).

Not surprisingly, inflation hit hard, particularly at the poorest segments of the population. The rise had become apparent even before the political transition of 1971—the cost of living increased by 10.3 percent in 1970–71 alone (Groupe de Recherches Nouvelle Optique 1972). Successive increases punctuated the tenure of Duvalier *fils*. If we take as a base (100) fiscal year 1975–76, the general cost of living index went from 53.07 in 1969–70 to 151.02 in 1980–81, to 206.98 in 1984–85 (IHSI 1986: 26). The World Bank itself acknowledged that even with the rise of the minimum wage to $3 *a day* in 1985, inflation caused a drop of 20 percent in real wages between 1981 and 1986 (Hooper 1987b: 35). That is, of course, for those who actually worked. In fact, these figures provide only a limited view of the crunch experienced by the lower classes, the peasantry, and especially the new lumpen swelling the slums of Port-au-Prince and the major provincial towns of Cap-Haïtien, Les Cayes, and Gonaïves.

Housing and food prices registered the most dramatic increase. The rise was due in part to the government's increased reliance on "internal" revenues and its effects on the peasantry, in part to the general movement from countryside to urban centers and from agricultural to industrial production. Urban housing prices registered more than a four-fold increase between 1970 and 1985. Housing prices in the capital increased even more dramatically (IHSI 1986: 26–28).

The government did not bother to compile comparative figures for the provinces, but having toured the most important towns of the country between February 1986 and July 1987, I suspect that increases in housing prices were substantially lower there, while increases in food prices may have been equal to—and in certain cases greater than—those in Port-au-Prince.

The reasons for the national increase in the price of food are easy to understand. Jean-Claude Duvalier's government pushed to new heights the insensitivity of the state toward the rural world. Its handling of the "creole pig" affair is a case in point. After an outbreak of African swine fever in 1981, on advice from the U.S. government, the regime ordered the slaughter of the entire population of native Haitian pigs. Between 1982 and 1984, it killed more than 1 million animals belonging primarily to low-income peasants, for whom pigs have always been a major form of investment. Few peasants understood the need to kill the pigs, and, despite promises, few received compensation. Those who did received pinkish U.S. pigs, soon baptized *kochon grimèl* ("light-skinned pigs") by the populace. The imported animals required imported food, which few peasants could afford, and they had none of the ritual value of the native black pig that they replaced. By 1984 pig-raising had become a bourgeois venture, and the price of all meat had increased greatly.

The neglect of the rural world removed a yet uncounted number of workers from both agricultural production and food distribution. The subcontracting industries use a primarily female labor force. But women have long constituted the backbone of the Haitian marketing system for local food crops (Mintz 1984). No one has yet established any systematic correlation between the use of a largely female labor force by subcontracting bosses, and the decline in the production and distribution of foodstuffs in the course of the last few years. But even if it could be proven that *none* of the day laborers at the Delmas industrial park were directly taken from the food production network, the very idea of wages that were more than ten times the income of the average peasant certainly increased the rural exodus. The growth of the urban population in turn contributed to the rise of food prices, especially since agricultural production remained stagnant in the countryside and the increase in food prices had to affect all segments of the population as the proportion of imported foodstuffs increased.

The value of imported food rose from $10.7 million in 1970 to $62.1 in 1976. By 1977, foodstuffs constituted 20 percent of Haiti's imports, at a cost of $89 million. Haiti's dependence on imported wheat and wheat products increased at a geometrical pace from 1970 to 1985 (IHSI 1986: 2; Hooper 1987b: 33). Further, as the volume and price of imported food rose, so did the price of locally produced food, which was now available in smaller quantities and more heavily taxed. Thus the average price of *all* foodstuffs more than doubled between 1975 and 1985, with such common items as sweet potatoes leading the increase. Millet, maize, goat meat, potatoes, yams, and beans also registered significant increases (IHSI 1986: 106).[14]

The yearly increases from 1980 to 1984 were small, however, compared to the inflationary wave that hit the country in the final twelve months of the dictatorship. Housing, fuel, and food prices reached new heights, with increases in the price of common food items leading an inflationary wave of unprecedented proportions. The Institut Haïtien de Statistiques particularly notes "millet, potatoes, yams, rice, and beans, which increased by 45.3 percent, 26.4 percent, 25 percent, 18.4 percent, and 18.3 percent respectively" in fiscal year 1984–85 (IHSI 1986: 8). Shortages of basic food items such as millet, flour, and rice accompanied the rise in prices in many provincial towns.

The government did nothing to stabilize prices or alleviate the plight of the urban poor. On the contrary, Jean-Claude Duvalier and his closest allies picked this very moment, when most citizens were having difficulty obtaining their daily ration of food, to flaunt their luxurious lifestyle. This alone was enough for some people to take to the streets.

8

The Interrupted March to Democracy

The first mass demonstrations against the regime, in 1984, were food riots during which provincial slum dwellers attacked customhouses and the warehouses of charitable organizations where food was stored or reported to be stored. It is no accident that the riots snowballed in the old port-city of Gonaïves, now a dusty provincial town wedged between a bay and two rocky chains of hills, and remarkable primarily for the size of its slums and its isolation from the hinterland that had once provided its daily food. The first slogans, prudently limited to "Aba lamizè! " ("Down with poverty! "), soon evolved into cries of "Aba Duvalier!" Well aware of the unbridled corruption that marked the Duvalier regimes, Haitians had for long placed the responsibility for their poverty on the dictatorship. Yet while some peasants could fall back on household production of a few garden crops—even if they still lived below the threshold of subsistence— the mushrooming lumpen of the towns, freshly born of that peasantry, had lost both their gardens and their sense of political isolation. Now that they were more conscious of a national life, they also paid more attention to the occupants of the National Palace.

THE PERCEPTION OF INDIFFERENCE

In the 1970s, Haitians had seen the young Duvalier as an indolent playboy who cared more about his cars, his girlfriends, and his music lessons than about the burdens of his office. Yet because of his youth, his style, and his reputation for being somewhat obtuse, and especially because he was visibly controlled by prominent figures of the Duvalierist old guard (including his mother and his sister Marie-Denise), Jean-Claude Duvalier enjoyed the indulgence of many otherwise disgruntled citizens. Criticism of his government in the press or on the streets during this "liberal" phase of his tenure often bypassed him personally.[1]

This perception changed sharply after Duvalier's marriage to Michèle Bennett in 1980. As he gradually removed the Duvalierist old guard from the centers of decision-making, he appeared increasingly responsible, if not for the unpopular decrees of his new appointees, at least for the fact of having appointed them. Further, and more important, his wife quickly came to symbolize his presidency in the eyes of the people.

The masses knew of the regime's indifference. Michèle Bennett worsened the regime's image with an exaggerated arrogance and a sense of wanton greed. The presidential couple and their new cronies of middle- and lower-middle-class origin tried to outdo in luxurious expenditures the traditional bourgeoisie with whom they now mixed. *Nouveaux riches* themselves, they spurned the *nouveaux riches* of the two preceding decades, whose position and insatiable consumption they had inherited. They chased out earlier Duvalierists, who looked too *"classes moyennes"* in their eyes. Led by the light-skinned First Lady, they systematically courted light-skinned individuals who had—or claimed— "bourgeois" connections.

The desire to act "bourgeois" overnight put the Bennett-Duvalier clan under a spotlight. Intimates of the presidential couple boasted of personal expenses covered by a Treasury increasingly dependent on consumption taxes and U.S. support. Everyone who cared knew how much it cost to remodel the couple's residential quarters or to maintain the bar at their weekend retreat. Such expenditures, and the "creole pig" affair, came to symbolize the regime's indifference to the masses. Ostentatious presidential parties, televised on presidential demand, showed officials and bourgeois alike flaunting expensive designer gowns, jewels, champagne, and caviar.[2] In the middle of still another food shortage, in 1985, Michèle Duvalier returned from a shopping spree in Paris accompanied by reports in the U.S. media that she had spent $1.7 million in two weeks. Those and similar reports spread more rapidly than even Mme. Duvalier might have wished: with the new national roads and major improvements in telecommunications, Haiti had become a truly "national space." Words and images meant to impress certain segments of the population now reached unintended audiences. In the streets of the provincial towns, despair turned into anger, and anger into defiance.

DEFYING THE GUNS

That defiance paralleled what many people saw as the growing independence of two national institutions formerly subdued by the Duvalierist state: the Catholic church and the army. Cornered by grassroots Protestant missions, which had made large inroads among the lower classes during the 1970s and early 1980s, Catholic bishops had allowed—more or less reluctantly—the spread of socially oriented ministries, and activities so markedly different from traditional Catholic practice that Haitians soon dubbed them *ti-legliz*—the little churches. During the 1960s, François Duvalier's offensive against the national institutions and the "nationalization" of the Haitian clergy had led to changes in the class composition of that clergy. Up until then, Haitian priests constituted a minority within the church, and most of them came from traditionally intellectual or professional families, well rooted in Port-au-Prince or the provincial towns. By 1980, a majority of the Catholic priests were Haitian, and a majority of these came from more modest backgrounds than their pre-Duvalier predecessors. They were at the forefront of the *ti-legliz* movement, increasingly steering Catholic discourse toward a message of social justice, a mild version of liberation theology adapted to the repressive character of the country. That message received an unexpected boost from Pope John Paul II during his 1983 visit. From then on, the Conférence Episcopale (the formal body that included all the Bishops) joined the *ti-legliz*. Religious radio stations, especially the Port-au-Prince-based Radio Soleil, undertook a systematic if modest politicization of the populace, infusing a civic discourse within the "national space" newly created by increased centralization and improvements in transport and telecommunications.

At the same time, the higher echelons of the army appeared increasingly neutral. Rumors of open disobedience to presidential orders, and even of impending coups d'état by some of the higher brass, spread in 1984 and 1985. Such rumors may have been wishful thinking on the part of those who spread them. But they were believed in part because many officers—

especially those of lower-middle-class origin who had risen from the rank-and-file during the first phase of Duvalierism—had lost their enthusiasm to defend at all costs a regime now symbolized by Michèle Bennett. Further, many among the higher ranks believed that the president's reactions to the early signs of disquiet only served to irritate the populace.

Indeed, Jean-Claude Duvalier, advised by his wife and his youngest and most ambitious ministers, at first chose to respond to the popular discontent only with increased repression. Soldiers and elite battalions of the militia shot point-blank at demonstrators and closed down radio stations, including Radio Soleil, which by then had become the key symbol of anti-Duvalierist resistance. This overreaction seemed counterproductive to both past and current allies. Some prominent colonels and some civilian members of the Duvalierist old guard, for instance, favored a two-pronged response that would include carefully hedged concessions to popular demands. Resident U.S. officials in turn reacted so ambivalently to the new developments that they were associated with the new wave of repression in the popular perception. In Washington, however, the State Department tried to distance itself from its client's latest tactics. As demonstrations grew in size and intensity in 1985, so did Washington's public disapproval.

Pressured by allies and foes alike, and surprised at the quiet withdrawal of many of his father's traditional collaborators, Jean-Claude Duvalier wavered. Momentum shifted irreversibly from the government to the demonstrators in the streets. Government measures were contradictory, shifting according to the fluctuating fortunes of individuals within the cabinet and the polyvalent reading of Washington's own contradictory signals. In early 1985, the government approved legislation allowing the existence of political parties, denied until then, and trumpeted the release of thirty-six political prisoners. Some press organs were allowed to function one week, and then closed down the next. In July 1985, mostly because of pressures from the U.S. Congress to hold new elections, Duvalier conducted a mock referendum, on the basis of which he claimed renewed legitimacy. Discontent failed to subside; so did repression.

Then, on November 27, the army shot four schoolchildren in the streets of Gonaïves. The murder not only acerbated demonstrators there—Gonaïves had been the site of one of the earliest food riots—but it fueled public protest throughout the country. The government's clumsy attempt on December 5 to stop the flow of information by once more shutting down the now legendary Radio Soleil misfired. As protests grew despite constant killings and beatings, what remained of the Duvalier team continued to waver. On December 31, 1985, Duvalier revamped the cabinet and, in early January, announced a 10 percent reduction in the price of basic commodities controlled by the state, notably flour, cooking oil, and diesel fuel. Demonstrations nevertheless continued unabated. On January 26, 1986, the government dissolved the "political police," the nucleus of a *makout* network that gathered information on dissidents and engineered many of the repressive tactics, and whose existence the regime had until then denied.

This was too little too late. Roadblocks had sprung up all over the country. Some provincial towns held demonstrations daily, in spite of indiscriminate shootings and beatings by the armed forces. On January 27, the day after the official disbanding of the political police, the number of demonstrators reached a reported peak of 40,000 in the northern town of Cap-Haïtien (pop. 65,000). Three days later, U.S. presidential spokesman Larry Speakes announced that the government of Haiti had collapsed and that the leadership, including Duvalier, had fled the country.

The Haitian president quickly denied the news and suggested, in a public message, that his regime was "as strong as a monkey's tail." In part to measure the depth of the dissent, in part to prove that he was still in control, on Monday, February 3, the president joined his wife in an impromptu tour of Port-au-Prince, the ultimate scene of all Haitian political struggle—and until then the only quiet urban area in the country. But a majority of the Port-au-Prince masses, emboldened by the false news of the government's collapse, had finally taken to the streets. On February 7, 1986, Jean-Claude Duvalier and his wife left Haiti with their immediate family and a small group of followers.

DUVALIERISM AFTER DUVALIER

Good news about Haiti has repeatedly been premature, beginning with Larry Speakes' curious announcement of January 1986. Duvalier was replaced by a National Council of Government (CNG), a military-controlled regime led by General Henri Namphy, the chief of the armed forces. Within a week, there were numerous announcements, notably by the U.S. State Department, that the CNG would lead Haiti on the road to democracy. President Reagan promised increased U.S. support "as this interim government moves forward to institute democracy." U.S. support indeed came, but history proved the prognosis about democracy hasty. The Reagan administration granted $2.8 million in military aid for the CNG's first year. A joint letter from human rights organizations to then U.S. Secretary of State George Schultz asserted later that the aid had only served "to strengthen the tendency of the CNG to violate the rights of the citizens." By April 1987, while signs of support from Washington increased, there were as many demonstrators in the streets of Port-au-Prince as there had been in the last days of Duvalier. By the end of its first year in office the CNG, generously helped by the U.S. taxpayers' money, had openly gunned down more civilians than Jean-Claude Duvalier's government had done in fifteen years.

The state was not alone in its use of violence. Popular calls for a *dechoukaj* (uprooting) of the former ruling team were followed by summary judgments and executions of Duvalierists openly carried out by a civilian mob. The *dechoukaj* also included the removal from office, by force or by popular demand, of known Duvalierists. But many observers and participants came to realize that this brand of popular "justice," which started in the few hours after Duvalier's departure and continued well into the hot months of July and August, touched only the small fry of the Duvalierist machine. Understandably, most of the vigilantes were from the urban slums; equally understandably, the most important supporters of the deposed president were not. The latter were protected from the former by the government or by relatives and friends. Reputed criminals were quietly allowed to take the road to exile; others felt so secure that they did not even bother to leave. Private "justice" continued to operate until at least the end of 1986, especially in the countryside, but it became increasingly clandestine. By February 1987, a year after Duvalier's departure, most citizens were disillusioned with the results of the transition (Chamberlain 1987; Hooper 1987a).

Then, in March 1987, upon discovering that the new "liberal" Constitution drafted by a majority of CNG appointees drastically curtailed the power of the presidency and explicitly forbade a Duvalierist return to power, many Haitians thought that the tide had finally turned. The Constitution was overwhelmingly approved by referendum. Presidential candidates revamped their speeches, but they could not raise much enthusiasm among an electorate that revealed itself both suspicious of all politicians and more issue-oriented than in any previous presidential contest. However, state-sponsored violence returned with a vengeance in the summer of 1987: more than fifty demonstrators were shot between late June and late July. Progressive clergymen were attacked by "unknown" aggressors; the premises of the nongovernment radio stations were vandalized. In August, a presidential candidate was killed by an unidentified gang; another was shot in October, in front of the country's most important police station. Hundreds of peasants were killed by retaliating Duvalierists. The renewed violence, and the perception that the new Constitution offered true safeguards, convinced an otherwise reluctant electorate that the presidential elections might lead to a political solution.

Thus hope filtered back into the countryside as the elections neared. The rhetoric of the political parties, the large number of international observers, and the optimism of the press gave many Haitians a spurious sense of security. Alas, when the polls opened on November 29, 1987, Duvalierist thugs, often backed by uniformed soldiers, openly shot at lines of waiting voters. Estimates of the number of deaths ranged from 39 to 200. Hundreds of people who had committed no other crime than standing in line to exert their electoral rights for the first time in a generation were seriously wounded. Expectations were crushed once again, so much so, in fact, that very few citizens bothered to take part in the army-run "elections" of January 17, 1988, that led to the installation of Leslie François Manigat as president of Haiti.

This time, humbled by the turn of events, pundits were reluctant to prognosticate. The situation was also harder to read. On the one hand, Manigat's accession to power was clearly illegitimate, and pressure from abroad against the new regime mounted rapidly, notably in Canada and the United States. On the other hand, some saw in the forced "election" of a man whose background and qualifications were at least equal to those of his competitors a momentary relief, and perhaps an alternative to even worse cataclysms. But even muted expectations that the Manigat government could lead to a new era in Haitian politics were at the very least premature. As Namphy begot Manigat, so Namphy brought down Manigat: on June 20, 1988, the general resumed power alone and forced Manigat into exile.

But this was not the end of the series of coups and countercoups. Namphy was in turn brought down by an army coup, whose instigators again hinted at a clean sweep. Hope was rekindled once more. Lower rank soldiers, reported to have masterminded Namphy's ouster, ran the show for a few days, demoting many officers known for their Duvalierist ties. Street justice started anew, claiming to complete the *dechoukaj* that had begun in February 1986. By December 1988, however, when it appeared that the new president, General Prosper Avril, former head of Jean-Claude Duvalier's Presidential Guard and former member of the CNG, was (at least temporarily) in control, many knew that the clean sweep had not yet come.

A MUDDLED SCENARIO

If the last two and a half years of Haitian politics look like a badly dubbed movie where the words and gestures do not always match, it is because something is wrong with the premises of the script that most observers chose to read. For different reasons, the U.S. government, the CNG, the Haitian urban elites, political parties of all tendencies, and large chunks of the Haitian masses have fancied the assumption that Baby Doc's departure was a clear step on the march to democracy, an immediate and inevitable consequence of the disturbances and massive riots of 1984–85. To be sure, the riots were a necessary factor in the end of the Duvalier dynasty: had the Haitian masses not defied the army and militia with their bare hands during a month of daily encounters in which many unarmed citizens were injured and killed, chances are that Jean-Claude Duvalier would still be ruling the country. But if the riots were necessary for Duvalier to leave, they certainly were not a sufficient condition for him to depart the way he did. It took something else to orchestrate his departure at that particular time, under those specific circumstances, and with a no less specific aftermath.

Thus the problem with the dominant version of Duvalier's downfall is not what it acknowledges but what it leaves out. Two series of events occurred on February 7, 1986: first, the departure of Duvalier; second, *the takeover of the state machinery by a group of apparently disparate individuals:* civilians and career army officers, Duvalierists and former opposition figures, past backers of repression and former human rights leaders. Missing from the dominant version, or at best viewed as secondary, are the negotiations—the tacit and explicit understandings between Haitian and U.S. politicians, in Haiti and in the United States, local and foreign military and intelligence personnel, ambassadors, power brokers, and bureaucrats—that led to, and tied together, the two sets of events. For what Haitians witnessed on February 7, 1986, was not the disorderly escape of an "entire leadership" pushed out by popular pressure, as portrayed in Larry Speakes' untimely announcement, but a transmission of power, orchestrated with absolute order—albeit against the background of a popular uprising.

Before dawn on that Friday, February 7, Jean-Claude Duvalier drove his favorite BMW to the airport—hardly the behavior of a deported captive. Awaiting him was a U.S. C-141 Starlifter cargo plane—despatched, according to rumor, from South Carolina or from Guantanamo but in any case presumably authorized at the highest levels of the U.S. Executive. The Duvaliers' belongings, and those of their companions, were already loaded onto the plane. Finally, while most Haitians did not know the time of the president's departure in advance—there had been no announcement— some diplomats and foreign reporters were waiting at the airport, cameras in hand, as if for an Oscar night. Some had arrived before the landing of the Starlifter. At 3:45 a.m. the plane left; so did the cameras.

Popular beliefs notwithstanding—and note that the masses were not at the airport—this was the most graceful exit of a dictator in Haitian history. No previous dictator, even one of the less hated ones, had left for exile in the midst of so much civility on the part of those who took him to his boat or plane. Fignolé, the last president removed by the army before François Duvalier took power, was handled rather roughly, according to one of the arresting officers (Pierre 1987). The two chiefs of state who left *after* Baby Doc, Henri Namphy and Leslie Manigat, were at least harassed by their captors, and some of Manigat's supporters were arrested the night he left. Yet three months after Duvalier's departure, not a single Duvalierist had been questioned by the "new" authorities.

The more time passes, the more the events surrounding Duvalier's departure appear at least partly staged. What accounts for Larry Speakes' "mistaken" announcement? Who tipped off so many journalists, and why? Who allowed Duvalier to take what Haitians report to be millions of dollars in cash from the Banque Centrale? Was that part of his compensation for leaving gracefully? Who decided on the composition of the team that replaced him? Yet the incongruities of the night soon vanished with the dictator. Soon after, under the cover of national jubilation, a new government was in place. Understandably happy with the end of the dynasty, few people in Haiti or abroad bothered to ask how the transition had been managed and what it was meant to hatch. Questions came later, in April and May 1986, but by then they were clouded by preparations for one more fruitless electoral campaign. Hence the events of February 7 continue to appear as an important landmark in an otherwise uninterrupted advance toward "democracy."

There is, however, a strong case for an alternative reading of the script, one that would see the supervision of Duvalier's departure and the constitution of the first CNG as a multinational exercise in "crisis management," a calculated break in the democratic path that the Haitian people had embarked upon. We may never learn the details of the negotiations, but negotiations there were. And we need not know these details, or fully investigate ex-U.S. Marine Colonel Oliver North's claim to have brought an end to Haiti's nightmare, to be certain of one crucial fact: Jean-Claude Duvalier was brought down by a high-level coup d'état executed with international connivance.[3] Further, the management of his departure, and of its aftermath, effectively prevented the complete *dechoukaj* that most Haitians were calling for.

Interestingly, Duvalier was one of the first to question the dominant version of his departure. From his viewpoint, his resignation was part of a covenant among friends designed to avoid further bloodshed. His apparently genuine surprise at the news that he had fled the country to escape a popular uprising was attributed to his notoriously slow thinking. Thus most observers missed the significance of the fact that Duvalier did not direct his anger at his traditional enemies, or even at the demonstrators, but at the people who had replaced him, most of whom were close friends. Duvalier's main disagreement with his former allies was, strangely enough, not their account of his government's misdeeds but their account of its downfall.

More curious still, Duvalier's successors replied in kind. On February 17, ten days after Duvalier's demise, the CNG put out an official bulletin that seemed odd at the time and appears even more bizarre in retrospect. It read in part: "The National Council of Government insists upon reaffirming that the ex-president's resignation and departure for abroad have been provoked by popular pressure." Just in case the people doubted.

The dominant version of the end of the Duvalier saga has not been openly challenged in part because of the political rhetoric stimulated by the end of the dynasty. Most Haitians were eager for a drastic change. Few, especially among the urban poor, were willing to admit that their "revolution" had been tampered with. The economic and political elites gained the most from this confusion, and also recovered much quicker. Many promptly understood the need to muffle the street power that had speeded up the pace of the political process until Duvalier's departure. To be sure, the public denunciation of prominent Duvalierists continued, off and on, until early 1989. To be sure, most politicians and political parties used the relative freedom of expression of those three years to engage in vehement anti-Duvalierist posturing. To be sure, a tiny minority went against the current to address some of the most troubling long-term issues that the nation faced. But they found little echo among the candidates of 1986 or, later, among the most prominent opponents or backers of the successive Manigat, Namphy, and Avril governments.[4] Three years after Jean-Claude Duvalier's departure, in spite of an extraordinary period of free expression—at least by Haitian standards—the dominant political discourse has shown few signs of dynamism. Post-Duvalier Haiti seems to be drifting aimlessly.

This aimlessness stems from an implicit understanding among the Haitian elites that goes beyond the immediate bargains made, broken, and renewed just before Duvalier's departure. The months following clearly indicated to religious, business, and political leaders, Duvalierists and non-Duvalierists alike, that what Haitians called the "democratic steamroller" might not stop at *their* door if the *dechoukaj* continued. First, the list of individuals condemned by association kept growing, despite the political gymnastics of many bourgeois and professionals, who suddenly claimed to be age-old opponents of the deposed dictator. More important, at many points mob violence threatened to go beyond political boundaries to associate perceived class positions and Duvalierism. Mobs of young people threatened the U.S. consulate in Port-au-Prince at least three times. Never too seriously, perhaps—but on one occasion at least they were stopped only by Haitian soldiers from the nearby barracks. Expensive cars were ransacked repeatedly in Port-au-Prince. Truck drivers twice closed down the only road linking Port-au-Prince and the suburban areas of Fermathe and Thomassin where prominent Duvalierists lived next door to merchants, diplomats, and foreign aid consultants. The road to suburbia had to be cleared with tanks from the army's elite battalions. Similarly, throughout 1986, crowds of peasants formed roadblocks on the national roads, exacting money from private motorists regardless of political identification.

In the midst of these alarming incidences of popular justice, many urbanites retreated to the time-honored leitmotif of the commercial bourgeoisie: the absurdity of Duvalierism. At times by design but more often because it was simply too convenient an excuse to forgo, middle-class political or religious leaders presented the Duvalier era as a monstrous phenomenon, a parenthesis after which Haitians could, presumably, pick up the reins of their history and proceed. On the basis of such an understanding, they endorsed an article of the constitution that forbade known Duvalierists from running for office—as if a stroke of the pen could erase the Duvalierist nightmare and the crisis on which it fed. Yet only a distorted presentation of the Haitian past and present can sustain the illusion that the crisis will subside spontaneously if and when the dictatorship it nurtured disappears. The Duvalierist state has its roots deep in the organization of Haitian society itself. Similar regimes will inevitably succeed each other unless the relation between state and civil society is reformulated.

EPILOGUE

If wishes alone sufficed, I would have ended on a more cheerful note. As things stand, this book is offered partly as a warning. For if the Duvalierists are understandably among the villains of the story, there is nevertheless no clear champion of the popular cause. To be sure, the founders of the Haitian state deserve great credit; theirs was the most visionary revolution of its times. To be sure, many nineteenth-century Haitian intellectuals lucidly addressed some of the most important issues facing their ostracized nation. Yet whenever they took part in the political process, their deeds consistently fell short of their stated intentions.

Throughout the twentieth century, and especially under the Duvalier dictatorships, the Haitian left, as well as many urban democratic or nationalist factions, endured death and injury at the hands of both foreign and local soldiers and thugs. No analyst has the right to disregard these deaths, or the individual sacrifices they represent. But it would be equally dishonorable to use them as an excuse for the dogmatic analyses prevalent among Haitian progressives, or for the middle-class contempt that most urban liberals feel toward the common people of Haiti. Moreover, though Haitian activists willingly acknowledge the need to redistribute the country's resources more equitably, most are reluctant to face the complex problems created by declining agricultural productivity. We can understand the emphasis on economic justice in a country where drafting and enforcing a graduated income tax package might be the most revolutionary measure imaginable in the near future. But if corruption and unequal taxation are still at the forefront of Haiti's problems, their elimination can only set the stage for the creation of policies that will improve conditions in the rural world.

For better or worse, the size and social resilience of the peasantry are important aspects of the uniqueness of Haiti as an American nation. While Haitian peasants cannot be blamed for the institutions that regulate the state or for the transfer of surplus out of the countryside, their inflexible attachment to a labor process that is unlikely to generate growth or increase productivity is certainly part of the Haitian dilemma. Ultimately, there is only one Haitian question: that of the peasantry. For it is in the contradictions of the peasantry that the resources, stakes, and predicaments of the nation intertwine. How to measure the limits and potential of this peasantry—whose diversity has barely been studied—against the economic, social, political, and cultural problems outlined in this book is probably beyond the means of any one politician or scholar. But any solution to the Haitian crisis must face the peasant question. It must find its roots in the resources of that peasantry, the very same resources that have contributed to the fortunes of thousands of Haitians and foreigners during a century and a half of unbridled exploitation. And to do this, Haitians must create institutional channels through which *all* sectors within the peasantry can participate in a political debate from which they have been too long excluded. Both steps in turn require that intellectuals, politicians, and planners—foreign and Haitian alike—talk less about (or "for") the peasantry and begin listening more attentively to what its diverse subgroups have said in the past and have to say now about their own future. The long overdue reconciliation of state and nation requires the fundamental understanding that, in Haiti, the peasantry *is* the nation.

Notes

INTRODUCTION

1. This summary does not exhaust Lundahl's work, which remains far above most of what has been written about Haiti from the viewpoint of traditional economics. For a critique of Lundahl's economic analysis, see Caprio (1979) and M.-R. Trouillot (1980).

2. I see an "organic" connection as one that is intrinsic to the object of study, aspects or parts of which can be separated or abstracted for methodological purposes. Kinship terms offer good examples of one type of organic connection: one term often presupposes another—as husband/wife, grandparent/grandchild easily demonstrate. This is the simplest form of organic connection (organic positional: one position implies another). The strongest organic connection that can be claimed is one in which an aspect of the object of study (e.g., political society) implies the other (e.g., civil society).

   To accuse Gramsci of conceptual slippage on this latter connection (which seems at times methodological and at times organic) and the related issue of coercion and hegemony (e.g., Anderson 1976-77; Hoffmann 1984) is both fair and easy. Gramsci's breakthrough remains germane, however, even though students of politics have yet to meet his theoretical challenge. Anthropologists now question the public/private dichotomy prevalent in the 1950s and 1960s, and those who work on so-called complex societies constantly verify the fact that there are aspects of human behavior that cannot be neatly boxed either in a "cultural" *qua* "civil" domain or, conversely, in a distinct political sphere. A hard look at marriage and divorce, at socialization and education, not to mention the history of science, the politics of race, gender, and religion, or electoral advertising, teaches us that the division between "political" and "civil" society is useful but nevertheless artificial. So is the distinction between consent and coercion. In that sense at least, we can revert to Gramsci's Hegelian language to describe "state" and "civil society" as "moments" of the same processes.

3. Many authors have stressed the need to look at the historical conditions under which specific states emerged as clues to their current character. Anthony Giddens (1985: 269) groups the states of the world according to a typology that combines circumstances of emergence, longevity, and contemporary characteristics. Similarly, Clive Thomas (1984) emphasizes the role of time in explaining important differences between states that obtained their independence in the nineteenth century (e.g., Latin America) and those that did so after World War II (e.g., the British West Indies). The Haitian case is a striking exception to typologies of this sort, even though time and conditions of emergence influenced the character of the state in Haiti as anywhere else.

1. NATIONALISM AND DEPENDENCY:
THE GENESIS OF STATE AND NATION

1. Private U.S. citizens did not influence Haiti's social life very much either, with the exception of a few Protestant preachers--notably James Theodore Holly-- who spread their version of Christianity in the coastal cities and parts of the countryside. This is all the more puzzling given the strong and favorable interest that many black Americans had in Haiti in the nineteenth century. We know that many free blacks in United States saw Haiti as something of a promised land before the Civil War, and that successive Haitian governments encouraged the immigration of U.S. blacks throughout the century. Alexander DuBois, W.E.B. DuBois' father, was born in Haiti, the son of the a light-skinned U.S. immigrant and (probably) a Haitian elite woman. DuBois' few pages on his grandfather's Haitian journeys seem to suggest that the immigrants encountered economic as well as cultural difficulties. Be that as it may, the U.S. diplomats clearly--and understandably perhaps--showed greater, even if not complete, political allegiance to the state they represented, even when they were emotionally inclined to support the black republic.

2. A REPUBLIC FOR THE MERCHANTS

1. Pétion's sole act of resistance to the merchants' demands was to pass a law that curbed the export of currency by renewing Dessalines' policy requiring consignment merchants to purchase export goods equal in value to their imports. But that law was forced upon him by the senate, in one of its very few shows of independence, prompted by the specter of an economic disaster (De Pradine 1886: 452–58, 496). Further, we know little about its enforcement.
2. Yet while the foreign merchant could threaten Haiti, the Haitian state had little hold on him when he was in Haiti and often no diplomatic recourse if he decided to leave. In 1896, a foreign merchant who had stolen between 80,000 and 90,000 piasters through illegal transactions "put the Atlantic Ocean between himself and President Salomon, thus escaping any obligation to pay restitution" (Un Patriote Haïtien 1887: 11).

3. THE RECURRING CRISIS

1. A minor qualification is necessary here. Georges Adam's classification of the different merchant groups is basically correct, but it is important to note that it refers to a structural level of organization. In real life, the same individual could occupy several such structural positions, either successively or at the same time. Such movement impeded systematic specialization among the agents of dependence, which might have allowed them to build more effective coalitions with specific segments of the political oligarchy. On the other hand, Brenda Gayle Plummer (1984, 1988) insists that private bankers did play a singular and specific role from about 1875 to 1915.
2. Besides Salomon's regime, one should also note that of Florville Hyppolite (1889–96), which managed to realize some major public works despite the president's despotism.

4. CULTURE, COLOR, AND POLITICS

1. In any given society, the somatic norm-image is likely to vary according to class and ethnic origins. In the extreme cases of societies with multiple ethnic

mixtures, such as Venezuela, Colombia, or Brazil, the category as defined by Hoetink could even turn out to be inoperative. But this is not the case in Haiti.

2. Indeed, foreign observers tend to make major mistakes in specifying the "color" of specific Haitians. One counts, among the most important gaffes, Leyburn's (1941: 316) classification of President Salnave as "dark" and, more recently, Ferguson's (1987: 72) branding of Simone Duvalier (François' wife) as a "mulatto"!

3. The Haitian school of ethnology, oriented toward folklore, has not touched on the complex relationship between culture and power. Only recently have a few works of cultural anthropology, published abroad, begun to sketch out paths of inquiry in this area (Amer and Coulanges 1974; Bebel-Gisler and Hurbon 1975; Hurbon 1979).

4. The preferred uses of Haitian varies with age, gender, and the context of communication among the elites, but there are social penalties for using French at the "wrong" time, just as there are penalties for the improper use of Haitian by French-competent speakers.

5. I thank Czerny Brasuell and Michel Acacia, who forced me to deal with this question.

6. One cannot make reference to the continued immigration of whites and *mulâtres* to explain the survival of persons considered "*clairs.*" White and *mulâtre* immigration certainly played a role, but it was more social than biological.

   Candler, during his visit of 1838–40, noted that "a large number among the class of *mulâtre* citizens residing in the capital were immigrants from the United States" (Candler 1842: 165). Later, white and light-skinned newcomers had different points of origin: Cuba, the Dominican Republic, France, the British West Indies, Austria, Corsica, Sicily, Syria, Lebanon, Germany, and especially Martinique and Guadeloupe. Many adapted quickly and formed prominent "Haitian" families (Aubin 1910). But the in-flow was too slow for this immigration alone to maintain the biological reproduction of a *clair* group. In addition, the migratory flow was not in one direction. The long regimes of Soulouque (1847–59) and of Salomon (1879–88), for instance, which were dominated by *noirs,* forced numerous *mulâtres* to leave the country.

7. Maxime Raybaud, who lived in Haiti during Acau's lifetime, gives a detailed version of the origins of this saying. It seems that during a demonstration Acau demanded that *all* the mulattoes be expropriated. A disapproving murmur came from the crowd, in which there were mulattoes in rags. Acau replied, "Oh! *These* are blacks!" Then, says Raybaud, "a black of about thirty years of age, who worked as a laborer in a rum plant, stepped forth and said to the crowd: 'Acau is right, because the Virgin said, "*Nèque rich qui connait lit et*

écri, cila mulâtre, mulâtre pauve qui pas connait li ni écri, cila nèque.''' [The rich black who knows how to read and write is a mulatto, the poor mulatto who does not know how to read or write is a black.] This black was named Joseph, and from that day on he called himself *Brother Joseph.* With a white kerchief on his head, dressed in a white shirt which gripped a pair of white pants, he walked, candle in hand, among Acau's troops, [repeating]: *'The rich black who knows how to read and write is a mulatto, etc.'''* (d'Alaux 1856: 112–13). Note the association of "reading" and "writing" to wealth and skin color in this early version of the saying.

8. The disappearance of poor mulattoes might also explain the double semantic twist in the term *mulâtre,* which has come to include darker and darker people but also to increasingly exclude individuals at the bottom of the social ladder. Today in the countryside there is a tendency to call a very light-skinned peasant *ti rouj, ti blan,* or simply *blan* (literally little red one, little white one, white) rather than *milat.* The same is done in the city for an artisan, a laborer, or a member of the lumpenproletariat.

9. Jacqueline Gautier and Evelyne Trouillot have both suggested to me that the assimilation of the Western-dominated aesthetic is stronger among Haitian males than among Haitian women, at least in the *petite bourgeoisie.* In other words, my example reversing the genders might not be completely justified. It is possible that the interiorization of the *mulâtre* aesthetic is more general among males, and that the emphasis on social promotion through the offspring is more systematic among women. Cultural anthropologists have yet to systematically study relations of alliance and kinship in urban Haiti and their influence on class reproduction.

10. The vast majority of political leaders who have consistently or temporarily utilized *noiriste* rhetoric have themselves chosen to have *clair* progeny, or at the very least, progeny more *clair* than they themselves. Salomon married a Frenchwoman; Estimé and François Duvalier married women less dark than themselves; Jean-Claude Duvalier had a child with a *mulâtresse* before he married Michèle Bennett, a *clair* though not a wealthy *mulâtresse,* as often claimed in the international press.

11. Price-Mars knew well that color prejudice could decide a candidate's lot. As a *noir,* he did not use it, and this speaks well of him (Antoine 1981: 190–91), but the maneuver was possible and it usually worked.

12. There were others who seemed much more qualified to be Estimé's heir, either because of their greater ideological allegiance to *noiriste* dogma, their greater partisan loyalty to Estimé, or their political preparation. According to Col. Pressoir Pierre, a personal friend of Duvalier, his success was due mainly to a palace coup, as it were, that took place within the ranks of the ex-president's

supporters after Estimé's death in exile. Some young officers (among them Pierre), profiting from support given by Estimé's widow, tipped the balance in favor of Papa Doc (Pierre 1987). It has also been said that Duvalier made a pact with several Estimist leaders, promising them that he would pass power on to them after his term was over.

5. THE TRANSITION TO DUVALIERISM

1. Among Haitian authors, Gérard Pierre-Charles (1967: 197–203; 1973; and especially 1979) is one of the exceptions, and the following survey has benefited from a reading of his work. In general, the traditional right, superseded by Duvalierism, only stressed "dictatorship" without making a qualitative distinction between Duvalier's dictatorship and preceding ones. Or it focused on "the color question." Foreign observers in turn have tended to emphasize the superficial peculiarities of a regime that seemed to them one more expression of the strangeness of the Haitian people. Few have focused on the impact of structural, economic, and sociopolitical problems on Duvalierism (but see Mintz 1984 and Lundahl 1979). Paul Moral (1959, 1961) perceived early on the dimensions of the crisis, although he did not to my knowledge use this word, or establish a relation between the structural crisis and the changes he was observing in state power.

2. Estimé's Financial Liberation Loan is a convincing example. Of a total of U.S. $7 million, $2 million were allotted to rebuilding the town of Belladère (a border town meant to impress Trujillo's Dominican Republic) and to building pavilions for the international fair celebrating the Port-au-Prince Bicentennial. The remaining $5 million went to cover the external debt (for a general survey of 1945–52, see Irving 1952).

3. As an officer in Estimé's presidential guard, Magloire "almost singlehandedly" had decided the terms of Lescot's "resignation" and of the formation of the military junta that ensured the transition from Lescot to Estimé (Pierre 1987: 11–13). Later, as chief of the presidential guard, he led the coup d'état that ended Estimé's hopes for a second term (Pierre 1987: 23–32). Uncontested leader of the transitional junta that replaced Estimé, Magloire campaigned without real competition and was elected in 1950.

4. Not all the officers were united behind him. In addition, his merchant allies were incapable of slowing down the momentum that the middle classes still

drew from the experience of 1946. Finally, Magloire himself recoiled before the possibility of massive bloodshed in Port-au-Prince.

5. Such hypotheses ignore the fact that the dominant classes are inherently heterogeneous under capitalism, and elections rarely express specific class alternatives even in advanced capitalist nations. In peripheral countries, that inherent heterogeneity is reinforced by economic dependence and clear political choices are rarer (Thomas 1984; Alavi 1982a, 1982b). Further, the hypothesis that class alternatives were represented in 1956–57 ignores the chronic lack of bona fide parties in Haiti.

6. The copious volumes of Clément Célestin (1958a, 1958b, 1959, 1960), which reproduce the most important campaign documents of 1956–57, and Bonhomme's book (1957) detail the chronology of the campaign (see also Pierre-Charles 1973, and Pierre 1987).

7. To be sure, political campaigns everywhere tend to impose their often superficial theatrics on the most important decisions, and there is no reason to believe that Haiti, of all places, would have escaped the superficiality. But the superficiality of political campaigns in the West, for instance, is often a "good" sign that those who want to be in control are already in control. Yet in 1956 Haiti, as mentioned before, the bourgeoisie confronted the crisis feverishly, with neither discourse nor organization.

   Poulantzas (1971: 122) reminds us that the Nazi state came about during a "particularly intense crisis of political organization proper" among the German bourgeoisie and in the absence of class-based political organization among the petty bourgeoisie and the small-holding peasantry. Establishing direct equivalence with the Haitian situation is out of the question, but note the enormous political weakness of the bourgeoisie after the demise of the Parti Libéral in the last quarter of the nineteenth century.

8. Sociocultural conditions also helped. Cheresky (1983) follows a Latin American sociological tradition in suggesting that political authoritarianism is more easily implanted in a society that is strongly hierarchical and accustomed to what can be called "social authoritarianism." The thesis has a long history and its numerous formulations have had their critics and their supporters. But provided that social authoritarianism exists, and provided that it can, at the very least, extend the possibilities of political authoritarianism, Haiti's case is not an exception. Family relations, the educational system, the etiquette (or absence of it) of meetings between people of different social origins, the attitude of Catholic priests (until then, mostly foreign whites), and a whole series of social codes engendered and constantly reinforced the belief that the only possible authority must be vertical and uncontested in its sphere of influence.

9. I will expand later, especially in Chapter 6, on the crucial difference between a militia member (*milisyen, milisyèn*) and a *tonton-makout.*

10. According to Pierre (1987: 139), Duvalier "used an incident of a sentimental nature to make Franck Beauvoir lose the unlimited confidence of the general that he had enjoyed." Then he pushed Kébreau to give Beauvoir—who also had sworn enemies of long standing—a sinecure as ambassador to Caracas. Kébreau, blinded by what he considered to be a major affront to his family's honor from his political ally, embraced the easy solution. Beauvoir kept his rank but was removed from Port-au-Prince. Duvalier made a friendly visit to Beauvoir's wife to reassure her that her husband was still in the good graces of those in power. Kébreau did not even realize that he had been robbed of his surest political ally.

6. STATE AGAINST NATION

1. Some may question my calling the Haitian state under Duvalier "totalitarian" because the term has increasingly been used in lay language to refer to Soviet-type (or Soviet-dominated) regimes. But the Duvalierist state does fit, for what it is worth, the dominant model: totalist ideology; single party led by one man; fully developed secret police; monopoly on mass communications, on operational weapons, and on all forms of organization. More importantly, the Duvalierist project was "total" in the original sense meant by the Mussolinists, that is, as a project for a political organism encompassing the civil society. (See Giddens [1985: 294–310] for an overview of totalitarianism, including a positive critique of the dominant model.)

2. In the United States, for example, Congress declares war, judges condemn criminals to the electric chair, and the president has the right to grant pardons. The state monopoly of force is thus divided between the three branches. This division, *ceteris paribus,* protects citizens against the extreme use of violence by the state. Though foreign military ventures by Western powers or police brutality in inner cities of North America and Europe suggest that the use of state violence in the so-called liberal democracies is not as fully controlled as is generally maintained, it would be wrong to suggest that governmental violence, because universal, is everywhere the same (see Thomas 1984).

3. As early as 1803, Dessalines ordered the execution of Sanite Belair, a female maroon leader who had fought beside her husband against Dessalines. A century later, under the government of Nord Alexis, the state paramilitary

minions used violence against women, although they were not killed (Jolibois 1986). As the totalitarian temptation grew in the time of Magloire and Kébreau, women were not spared during the army's beating sprees (Bonhomme 1957; Célestin 1958a, 1958b, 1959). But even Kébreau did not dare to use state violence openly against middle- and upper-class women. Obviously, the mingling of class/color, gender, sexuality, and politics in Haiti before and under the Duvaliers deserves more study.

4. The indiscriminate use of violence by the state preceded François Duvalier's presidency (Jolibois 1986; Gaillard 1974–84) and grew under Magloire. However, it was publicly condemned, and was not systematized before 1961.

5. The renewal of the personnel of the apparatus and the—sometimes explicit—formulation of the new political morality underlines the systematic nature of the Duvalierist enterprise. For if the totalitarian solution had been due only to the frenzied passions of a few men, it would have softened or disappeared when they fell or died (for example, when Clément Barbot, the first chief of the secret police, died in 1963, or after Kébreau's exile). However, the repressive machinery found new individuals to replace them. Some of the newcomers had not even supported Duvalier in 1957, either because they were in one of the other camps or because they had been too young.

6. The only case where the pursuers would carry on without hesitation would be one in which the political status of the household cancelled out the thief's political claim—for instance, if the master was a well-known *makout*. But again, few thieves would dare to enter such a house.

7. Within the last twelve years, one of the most stimulating developments of a Haitian diaspora still trying to define its role vis-à-vis the home country has been the creation of numerous organizations that regroup immigrants coming from the same provincial towns. Their economic contribution to the areas of origin varies, however; some are mere social clubs while others have a beneficial (though limited) impact on the local distribution of power. At any rate, their very existence suggests the demographic importance of the provincial towns among Haitian expatriates.

7. THE CONTINUITIES OF DUVALIERISM

1. On the connection between Duvalierism and Haitian history and social structure, see also Pierre-Charles 1967, 1973, 1979; Lundahl 1979, 1983; Nicholls 1979; Honorat 1974; Mintz 1984; and chapters 5 and 6.

2. The closest competitor is the political pair formed by the regimes of Pétion (1807–18) and Boyer (1818–43), which can be seen as part of a twofold progression in the executive branch of government. But Pétion ruled over only part of Haiti. Further, Boyer's regime did not stress formal continuities with that of Pétion the way Jean-Claude Duvalier's regime clearly presented itself as a phase of Duvalierism. Boyer still holds the record for the longest presidency of Haiti, followed by Jean-Claude and François Duvalier, in that order.

3. Among the few writers to take Duvalierist discourse seriously, see Laforest 1972, Hurbon 1979, and especially Lévèque 1971. For a widely publicized defense of the regime by a renowned intellectual, see Piquion 1972.

4. Toussaint Louverture was the first politician to baptize himself "Father" (M.-R. Trouillot 1977). Nicknames such as "Papa Dessalines," "Papa Bon Coeur" (for Pétion), "Papa Vincent," and "Papa Fignolé" all suggested positive relationships between those in power and certain segments of the masses. To this Duvalier added the positive-sounding appellation "Doc," familiar nickname for beloved and respected doctors.

5. Haitian historiography dates the creation of the first Haitian flag—blue and red, vertically placed—to May 18, 1803, when Dessalines reportedly tore the white stripe off a French flag. Dessalines' Imperial Constitution of 1805 replaced the blue band with a black one, supposedly to symbolize the union of blacks and mulattoes. After Dessalines' murder, while Christophe used the black and red flag in the North, Pétion reinstated the color blue, placing both bands horizontally (De Pradine 1886: 56–57). After Christophe's death, that blue and red flag became the sole Haitian banner and it remained so until Duvalier reinstated Dessalines' flag in 1964, to symbolize the alleged "Dessalinian heritage" of Duvalierism. In 1986, under pressure from the urban masses who associated the black and red flag with the Duvaliers, the junta that succeeded Jean-Claude returned to the very first flag of 1803.

6. For example, under Jean-Claude Duvalier, ministerial numbers-juggling was to the advantage of the *mulâtres,* more of whom came to participate in the government. Further, many of the young president's playmates and girlfriends were visibly *mulâtres.* The black pillars of the regime had not lost any of the economic advantages won under François Duvalier, however, and a dispassionate observer might well suggest that acceptance by the *mulâtres* had always been high on the *noiriste* political agenda. Another superficial change was the decline of the populist-nationalist discourse which had allowed the regime to keep the bourgeoisie at bay during the years when François Duvalier was consolidating his power. Then again, the cynical observer might suggest that cultural nationalism was much less useful to the regime during Jean-Claude's years than it had been during his father's rule.

7. Significantly, a 1985 World Bank report repeated Papa Doc's statement almost word for word:

> Haiti could enjoy a better place in the world. . . . Industry as a whole can take advantage of the factors that have so attracted the largely foreign firms: productive low-cost labor, proximity to the United States, functioning basic infrastructure, pro-business atmosphere, and political stability. (Cited in Hooper 1987b: 33.)

8. Haiti's electric production grew from 21.6 million kilowatts/hour in the fourth quarter of 1969–70 to 108.6 million in the last quarter of fiscal year 1984–85 (IHSI 1986: 22), a five-fold increase. The official figures for per capita consumption grew accordingly: they doubled in less than ten years.

9. Note that in comparison the average Haitian peasant paid at least 30 per cent of his income in various taxes on coffee—though his income was thousands of times smaller (Tanzi 1976).

10. Recently declassified State Department documents support this and the following assertions on the relation between the Duvalier dictatorship and the U.S. government. See, for instance, *Haiti Beat* (August 1988).

11. One suspects, though, that some U.S. firms were "privately" encouraged. Lady Bird Johnson reportedly had an interest in the Texan firm that controlled HAMPCO (Haitian American Meat Packing Company), an outfit that exported Haitian meat to the United States.

12. The PUCH itself never represented a serious military threat. Even though most units of the Haitian army were poorly trained, the elite battalions controlled directly by the Executive and financed and trained by the United States were quite capable of dealing with a few Communist infiltrators.

13. The scarcity of dollars, the increase in the rate of exchange, and the monopoly shared by civilian and military officials and merchants in the currency market has survived the Duvaliers. By January 1989 the gourde was 30 percent below the official rate of 5:1.

14.
Cost-of-Living Index and Food Index
in the Years of Jean-Claudisme, 1972–1985
(Base 1975–76 = 100)

Years	General index	Food index
1972–73	70.23	71.30
1976–77	107.43	107.71
1980–81	151.02	159.06
1984–85	206.98	217.50

The table is based on calculations of the Institut Haïtien de Statistiques (IHSI 1986: 26, 106), which used fiscal year 1975–76 as a base. But note that the pre-1971 figures reveal even more clearly the inflationary cost of the light assembly strategy. On a 1975–76 base, the general price index for 1969–70 is only 53.07, and the food index 49.59.

8. THE INTERRUPTED MARCH TO DEMOCRACY

1. The "liberal" phase of Jean-Claudisme which lasted from about 1975 to 1980, was part condition and part effect of the light industry strategy. In more immediate terms, it was also a positive result of the Carter administration's emphasis on human rights in the Americas—including the limited amnesty trumpeted by the regime in 1977 and the creation of the Haitian Human Rights League in 1978. That phase ended abruptly on November 20, 1980, with a wave of arrests, the expulsion of many journalists, and the closing down of independent press organs. We cannot help but notice that the change came six months after the president's wedding; but it is more important to point out that it occurred less than three weeks after the 1980 U.S. elections. No matter who actually gave the orders, the new wave of repression expressed the Haitian government's reading of the implications of the Reagan landslide for human rights in Latin America and the Caribbean.

2. The most publicized of these parties was a $500-a-plate dinner in which the *crème* of the bourgeoisie, the *nouveaux riches* of the regime, and many foreign officials and entrepreneurs took part. It was supposedly a fundraising event for a charitable foundation headed by the First Lady. Indeed, Michèle Bennett tried to counter rumors of her unscrupulous ambition with a philanthropic image. This worked for the first few months after her wedding, but the image later disintegrated, despite the public accolade Mother Theresa gave to the Haitian First Lady. By the time of the celebrated dinner, no one cared about the charitable pretext for the extravagant party.

3. Colonel North's Haitian connection received little attention in the U.S. press. Nevertheless, according to the *Village Voice* (29 December 1987), before the Iran-Contra affair became public, "In Washington, Duvalier's removal became yet another feather in the rakish cap of a mysterious marine colonel named Oliver North, abetted by his State Department sidekick, Elliott Abrams."

4. A good case in point is the issue of decentralization. That issue was born in the

grassroots struggle, at a time when, in contrast to the deafening silence from Port-au-Prince, the entire population of many provincial towns had clearly gambled with their lives by defying the regime. Had Duvalier survived, these provincials would have paid dearly for it. The 1964 Jérémie massacres showed how Duvalierism could punish an entire town. The provincial slum-dwellers also knew that, and by January 1986 it had become clear in places like Gonaïves and Cap-Haïtien that the entire community's survival depended on the government's fall. In the midst of Port-au-Prince's silence, the issue of decentralization found fertile ground in the provinces. After Duvalier's fall and up until April and May 1986, the provincials loudly denounced Port-au-Prince's unfair share of the national revenues. Yet the illusion of an undisturbed march toward democracy defused that particular issue until the drafting of the Constitution, when the problem was solved brilliantly by the bureaucrats. . . . on paper at least. Yet the people hardly noticed, and the bureaucrats failed to remind them, that numerous reports and dossiers had "solved" that problem many times in the past.

Bibliography

Ahmad, Eqbal
  1980. "The Neo-Fascist State: Notes on the Pathology of Power in the Third World." *International Foundation for Development Alternatives:* 19:15–26.

Alavi, Hamza
  1982a. "State and Class under Peripheral Capitalism." In H. Alavi and T. Shanin, eds., *Introduction to the Sociology of "Developing" Societies*, pp. 289–307.
  1982b. "The Structure of Peripheral Capitalism." In H. Alavi and T. Shanin, eds., *Introduction to the Sociology of "Developing" Societies*, pp. 172–92.

Alavi, Hamza and Teodor Shanin, eds.
  1982. *Introduction to the Sociology of "Developing" Societies.* New York: Monthly Review Press; London: Macmillan.

Amer, Michel and J. Coulanges
  1974. "Mini-Jazz: sens et significations." *Lakansièl* 2: 8–20.

Amin, Samir
  1980 [1979]. *Class and Nation, Historically and in the Current Crisis.* New York: Monthly Review Press.

Anderson, Benedict
  1983. *Imagined Communities: Reflections on the Origins and Spread of Nationalism.* London: Verso.

Anderson, Perry
  1976–77. "The Antinomies of Antonio Gramsci." *New Left Review* 100: 4–77.

Anglade, Georges
　　1982. *Espace et liberté en Haïti.* Montreal: Etudes et Recherches Critiques d'Espace, Université du Québec à Montréal et Centre de Recherches Caraïbes, Université de Montréal.

Antoine, Jacques Carmeleau
　　1981. *Jean Price-Mars and Haiti.* Washington, D.C.: Three Continents Press.

Ardouin, A. Beaubrun
　　n.d. [1843?] *Réponse du Sénateur Beaubrun Ardouin à un écrit intitulé Apologie des destitutions . . .* Port-au-Prince: Imprimerie Pinard. [New York Public Library, Special Collections, Haitian Papers.]
　　1958 [1853–60]. *Etudes sur l'Histoire d'Haïti.* Port-au-Prince: François Dalencour, éditeur.

Aubin, Eugène
　　1910. *En Haïti. Planteurs d'autrefois, nègres d'aujourd'hui.* Paris: Armand Colin.

Auguste, Claude B. and Marcel B. Auguste
　　1985. *L'expédition Leclerc, 1801–1803.* Port-au-Prince: Imprimerie Henri Deschamps.

Balch, Emily Greene, ed.
　　1927. *Occupied Haiti.* New York: Writers Publishing Co.

Bebel-Gisler, Dany and L. Hurbon
　　1975. *Cultures et pouvoir dans la Caraïbe.* Paris: L'Harmattan.

Benoit, Pierre V.
　　1954. *Cent cinquante ans de commerce extérieur d'Haïti, 1804–1954.* Port-au-Prince: Imprimerie de l'Etat.

Blassingame, John W.
　　1969. "The Press and American Intervention in Haiti and the Dominican Republic, 1904–1920." *Caribbean Studies* 9, no. 2: 27–43.

Bonhomme, Colbert
　　1946. *Les Origines et les leçons d'une révolution profonde et pacifique.* Port-au-Prince: Imprimerie de l'Etat.
　　1957. *Révolution et contre-révolution en Haïti, de 1946 à 1957.* Port-au-Prince: Imprimerie de l'Etat.

Brisson, Gérald
1968. Les Relations agraires dans l'Haïti contemporaine. Mimeographed. Mexico.

Brown, Jonathan
1971 [1837]. *The History and Present Condition of St. Domingo*. Rept. ed. London: Frank Cass.

Bruno, Camille et al.
1909. *Rapport relatif à l'emprunt de 1896 de 50.000.00 de francs*. Port-au-Prince: Imprimerie Nationale.

Buci-Glucksmann, Christine
1969. "A propos de la théorie marxiste de l'Etat capitaliste: vers une conception nouvelle de la politique." *L'Homme et la société* 11: 199–207.
1975. *Gramsci et l'Etat. Pour une théorie matérialiste de la philosophie*. Paris: Fayard.

Buci-Glucksmann, C., ed.
1983. *La gauche, le pouvoir, le socialisme. Hommage à Nicos Poulantzas*. Paris: Presses Universitaires de France.

Bureau of the American Republics
1893. *Haiti*. Washington, D.C.: Bureau of the American Republics, Bulletin No. 62 (rev. ed.).

Calixte, Colonel D.P.
1939. *Haiti: The Calvary of a Soldier*. New York: Wendell Malliet & Co.

Calvet, Louis-Jean
1974. *Linquistique et colonialisme. Petit traité de glottophagie*. Paris: Payot.

Candler, John
1842. *Brief Notices of Hayti: with Its Conditions, Resources, and Prospects*. London: Thomas Ward & Co.

Caprio, Giovanni
1979. "Un livre de Mats Lundahl: Les Paysans et la Pauvreté: une étude sur Haïti," *Le Nouveau Monde*, 5 August 1979.

Castor, Suzy
1971. *La Occupacion norteamericana de Haiti y sus consecuencias (1915–1934)*. Mexico: Siglo XXI.

C.E.G.E.T. (Centre d'Etudes de Géographie Tropicale) et Université de Bordeaux
1985. *Atlas d'Haïti*. Talence: CEGET-CNRS et Université de Bordeaux 3.

Célestin, Clément
  1958a. *Compilations pour l'histoire*. Vol. 1. *Les Gouvernements provisoires, 6 décembre 1956 au 25 mai 1957*. Port-au-Prince: Imprimerie N.A. Théodore.
  1958b. *Compilations pour l'histoire*. Vol. 2. Port-au-Prince: Imprimerie N.A. Théodore.
  1959. *Compilations pour l'histoire*. Vol. 3. *Conseil Militaire de Gouvernement*. Port-au-Prince: Imprimerie N.A. Théodore.
  1960. *Compilations pour l'histoire*. Vol.4. *Les évènements des 28 et 29 juillet 1958 et les grands procès politiques de 1958*. Port-au-Prince: Imprimerie N.A. Théodore.

C.E.P.A.L. (see United Nations)

Chamberlain, Greg
  1987. "Up by the Roots." *NACLA Report on the Americas* 21, no. 3: 14–23.

Chassagne, Albert D.
  1977. *Bain de sang en Haïti. Les macoutes opèrent à Jérémie en 1964*. 2nd ed. New York: Cohen Offset Printing.

Cheresky, Isidoro
  1983. "Conflits à l'intérieur des régimes autoritaires et mobilisation démocratique." In C. Buci-Glucksmann, ed., *La gauche, le pouvoir, le socialisme*, pp. 271–87.

Un citoyen privé
  n.d. [1843?] *Apologie des destitutions pour opinions politiques ou dogme de l'obeissance passive preché aux fonctionnaires publics, par un Sénateur et réfuté par un citoyen privé*. New York Public Library, Special Collections, Haitian Papers.

Cliffe, Lionel
  1982. "Class Formation as an 'Articulation Process': East African Cases." In H. Alavi and T. Shanin, eds., *Introduction to the Sociology of "Developing" Societies*, pp. 262–78.

Collectif Paroles
  1976. *1946–1976, Trente ans de pouvoir noir en Haïti*. La Salle, Canada: Collectif Paroles.

Bibliography   249

Corvington, Georges
1984. *Port-au-Prince au cours des ans. La capitale d'Haïti sous l'occupation: 1915–1922.* Port-au-Prince: Imprimerie Henri Deschamps.

d'Alaux, Gustave [Maxime Raybaud]
1856. *L'empereur Soulouque et son empire.* Paris: Michel Lévy Frères.

Danache, B[ertomieux]
1950. *Le Président Dartiguenave et les américains.* Port-au-Prince: Imprimerie de l'Etat.

Debien, Gabriel
1956. *Les Colons de St. Domingue et la révolution. Etudes antillaises.* Paris: Armand Colin & Cahiers des Annales.

De Catalogne, Gérard
1966. Preface to François Duvalier, *Oeuvres essentielles,* vol. 1.

De la Rue, Sidney
1930–1933. *Annual Reports of the Financial Adviser-General Receiver.* 3 vols. Port-au-Prince: Imprimerie de l'Etat: Imp. du Service Technique.

Delince, Kern
1979. *Armée et politique en Haïti.* Paris: L'Harmattan.

Delorme, Demesvar
1873. *Reflexions diverses sur Haïti. La misère au sein des richesses.* Paris: F. Dentu.

Denis, Lorimer and F. Duvalier
1938. *Le Problème des classes a travers l'histoire d'Haïti.* Port-au-Prince.

De Pradine, Linstant
1886. *Receuil général des lois et actes du gouvernement d'Haïti depuis la proclamation de son indépendence.* Vol. 1, 1804–1808. Paris: A. Durand-Pédone-Lauriel, sr.

Dorsinville, Roger
1965. *Toussaint Louverture ou la vocation de la liberté.* Paris: Julliard.
1972. "1946 ou le délire opportuniste." *Nouvelle Optique* 6: 117–40.
1985. "Dans le fauteuil de l'histoire." Interview with Michel Adam and Edgard Th. Gousse. *Etincelles* 1, no. 10: 18–21.

Du Tertre, Jean-Baptiste
1667. *Histoire générale des Antilles habitées par les français.* Paris: Th. Jolly.

Duvalier, François
    1966a. *Oeuvres essentielles.* Vol. 1. *Elements d'une doctrine.* Port-au-Prince: Presses Nationales d'Haïti.
    1966b. *Oeuvres essentielles.* Vol. 2. *La Marche à la présidence.* Port-au-Prince: Presses Nationales d'Haïti.
    1967. *Bréviaire d'une révolution.* Port-au-Prince: Presses Nationales d'Haïti.
    1969. *Mémoires d'un leader du Tiers-Monde, ou mes négociations avec le Saint-Siège.* Paris: Hachette.

Eaton, John
    1966. *Political Economy.* New York: International Publishers.

Ferguson, James
    1987. *Papa Doc, Baby Doc: Haiti and the Duvaliers.* Oxford and New York: Basil Blackwell.

Firmin, Anténor
    1885. *De l'Egalité des races humaines.* Paris.

Fontaine, Jean-Marc et al.
    1983. "Répression: emprise, dérive, violence." *L'Homme et la société* 67–68 (Special issue, January–June 1983).

Fossaert, Robert
    1981. *La Société.* Vol. 5. *Les Etats.* Paris: Seuil.

Fouchard, Jean
    1972. *Les Marrons de la liberté.* Paris: L'Ecole. In English as *The Haitian Maroons: Liberty or Death* (New York: Blyden Press, 1981).
    1975. *La Méringue: danse nationale d'Haïti.* Montreal: Editons Lemeac.

Franklin, James
    1971 [1828]. *The Present State of Hayti (Saint Domingo), with Remarks on its Agriculture, Commerce, Laws, Religion, Finances, and Population.* Rept. ed. London: Frank Cass.

Frostin, Charles
    1975. *Les Révoltes blanches à Saint-Domingue aux XVII et XVIII siècles.* Paris: L'Ecole.

Gage, Thomas
    1958 [1648]. *Thomas Gage's Travels in the New World.* Edited with an introduction by J. Eric Thompson. Norman: University of Oklahoma Press.

Gaillard, Roger
1974–84. *Les Blancs débarquent.* 5 vols. Port-au-Prince: Presses Nationales, Imprimerie Le Natal.

Gellner, Ernest
1983. *Nations and Nationalism.* Oxford and New York: Basil Blackwell.

Georges Adam, André
1982. *Une Crise haïtenne: 1867–1869, Sylvain Salnave.* Port-au-Prince: Editions Henri Deschamps.

Giddens, Anthony
1985. *The Nation-State and Violence.* Berkeley: University of California Press.

Girault, Christian A.
1981. *Le Commerce du café en Haïti: habitants, spéculateurs et exportateurs.* Paris: C.N.R.S.

Goulbourne, H., ed.
1979. *Politics and the State in the Third World.* London: Macmillan.

Graham, Norman A. and K.L. Edwards
1984. *The Caribbean Basin to the Year 2000: Demographic, Economic, and Resource-Use Trends in Seventeen Countries: A Compendium of Statistics and Projections.* Boulder and London: Westview Press.

Gramsci, Antonio
1971. *Selections from the Prison Notebooks.* Edited and translated by Q. Hoare and G.N. Smith. New York: International Publishers.

Groupe de Recherches Nouvelle Optique
1972. "Haïti: Porto Rico 2? Notes sur la conjoncture économique." *Nouvelle Optique* 8: 1–15.

Haiti Beat, no. 1, August 1988.

Hobsbawm, Eric
1975. *The Age of Capital.* London and New York: New American Library.

Hobsbawm, Eric and T. Ranger, eds.
1983. *The Invention of Tradition.* Cambridge: Cambridge University Press.

Hoetink, Harry
1967. *The Two Variants in Caribbean Race Relations*. London: Oxford University Press.

Hoffman, John
1984.˙ *The Gramscian Challenge: Coercion and Consent in Marxist Political Theory*. Oxford and New York: Basil Blackwell.

Honorat, Jean-Jacques
1974. *Enquête sur le développement*. Port-au-Prince: Imprimerie Centrale.

Hooper, Michael S.
1986. *Duvalierism Without Duvalier*. New York: National Coalition for Haitian Refugees and Americas Watch.
1987a. "The Monkey's Tail Still Strong." *NACLA Report on the Americas* 21, no. 3:24–31.
1987b. "Model Underdevelopment." *NACLA Report on the Americas* 21, no. 3:32–38.

Hurbon, Laënnec
1979. *Culture et dictature en Haïti. L'Imaginaire sous contrôle*. Paris: L'Harmattan.

IHSI (Institut Haïtien de Statistique et d'Informatique. Ministère de l'Economie et des Finances.)
1985. *Bulletin trimestriel de statistique*, no. 137.
1986. *Indicateurs de la conjoncture*. September 1986.

Irving, D.J. Mill, ed.
1952. *Hayti. Economic and Commercial Conditions in Hayti*. London: HMSO, Overseas Economic Surveys, Board of Trade.

James, C.L.R.
1962 [1938] *The Black Jacobins: Toussaint Louverture and the San Domingo Revolution*. 2nd ed. New York: Viking.

Janvier, Louis-Joseph
1886. *Les Constitutions d'Haïti, 1801–1885*. 2 vols. Paris: C. Marpon et E. Flammarion.

Jean-Luc [Yves Montas]
1972. "Sur la diffusion du marxisme en Haïti." *Nouvelle Optique* 6: 89–104.
1976. *Structures économiques et lutte nationale populaire en Haïti*. Montréal: Editions Nouvelle Optique.

Jolibois, Gérard
1986. *L'Exécution des frères Coicou.* Port-au-Prince: Imprimerie Le Natal.

Justin, Joseph
1915. *Les Réformes nécessaires: questions haïtiennes d'actualité.* Port-au-Prince: Imprimerie Edmond Chenet.

Kaplan, Marcos
1984. *Estado y sociedad en America Latina.* Oaxaca: Editorial Oasis.

L.A.B. (Latin American Bureau)
1985. *Haiti: Family Business.* London: LAB.

Labelle, Micheline
1976. "Témoignages sur la question de couleur." *Lankansièl* 5: 25–43.
1978. *Idéologie de couleur et classes sociales en Haiti.* Montreal: Les Presses de l'Université de Montréal.

Laforest, Jean-Richard
1972. "Notes à propos d'un article de René Piquion." *Nouvelle Optique* 8: 118–24.

Lamartinière, Jacqueline
1976. *Le Noirisme.* Paris: MHL.

Langley, Lester D.
1980. *The United States and the Caribbean, 1900–1970.* Athens: The University of Georgia Press.

Laroche, Dr.
1908. *Un Coup de clairon.* Cap-Haïtien.

Léger, Abel-Nicolas
1930. *Histoire diplomatique d'Haïti.* Vol. 1. Port-au-Prince: Imprimerie Auguste A. Héraux.

Lepkowski, Tadeusz
1968–69. *Haití.* 2 vols. Havana: Casa de las Americas.

Lévèque, Karl
1971. "L'Interpellation mystique dans le discours duvaliérien." *Nouvelle Optique* 1, no. 4: 5–32.

Lewis, Gordon
1983. *Main Currents in Caribbean Thought.* Baltimore and London: The Johns Hopkins University Press.

Leyburn, James G.
1941. *The Haitian People.* New Haven: Yale University Press.

Lundahl, Mats
1979. *Peasants and Poverty: A Study of Haiti.* New York: St. Martin's Press, London: Croom Helm.
1983. *The Haitian Economy: Man, Land, and Markets.* New York: St. Martin's Press.

Macciocchi, Maria-Antonietta
1974. *Pour Gramsci.* Paris: Editions du Seuil.

Mackenzie, Charles
1830. *Notes on Haiti Made during a Residence in that Republic.* 2 vols. London.

Madiou, Thomas
1981 [1847]. *Histoire d'Haïti, 1804–1807.* Rept. ed. Port-au-Prince: Editions Fardin.

Makandal (Montreal)
1971. Various issues.

Manigat, Charles, C. Moïse, and E. Ollivier
1975. *Haïti: quel développement? Propos sur "l'Enquête . . ."* de Jean-Jacques *Honorat.* Montreal: Collectif Paroles.

Manigat, Leslie F.
1971. *Status quo en Haïti.* Paris: La Technique de Livre.
1977. "The Relationship Between Marronage and Slave Revolts and Revolution in St. Domingue-Haiti." In V. Rubin and A. Tuden, eds., *Comparative Perspectives on Slavery in New World Plantation Societies.* New York: Annals of the New York Academy of Sciences.

McCrocklin, James H.
1956. *Garde d'Haïti.* Annapolis: U.S. Naval Institute.

McNeill, William H.
1986. *Poly-ethnicity and National Unity in World History.* Toronto: University of Toronto Press.

Michel, Antoine
1932. *L'Avènement du général F.N. Geffrard à la présidence d'Haïti.* Port-au-Prince.

Millet, Kethly
1978. *Les Paysans haïtiens et l'occupation américaine, 1915–1930.* La Salle, Canada: Collectif Paroles.

Miliband, Ralph
1973. *The State in Capitalist Society.* New York: Basic Books.

Mintz, Sidney W.
1960a. "A Tentative Typology of Eight Haitian Marketplaces." *Revista de ciencas sociales* 4: 15–57.
1960b. "Le Système du marché rural dans l'économie haïtienne." *Bulletin du Bureau d'Ethnologie 3.*
1961. "Pratik: Haitian Personal Economic Relationships." *Proceedings of the 1961 Annual Spring Meetings of the American Ethnological Society,* pp. 54–63.
1979. "Slavery and the Rise of Peasantries." *Historical Reflections/Reflexions Historiques* 6, no. 1: 213–42.
1984 [1974]. *Caribbean Transformations.* Baltimore and London: The Johns Hopkins University Press.

Moral, Paul
1959. *L'Economie haïtienne.* Port-au-Prince: Imprimerie de l'Etat.
1961. *Le Paysan haïtien: étude sur la vie rurale en Haiti.* Paris: Maisonneuve & Larose.

Moreau de Saint-Méry, Médéric-Louis-Elie
1958 [1797]. *Description topographyque, physique, civile, politique et historique de la partie française de l'Isle Saint-Domingue.* Paris: Société de l'Histoire des Colonies Françaises.

Murray, Gerald F.
1977. *The Evolution of Haitian Peasant Land Tenure: Agrarian Adaptation to Population Growth.* Ph D. dissertation, Columbia University.

Nicholas, Hogar
n.d. [1955?]. *L'Occupation américaine d'Haïti: la revanche de l'histoire*. Madrid: Industrias Graficas Espana.

Nicholls, David
1979. *From Dessalines to Duvalier: Race, Colour, and National Independence in Haiti*. Cambridge: Cambridge Unversity Press.

Padgett, James
1940. "Diplomats in Haiti and Their Diplomacy." *Journal of Negro History* 25, no. 3: 265–330.

Un Patriote Haïtien
1887. *Les Finances d'Haïti sous le Président Salomon . . .* , n.1.

Paul, Edmond
1876. *De l'Impôt sur le café*. Kingston, Jamaica: Imprimerie de Cordoba.
1882. *Les Causes de nos malheurs. Appel au peuple*. Kingston, Jamaica: Geo. Henderson & Co.

Péan, Marc
1978. *L'Illusion héroique: vingt-cinq ans de vie capoise, 1890–1902*. Port-au-Prince: Henri Deschamps.

Le Petit Samedi Soir (Port-au-Prince)
(1975–1980)

Pierre, Guy
1971. "Bilan économique du duvaliérisme." *Nouvelle Optique* 1, no. 4: 33–49.

Pierre, Pressoir
1987. *Témoignages: 1946–1976, l'espérance déçue*. Port-au-Prince: Imprimerie Henri Deschamps.

Pierre-Charles, Gérard
1967. *L'Economie haïtienne et sa voie de développement*. Paris: Editions G.P. Maisonneuve et Larose.
1973. *Radiographie d'une dictature: Haïti et Duvalier*. Montreal: Editions Nouvelle Optique.
1979. *Haití: la crisis interrumpida, 1930–1975*. Havana: Casa de las Americas.

Piquion, René
1972. "Nouvelle ou ancienne optique." *Nouvelle Optique* 8: 107–112.

Plummer, Brenda Gayle
1981. "Race, Nationality, and Trade in the Caribbean: The Syrians in Haiti, 1903–1934." *The International History Review* 3, no. 4: 517–39.
1984. "The Metropolitan Connection: Foreign and Semi-Foreign Elites in Haiti, 1900–1915." *Latin America Research Review* 19, no. 2: 119–42.
1988. *Haiti and the Great Powers.* Baton Rouge: Louisiana University Press.

Poulantzas, Nicos
1971 [1969]. *Pouvoir politique et classes sociales.* Paris: Maspéro.

Price, Hannibal
1900. *De la Réhabilitation de la race noire par la République d'Haïti.* Port-au-Prince.

Price-Mars, Jean
1983 [1928]. *So Spoke the Uncle.* Washington, D.C.: Three Continents Press.
n.d. [1979?]. *Anténor Firmin.* Port-au-Prince: Imprimerie Séminaire Adventiste.

Radio Nationale (4 VRD)
1979. *Dossier provinces.* Port-au-Prince: Ateliers Fardin.

Recherches Haïtiennes
1980. *Espace rural et société agraire en transformation: des jardins haïtiens aux marchés de Port-au-Prince* 2 (Special issue, December 1980.)

Roy, Hérard
1902. *Mes Comptes, mes paroles et mes actes.* Port-au-Prince: Imprimerie J. Verrollot.

St. John, Spencer
1889. *Hayti, or The Black Republic.* 2nd ed. London: Smith, Elder & Co.

Schmidt, Hans
1971. *The U.S. Occupation of Haiti, 1915–1934.* New Brunswick, N.J.: Rutgers University Press.

Tanzi, Vito
1976. "Export Taxation in Developing Countries: Taxation of Coffee in Haiti." *Social and Economic Studies* 25, no. 1: 66–76.

Tarrade, Jean
1972 [1969]. *Le Commerce colonial de la France à la fin de l'ancien régime: l'évolution du système de l'exclusif de 1763 à 1789.* 2 vols. Doctoral thesis, Université de Paris, Faculté des Lettres et des Sciences Humaines.

Le Télégraphe (Port-au-Prince)
(1819–1843)

Thomas, Clive Y.
1984. *The Rise of the Authoritarian State in Peripheral Societies.* New York: Monthly Review Press; London: Heineman.

Thoumi, Francisco E.
1983. "Social and Political Obstacles to Economic Development in Haiti." In P. Henry and C. Stone, eds., *The Newer Caribbean: Decolonization, Democracy, and Development.* Philadelphia: ISHI.

Touraine, Alain
1973. *Production de la société.* Paris: Editions du Seuil.
1978. *La Voix et le regard.* Paris: Editions du Seuil.

Trollope, Anthony
1985 [1859]. *The West Indies and the Spanish Main.* Gloucester: Alan Sutton.

Trouillot, Ernst and E. Pascal-Trouillot
1978. *Code de lois usuelles.* Port-au-Prince: Editions Henri Deschamps.

Trouillot, Hénock
1960. "La République de Pétion et le peuple haïtien." *Revue de la Société Haïtienne d'Histoire, de Géographie et de Géologie* 31, no. 107: 16–157.
1963. *Les Anciennes sucreries coloniales et le marché haïtien sous Boyer.* Port-au-Prince: Imprimerie de l'Etat.
1974. *Le Gouvernement du roi Henri Christophe.* Port-au-Prince: Imprimerie Centrale.

Trouillot, Michel-Rolph
1977. *Ti difé boulé sou Istoua Ayiti.* New York: Koléksion Lakansièl.
1980. Review of Peasants and Poverty by Mats Lundahl. *Journal of Peasant Studies* 8, no. 1: 112–16.

1982. "Motion in the System: Coffee, Color, and Slavery in Eighteenth-Century Saint-Domingue." *Review* 5, no. 3: l 331–88.

1985. *Nation, State, and Society in Haiti, 1804–1984.* Washington, D.C.: The Woodrow Wilson International Center for Scholars.

1986a. *Les Racines historiques de l'état duvaliérien.* Port-au-Prince: Editons Henri Deschamps.

1986b. Review of *So Spoke the Uncle* by J. Price-Mars. *Research in African Literatures* 17, no. 4: 596–97.

1988. *Peasants and Capital: Dominica in the World Economy.* Baltimore and London: The Johns Hopkins University Press.

Turnier, Alain
1955. *Les Etats-Unis et le marché haïtien.* Washington, D.C.

n.d. [1979?] *Avec Mérisier Jeannis: une tranche de vie jacmélienne et nationale.* Port-au-Prince: Imprimerie Le Natal.

United Nations, United Nations Development Program
1980. *Rural Women's Participation in Development.* New York: U.N.D.P., Evaluation Study No. 3.

United Nations, C.E.P.A.L.
1982. *Economic Survey of Latin America.* Santiago de Chile.

United Nations, Department of International Economic and Social Affairs
1983. *Population and Vital Statistics Report.* New York: Statistical Papers, A, vol. 35.

Vibert, Paul
1895. *La République d'Haïti, son présent, son avenir économique.* Paris: Berger-Leverault et Cie.

Viré, Armand
1942. *En Haïti: Notes de voyage et prospections radiesthesiques.* Paris: Editions de la Maison de la Radiesthesie.

Wallerstein, Immanuel
1987. "La Construction des Peuples: Racisme, Nationalisme, Ethnicité." *Actuel Marx* 1: 11–27.

Woodson, Drexel
n.d. "Tout mounn se mounn, men tout mounn pa menm: Microlevel sociocultural aspects of land tenure in a northern Haitian locality." Mss.

World Bank (International Bank for Reconstruction and Development)
   1984. *World Tables*. Baltimore and London: Published for the World Bank by
   The Johns Hopkins University Press.

Worsley, Peter
   1984. *The Three Worlds: Culture and World Development*. Chicago: University
   of Chicago Press.

Index